IMPOSTOR

IMPOSTOR

HOW **GEORGE W. BUSH** BANKRUPTED AMERICA AND BETRAYED THE REAGAN LEGACY

BRUCE BARTLETT

DOUBLEDAY

New York London Toronto Sydney Auckland

PUBLISHED BY DOUBLEDAY

A division of Random House, Inc.
1745 Broadway, New York, New York 10019

DOUBLEDAY and the portrayal of an anchor with a dolphin are
trademarks of Doubleday, a division of Random House, Inc.

Cataloging-in-Publication Data is on file with the Library of Congress.

ISBN 0-385-51827-7

Book design by Tina Henderson

Printed in the United States of America

FIRST EDITION

10 9 8 7 6 5 4 3 2 1

Contents

CHAPTER 1

I Know Conservatives, and
George W. Bush Is No Conservative   1

CHAPTER 2

The End of Serious Policy Analysis   20

CHAPTER 3

Why the Bush Tax Cuts Didn't Deliver   44

CHAPTER 4

The Worst Legislation in History?   64

CHAPTER 5

The Worst Record on Trade Since Hoover?   82

CHAPTER 6

Is Enron a Metaphor for Bush's
Economic Policy?   102

CHAPTER 7

On the Budget, Clinton Was Better   121

CHAPTER 8

IS BUSH ANOTHER NIXON?   141

CHAPTER 9

THE INEVITABLE TAX INCREASE   157

CHAPTER 10

THE SHAPE OF TAXES TO COME   175

CHAPTER 11

THE POST-BUSH ERA:

REPUBLICAN OR DEMOCRATIC?   192

APPENDIX I: PRESIDENTIAL VETOES   211

APPENDIX II: PORK BARREL SPENDING   213

APPENDIX III: LEGISLATED TAX CHANGES

   BY RONALD REAGAN AS OF 1988   214

APPENDIX IV: VAT RATES IN OECD COUNTRIES

   ESTABLISHING VATS BEFORE 1975   215

APPENDIX V: VAT RATES IN OECD COUNTRIES

   ESTABLISHING VATS AFTER 1975   216

NOTES   217

REFERENCES   248

INDEX   297

IMPOSTOR

I Know Conservatives, and George W. Bush Is No Conservative

GEORGE W. BUSH IS WIDELY CONSIDERED TO BE ONE OF THE most politically conservative presidents in history. His invasion of Iraq, his huge tax cuts, and his intervention in the Terri Schiavo case are among the issues where those on the left view him as being to the right of Attila the Hun. But those on the right have a different perspective—mostly discussed among themselves or in forums that fly below the major media's radar. They know that Bush has never really been one of them the way Ronald Reagan was. Bush is more like Richard Nixon—a man who used the right to pursue his agenda, but was never really part of it. In short, he is an impostor, a pretend conservative.

I write as a Reaganite, by which I mean someone who believes in the historical conservative philosophy of small government, federalism, free trade, and the Constitution as originally understood by the Founding Fathers. On that basis, Bush clearly is not a Reaganite or "small c" conservative. Philosophically, he has more in common with liberals, who see no limits to state power as long as it is used to advance what they think is right. In the same way, Bush has used government to pursue a "conservative" agenda as he sees it. But that is something that runs totally contrary to the restraints and limits to power inherent in the very nature of traditional conservatism. It is inconceivable to traditional conservatives that there could ever be such a thing as "big government conservatism," a term often used to describe Bush's philosophy.[1]

Perhaps the greatest sin of liberals is their belief that it is possible for them to know everything necessary to manage the economy and society. To conservatives, such conceit leads directly to socialism and totalitarianism. At a minimum, it makes for errors that are hard to correct.[2] By contrast, conservatives like Ronald Reagan understand that the collective knowledge of people as expressed in the free market is far greater than any individual, government bureau, or even the most powerful computer can possibly have.[3] And in politics, they believe that the will of the people as expressed through democratic institutions is more likely to result in correct policies than those devised by Platonic philosopher kings.[4] Liberals, on the other hand, are fundamentally distrustful of the wisdom and judgment of the people, preferring instead the absolutism of the courts to the chaos and uncertainty of democracy.[5]

Traditional conservatives view the federal government as being untrustworthy and undependable. They utilize it only for those necessary functions like national defense that by their nature cannot be provided at the state and local level or privately. The idea that government could ever be used actively to promote their goals in some positive sense is a contradiction in terms to them. It smacks too much of saying that the ends justify the means, which conservatives have condemned since at least the French Revolution.

George W. Bush, by contrast, often looks first to government to solve societal problems without even considering other options. Said Bush in 2003, "We have a responsibility that when somebody hurts, government has got to move."[6] A more succinct description of liberalism would be hard to find.

My main concern is with Bush's economic policy because that is my field of expertise. But it doesn't mean that I am content with the rest of his program. I am deeply concerned about the Iraq operation, which has more in common with Woodrow Wilson's policy of making the world safe for democracy than with traditional conservative foreign policy, which is based on defending the American homeland and avoiding unnecessary political and military entanglements with other countries— a view best expressed in George Washington's Farewell Address.[7]

I am also concerned with Bush's cavalier attitude toward federalism and his insistence on absolute, unquestioning loyalty, which stifles honest criticism and creates a cult of personality around him that I find disturbing. As former Reagan speechwriter John Podhoretz, author of a sympathetic book about Bush, has observed, "One of the remarkable aspects of this White House has been the fanatical loyalty its people have displayed toward Bush—even talking to friendly journalists like me, it's been nearly impossible to get past the feel-good spin."[8]

For example, in 2002, the White House directly ordered the firing of former Republican congressman Mike Parker of Mississippi as head of the Army Corps of Engineers because he publicly disagreed with the administration's budget request for his agency.[9] In 2005, it ordered the demotion of a Justice Department statistician who merely put out some data that the White House found inconvenient.[10] This micromanagement of such low-level personnel is extraordinary in my experience. Columnist Robert Novak referred to this sort of thing as the Bush White House's "authoritarian aura."[11]

In White Houses filled with high-caliber people, dissent invariably arises and becomes known. The apparent lack of dissent in this White House, therefore, is an indication to me of something troubling—an unwillingness to question policies even behind closed doors, an anti-intellectual distrust of facts and analysis, and blind acceptance of whatever decisions have been made by the boss.

The only alternative is something equally bad—fear of telling Bush something he doesn't want to hear. When asked whether he ever disagreed with him, Mark McKinnon, Bush's chief campaign media adviser in 2004, said, "I prefer for others to go into the propeller first."[12] This is the sort of thing that has gotten many big corporations like Enron in trouble in recent years, and I fear similar results from some of

Bush's ill-considered policies, especially the disastrous unfunded expansion of Medicare.

In thinking about Bush, I keep coming back to Ronald Reagan. Although derided as an amiable dunce by his enemies, it is clear from recent research that his knowledge and intellect were far deeper than they imagined. Articles and speeches drafted in his own hand leave no doubt that Reagan was exceptionally well read and had an excellent grasp of both history and current issues, including highly technical matters and complex statistics.[13] This knowledge was honed by decades of reading the classics of conservative thought and having spent much of his life publicly debating those whose views were diametrically opposed to his.

By contrast, George W. Bush brags about never even reading a daily newspaper.[14] Having worked in the White House, I know how cloistered the environment can be and how limited its information resources are—much of what White House staffers know about what is going on in the White House actually comes from reporters and news reports rather than inside knowledge, which is frequently much less than reporters imagine. It's distressing to contemplate the possibility that the president's opinion about the worthlessness of outside information sources is widely held within the White House. Unfortunately, I know from experience that the president sets the tone and style for everyone in the White House, suggesting that it is more likely than not that this view does indeed permeate the West Wing—a suspicion confirmed by the memoirs of those who have worked in this White House.[15]

Reagan, on the other hand, had a conservative distrust of his own ability to know all the facts and arguments before making important decisions. That is one reason why he was so tolerant of leaks from the White House during his administration. Reagan knew that this was an important safety valve that allowed dissenting viewpoints to reach him without being blocked by those with their own agendas. Deputy Chief of Staff Dick Darman, who controlled the paper flow in and out of the Oval Office, for example, was often accused of preventing Reagan from seeing memos that argued against positions Darman favored.[16]

I was involved in one very small effort to get around Darman myself. One day early in the Reagan Administration, while I was still working on Capitol Hill, a midlevel White House staffer whom I knew called me. He had written a memo to the president that he couldn't get through the bureaucracy. Knowing that Reagan was an avid reader of *Human Events,* the conservative weekly newspaper, my friend suggested that I take his memo, put my name on it, and publish it as an article in *Human Events.* I did, thereby getting the information and analysis to the president that my friend thought he needed.[17] Others in the White House frequently did the same thing by leaking memos to the *Washington Post* or the *New York Times* that appeared as news stories.

By contrast, the Bush White House is obsessive about secrecy, viewing leaks of even the most mundane information as the equivalent of high treason.[18] Ironically, this attitude can be self-defeating, since "leaks" are a very effective way of getting one's message out—as the Clinton White House often demonstrated. Think of it as giving an exclusive story to a reporter who has no choice but to accept the leaker's "spin." In this way, a leak can garner more and better press for a White House initiative than more conventional means like press releases. Leaking, in short, is not a moral issue, but can be a useful public relations technique.

CONSERVATIVE DOUBTS

TRADITIONAL CONSERVATIVES HAD grave doubts about George W. Bush since day one. First, he was his father's son. George H. W. Bush ran as Reagan's heir, but did not govern like him. Indeed, the elder Bush signaled that there would be a sharp break with Reagan-style conservatism in his inaugural address, when he spoke of being "kinder" and "gentler." Conservatives immediately asked themselves, "Kinder and gentler than whom?" To them, the answer was obvious: Ronald Reagan. In effect, Bush was accusing his predecessor and the philosophy he stood for as being the opposite of kind and gentle—nasty and brutish, perhaps. As columnist George Will later put it, Bush was deter-mined "to distinguish himself from Reagan by disparaging Reagan."[19]

George H. W. Bush's break with Reagan quickly became apparent in other ways as well. For instance, he fired virtually every Reagan political appointee in the federal government just as thoroughly as if he had been a Democrat. Of course, the Reagan appointees all knew that they were liable to be replaced at some point, but the suddenness and thoroughness of the purge caught them all by surprise—there had been no forewarning before Inauguration Day. It created a lot of ill will that came back to haunt the elder Bush when he got into political trouble later on. Most of the Reagan people sat on their hands rather than come to his aid.[20]

I was spared the purge only because Reagan had appointed Treasury Secretary Nicholas Brady in the last days of his administration, knowing that he was a close friend of then–Vice President Bush. Since Brady stayed on, that spared Treasury the "transition" that other departments under-went and thus avoided a purge. Within a year or so, most of the senior political appointees moved on anyway and Bush had his chance to appoint their successors. The same thing would have happened in all the other departments, too, thereby saving Bush a lot of unnecessary antagonism from the Reagan crowd. It would have helped Bush govern as well, since many of the purged positions remained vacant for some time for various reasons and were often filled with less competent and experienced replacements. Moreover, many of the so-called Bush people turned out to have no meaningful connection to him and were nothing more than friends of friends, serving in government just to get a line on their résumés and not because they had anything to accomplish in terms of policy.

One of the first things I noticed when the new crowd came in in 1989 was that they would very seldom mention Ronald Reagan's name. When necessary, they always referred to the "previous administration." And it was quite clear that they viewed Reagan's "hard-line" conservatism as passé and counterproductive to governing. They, on the other hand, thought themselves to be much more politically astute and believed that they would be far more effective by jettisoning Reagan's ideological baggage.

The problem was that having abandoned Reagan's principles, they had nothing to replace them with except political expediency. This culminated in the infamous abandonment of the no-new-taxes pledge in 1990. The Bush people thought they were being so clever by simply posting a notice in the White House pressroom on June 26, 1990, which said that budget negotiations with congressional Democrats would take place and include discussion of "tax revenue increases." They seem to have thought that no one would notice this fundamental reversal of Bush's position on taxes. Needless to say, it was noticed instantaneously, causing an almost immediate decline in Bush's poll ratings.[21]

I was told by one of the key participants in this decision that they never intended it as a repudiation of the pledge, but merely as an acknowledgment that in a growing economy taxes automatically rise.[22] If this is true, it certainly is not evidence of political sophistication, but rather its opposite. Being the only Reaganite left in the Treasury Department, apparently I was the only one who knew how negatively Bush's concession would be perceived by the Republican rank and file.[23] Unfortunately, no one asked my opinion before the decision was made.

I bring all this up because when George W. Bush first came on the radar screen as a potential presidential candidate, all that most conservatives knew about him was that he was the son of a president who had abandoned a successful conservative governing philosophy in favor of what they saw as squishy moderation, and was appropriately punished by voters for his sins. So when the younger Bush started talking about "compassionate conservatism," therefore, traditional conservatives immediately were suspicious of another Bush betrayal. As Richard Miniter wrote in the conservative *Manchester Union Leader,* "Bush's 'compassionate conservatism' strikes some as insulting and signals a return to his father's 'kinder and gentler' conservatism, which led to tax hikes and the loss of the White House."[24]

As *National Review*'s Andrew Stuttaford later put it, compassionate conservatism is an idea that should have been "strangled in the cradle."

To even call it an idea is "flattery," he said. For the most part, it is little more than "pork wrapped up in schmaltz."[25]

Right from the beginning, George W. Bush made it clear that he was not a conservative in the Reagan mold. In a speech in Indianapolis on July 22, 1999, he called the idea that our problems would be better solved if government would just get out of the way a "destructive mind-set." Government is "wasteful and grasping," Bush said, but "we must correct it, not disdain it."[26] Commenting on this speech, Cato Institute president Ed Crane said it could have come straight out of the Progressive Policy Institute, a think tank allied with the Democratic Party.[27]

Even in front of explicitly conservative audiences, Bush continued his theme that government was not the enemy, but just wasn't being used for the proper ends. In a speech to the Manhattan Institute on October 5, 1999, Bush put it this way: "Too often, my party has confused the need for limited government with disdain for government itself." He went on to complain that the government was too weak to do what was needed. It was "grasping" and "impotent," he said.[28]

BUSH IN OFFICE

GIVEN THE CHOICE between Al Gore and George W. Bush, conservatives had no choice but to back Bush, especially since Gore foolishly moved to the left of Bill Clinton during the campaign, effectively repudiating the most successful Democratic political program since Franklin D. Roosevelt.[29] Had Gore simply run as if he would fulfill his predecessor's third term, as George H. W. Bush did in 1988, he probably would have won easily. Why he didn't is a mystery.

In his first year in office, conservatives cheered Bush's tax cut but were deeply concerned about his education bill, widely viewed as essentially having been written by Ted Kennedy, and other compromises. By midyear there were growing complaints about Bush's flip-flops and governing style. Republicans on Capitol Hill and movement conservatives frequently voiced frustration with White House drift and lack of focus.[30] "Bush is a conviction politician until he isn't, whereupon he surrenders with brutal, almost jarring dispatch," wrote Paul Gigot, now editorial page editor of the *Wall Street Journal,* in a June 2001 column.[31]

But all of this came screeching to a halt on September 11, 2001. Conservatives and most liberals as well unified behind Bush in the wake of the World Trade Center and Pentagon attacks, and all concerns about him from the right were put on hold, at least temporarily.[32]

In early 2002, however, conservatives became alarmed by Bush's support for campaign finance reform, with virtually all of them viewing it as an unconstitutional abridgment of free speech. Columnist George Will was especially contemptuous of Bush's violation of his oath of office, which Will saw as nothing but a cynical political ploy for Bush to get good press in the liberal media while gaining a momentary advantage over the Democrats, owing to the modest increase in contribution limits, which was thought to benefit Republicans.[33]

Since Bush had previously said he would veto a campaign finance bill exactly like the one he ultimately signed, this revived the question of his consistency and commitment to principle.[34] Combined with his support for steel tariffs and proposed amnesty for illegal immigrants, this made conservatives increasingly restless. As the *Washington Times* reported, "Conservatives say that up to now they have been giving Mr. Bush a pass on some issues such as his education bill, which has put the government more deeply into state and local school policy than ever before. But the cumulative impact of his more recent moves has many of them raising their voices in protest for the first time."[35]

By spring, Republicans in Congress were complaining that Bush's actions were dragging them down with the party's base, threatening their own reelections.[36] Although liberals still saw Bush as an archconservative, some were starting to recognize that he was a very different type of conservative than Ronald Reagan had been—one who embraced government rather than disdaining it.

The *Washington Post's* David Broder argued that Bush was redefining the whole nature of conservatism. "The word, as this president uses it," Broder wrote, "has little or nothing to do with the traditional conservative inclination to preserve the status quo. Instead, it suggests a very bold and risk-taking readiness to reexamine, revise and restate basic tenets of government. It is a pattern that now pervades Bush's economic, social and foreign policy and makes this, in some respects, a truly radical government."[37]

The invasion of Iraq, like the World Trade Center and Pentagon attacks, tended to dampen conservative criticism of Bush in early 2003. Most traditional conservatives had deep misgivings about the war, which was driven mainly by neoconservatives, a conservative offshoot established by former liberals.[38] However, traditional conservatives tended to give Bush the benefit of the doubt as long as the threat of weapons of mass destruction in Iraq seemed genuine.

But by midyear, one could detect growing unease among conservatives, many of whom were starting to link Bush's expansive foreign policy with his expansive domestic policy. In a July essay, Sam Tanenhaus, author of a sympathetic biography of conservative hero Whittaker Chambers, asked whether Bush even deserved to be called a conservative at all:

> Just how conservative is the Bush administration? This is a question liberals have no trouble answering. They point to many items on an agenda long associated with the activist wing of the Republican Party: a parade of ideologically driven judicial nominees, a tax plan that rewards the rich even as the working poor are being lopped off employment rolls and, above all, a go-it-alone America-first foreign policy.
>
> But one notable group of critics has serious doubts about the administration's commitment to conservative ideals: American conservatives. For months now, a chorus on the right, growing in volume and clarity, has been challenging the White House's motives and aims. . . .
>
> What alarms these conservatives, young and old, is not so much the specific policies of the Bush administration as its appetite for an ever-enlarging, all-powerful government, a post-9/11 version of statism, the

bête noire of conservatism and the subject of one of the movement's founding texts, Albert Jay Nock's "Our Enemy, the State."[39]

That same month brought forth a host of conservative criticisms of Bush. George Will charged that he had somehow managed to alienate every faction of conservatism simultaneously.[40] Robert Novak accused Bush of smugness and arrogance.[41] *National Review* magazine's rather lame defense of Bush was that he never pretended to be a conservative in the first place.[42] Conservative columnist John Podhoretz of the *New York Post* argued that the war on terror trumped the war on big government.[43] Fred Barnes of the *Weekly Standard* simply conceded the point: "He's a big government conservative."[44]

By year-end 2003, frustration with Bush was becoming palpable among movement conservatives. A page 1 article in the conservative *Washington Times* cited a long list of conservative leaders who were becoming actively hostile to Bush, including direct-mail guru Richard Viguerie, National Taxpayers Union president John Berthoud, New York Conservative Party chairman Michael Long, and Don Devine of the American Conservative Union.[45] I myself basically gave up on Bush in November of that year, when he used all the power of his office to ram a massive new, unfunded spending program for prescription drugs through a Republican Congress. I will never forgive him for that.

REELECTION AND AFTER

CONSERVATIVE DOUBTS ABOUT Bush were strong going into 2004. The weight of the education bill, campaign finance reform, steel tariffs, drug legislation, failure to veto pork barrel spending, lack of WMDs in Iraq, concerns about illegal immigration, and other issues were clearly eroding his standing among conservatives, both inside the Beltway and at the grass roots.[46] In January the *Washington Times* quoted one unnamed Republican lobbyist who had given up on Bush.

Said the lobbyist, "In the administration's anxiousness to get an education bill, they gave away vouchers. In their anxiousness to get an energy bill, they gave away ANWR. In their anxiousness to get a campaign reform bill, they gave away free speech, unless you happen to be a media organization. If history is prologue, you would have to imagine there is nothing that will not be negotiated."[47]

In February, former White House speechwriter Daniel Casse tried to convince conservatives that Bush really was a conservative. The fact that he thought such a thing necessary was itself an indictment of Bush's weak position on the right—no one ever had to write any articles defending Ronald Reagan's conservatism. But Casse's effort was ultimately unsuccessful. It boiled down to saying that Bush's abandonment of principle had been compelled by political necessity and that leftists hated him with undisguised venom, which meant that he must have been doing something right.[48] Instead of guilt by association, we had the enemy of my enemy is my friend.

But old Reagan hands weren't buying it. In March, one of the oldest of the old Reagan hands, Lyn Nofziger, warned Bush that he had "not secured the support of that part of his conservative base still inspired by former President Ronald Reagan, which has been slipping away from him for more than a year." He chided Bush for "moving leftward in efforts to woo more moderate supporters." Nofziger warned that when his father had done that, it led many conservatives to stay home on Election Day.[49]

In April, the American Conservative Union, the nation's oldest and largest conservative organization, ran an entire issue of its online magazine seriously asking the question of whether conservatives should support Bush or oppose him in November. Editor Don Devine, a former political science professor at the University of Maryland who had been director of the Office of Personnel Management under Ronald Reagan, pointed out that voting Republicans out of the White House was not always a bad thing for conservatives. Gerald Ford's defeat in 1976 paved the way for Reagan's victory four years later, he said.

Going down a list of seven key issues, Devine put Bush ahead of Kerry in only four. Writing in the same issue, other conservatives decided that Bush had moved too far from their position on too many issues and that they would not vote for him in November. [50]

It was soon apparent that other Republicans felt the same way. In May, the *Washington Post*/ABC News poll found that all of Bush's fall in popularity was attributable to a decline in support among Republicans, which had dropped eight points in the previous month.[51] Ironically, Bush's own campaign commercials appear to have contributed to his weak support among conservatives, since he was emphasizing things like the education and Medicare bills that most of them had opposed.[52] Members of the Club for Growth, which makes large campaign contributions to candidates supporting free market policies, announced that they would not support Bush's campaign because he had strayed too far from their position.[53]

By midyear, growing numbers of conservative leaders were voicing doubts about the Iraq operation.[54] *National Review* founder William F. Buckley was one. "With the benefit of minute hindsight," he said, "Saddam Hussein wasn't the kind of extraterritorial menace that was assumed by the administration one year ago. If I knew then what I know now about what kind of situation we would be in, I would have opposed the war."[55]

As the campaign continued and despite the closeness of the race, more and more conservatives and libertarians spoke out publicly against Bush's reelection. A common theme was the idea that with John Kerry in the White House, congressional Republicans would go back to opposing new spending, as they had done during the Clinton years, which was a key reason for the emergence of budget surpluses.[56] Among those making this case were former special assistant to President Reagan Doug Bandow, *Reason* magazine editor Brian Doherty, *New York Post* editorial writer Robert George, and the editorial page of the *Tampa Tribune,* which had strongly endorsed Bush four years earlier.[57]

Bush won, of course, but by an exceedingly narrow margin given the relatively good state of the economy on Election Day. Yale University economist Ray Fair's computer model had predicted that Bush would win 57.7 percent of the two-party vote, based on how incumbent presidents had previously done when economic conditions were as good.[58] Instead, Bush won only 51.5 percent—a rather pathetic result by historical standards. The closeness of the result is partially explained by the fact that only 82 percent of self-described conservatives voted for Bush, with 18 percent voting instead for John Kerry, according to exit polls.[59]

As Lyn Nofziger observed, "The president and his people are deluding themselves if they think his victory signified general approval of his record, even within the Republican Party. It was fear of Senator John Kerry's liberal record that brought many critical Republicans back into the Bush camp on Election Day even though they were decidedly unhappy with his record of deficit spending, his increases in the size and scope of government, his lax immigration policies and his handling of postwar Iraq."[60]

In the end, it appears that none of Bush's deviations from conservative orthodoxy did him any good politically—not the drug bill, not the education bill, not his lenient policy on immigration designed to attract Hispanic voters.[61] In a case of delicious irony, his support for campaign finance reform, which appears to have been motivated primarily by a belief that it would give a small tactical advantage to Republicans in fund-raising, backfired. Democrats reacted by setting up so-called "527 groups" that raised millions of dollars from wealthy Bush-haters like financier George Soros. As George Will noted, all of this was perfectly predictable, proving once again that good policy is good politics.[62]

After the election, there was a noticeable shift in tone among many conservatives. They no longer felt they had to support Bush down the line, lest they give aid and comfort to the enemy. As John Fund of the *Wall Street Journal's* editorial board put it in a January column, "In the aftermath of 9/11, conservatives bottled up their frustrations over some of President Bush's policies. Then they muted their criticism during the presidential campaign. But now it is spilling out in all directions."[63]

At the same time, Bush no longer felt that he had to keep the conservative base happy, since he no longer needed their votes for reelection.[64] This became apparent when he used the first budget of his second term to pursue still more big government initiatives. As the *Washington Post* reported, "In many ways, Bush is . . . accelerating the trend toward a bigger, more activist government that was started early in his presidency."[65]

In February, White House Deputy Chief of Staff Karl Rove tried to calm the waters by speaking before the annual Conservative Political Action Conference. He argued that Bush had pushed conservatism past being "reactionary" to being "forward looking."[66] This raised again the question—whose conservatism was he referring to when he called it reactionary? To many conservatives, it could not mean anyone other than Ronald Reagan.

Although Bush got cheers from most conservatives for his effort to reform Social Security in 2005, it wasn't enough to compensate for growing complaints about his drift from conservative principles, lack of competence when conservative policies were pursued, and Bush's inability to hold together the disparate branches of the conservative coalition as Reagan had done. There was more and more talk of a "conservative crack-up."[67]

As former Reagan speechwriter Peggy Noonan put it, "President Bush is under pressure from various parts of his constituency, but there is little sign he's noticed. Among conservatives there is rising frustration over immigration, government spending and the gradual, slow-mo, day-by-day redefining of what modern conservatism is and what the Republican Party stands for that has taken place during the Bush presidency. That is in fact the big, largely unspoken fact of the Bush presidency."[68]

Said Andrew Ferguson in the *Weekly Standard,* "Conservative reform . . . turns out to be a lot like liberal reform. Each involves a whirlwind of government activity. Each is a formula for politics without end— splendid indeed for politicians and government employees, but a bit tiring for the rest of us. Who can blame the public for beginning to show its weariness? . . . Bush and his Republicans are close to proving that busybodyism can become a creature of the right as well as the left."[69]

Bush reacted by clamping down on dissent. By midyear, one was hearing more and more complaints about White House arrogance and impatience with any Republican not toeing the party line, no matter what the issue. In one case, Veterans Affairs Secretary Jim Nicholson publicly berated Congressman Chris Smith (R-NJ) for complaining about a shortfall in veterans program spending—a shortfall long denied by the administration, but eventually confirmed and rectified. Commenting on this incident, columnist Robert Novak said, "Nicholson represents an administration that operates on the principle that being in power means never having to admit being wrong."[70]

ASSESSMENT

THE PURPOSE OF this book is to disabuse people of the idea that George W. Bush is a conservative president who has relentlessly pursued a conservative agenda. Those in the conservative movement know better. They know that he is not a conservative in any meaningful sense of the term philosophically. He is simply a partisan Republican, anxious to improve the fortunes of his party, to be sure. But he is perfectly willing to jettison conservative principles at a moment's notice to achieve that goal.

The extraordinarily frustrating thing about this finger-in-the-wind style of conservatism is how manifestly unsuccessful it has been. Perhaps if Bush really had bought the long-term allegiance of the elderly with his drug benefit or the Hispanic community with his immigration program, then maybe one could rationalize it as a means of gaining the votes to pursue important but difficult-to-attain conservative goals, such as Social Security reform.

That has not been the case. Arguably, all of Bush's clever political ploys, in which he abandoned long-held conservative principles, ended up only hurting him politically. He would have done just as well electorally and possibly much better if he had stuck to those principles.

Whatever he gained at the margin by winning the votes of those who simply sell to the highest bidder, he lost at the conservative base. Moreover, in some cases he has virtually guaranteed that the Republican Party will suffer down the road, when someone must deal with the consequences of out-of-control Medicare spending, an Iraq operation that will probably drag on for decades, and an unconstitutional campaign finance bill that may be used to stifle alternative media outlets like blogs that have been so helpful to Republican candidates.[71]

Another problem is the creeping corruption inherent in "big government conservatism," which the New Republic's Jonathan Chait defines as "initiatives that benefit economic elites without using free-market mechanisms."[72] Since it is devoid of principle, it too easily becomes an excuse to lavish gifts on those with Republican connections. Chait points to people like lobbyist Jack Abramoff, once a foot soldier in the Reagan Revolution as head of the College Republicans, later accused of using his connections to bilk Indian gambling interests out of millions of dollars. In August 2005, Abramoff was indicted by a Florida grand jury on conspiracy and wire fraud in connection with these activities.[73]

Journalist Jacob Weisberg correctly noted that Republicans had simply taken the liberal spoils system and converted it to their own purposes. The result, he said, is "the curious governing philosophy of interest-group conservatism: the expansion and exploitation of government by people who profess to dislike it."

"In the daily business of Washington," Weisberg went on to say, "the old pattern remains in place, only with the substitution of these new supplicants and their new benefactors in the GOP. As in the old days, lobbyists work the halls of Congress and the regulatory agencies, functioning like carpenter ants to build a federal government ever bigger in size and more intrusive in scope."[74]

American University historian Allan Lichtman saw this as a "political revolution in the United States, creating a form of conservative big government that promotes not the general interests of ordinary Americans but the special interests of big corporations."[75]

This book will discuss in detail some of the ways in which I believe that George W. Bush has seriously hurt the country and set up conditions that will almost certainly lead to consequences that conservatives will find abhorrent. For example, his unwillingness to control spending and willingness to add significantly to it guarantees that there will be a massive tax increase at some point in the near future. I believe that the fiscal hole is so large that only a huge new revenue source like the value-added tax can fill it.

I think it is telling that Bush's Democratic predecessor, Bill Clinton, was far better on the budget than he has been. Clinton vetoed bills because they spent too much. Bush never does. Clinton not only reduced the deficit, but he actually cut spending. Bush has increased both. Clinton abolished an entitlement program. Bush created an extremely expensive new one. One can still argue about whether Clinton was a better president or a better man than Bush, but on the budget there is no ambiguity. Clinton was much better.

I believe there are gathering clouds of risk in the economy—the housing bubble, international imbalances, and such—that could bring a flood of trouble at a moment's notice. When one of these problems reaches storm strength and brings on a market crash, such as those in 1987 and 1989, I believe that the political climate will change overnight. All of a sudden there will be no more talk of tax cuts, but of budget deals and tax increases.

I believe that the tax cuts—Bush's signature domestic issue—have been far less effective than they could have been, owing in large part to his unwillingness to properly utilize the traditional policy development process. I believe this is also at the heart of the failure of his Social Security proposal and possibly the Iraq operation as well. It bothers me a great deal that Bush has driven away and even humiliated the few intellectuals in his midst, preferring instead the company of overrated political hacks whose main skills seem to be an ability to say "yes" to whatever he says and to ignore the obvious.

I believe that Bush may have the worst record on international trade of any president since Herbert Hoover. Although he initiated many small, bilateral trade agreements, they do not and cannot compensate for the failure of the Doha Round of multilateral trade talks, which was the direct result of Bush's ill-considered agriculture subsidies and steel tariffs.

It is my hope that those who remain in the Reagan wing of the Republican Party can come together to support a candidate in 2008 who will repudiate Bush's cynical policies, as Reagan repudiated those of another Republican president, Richard Nixon, whose methods so closely resemble Bush's. Nixon also thought he could buy off his enemies by selling out his friends. It didn't work for him and it won't work for Bush, either. Unfortunately, at this moment in time, there is no Reagan on the horizon who can pull disaffected conservatives together. But there is still a great opportunity there for the person who can, I think.

In my opinion, Republicans are better off having a debate about the consequences of Bush's policies sooner rather than later. There is always the danger that the Democrats will come to their senses and repudiate the left-wing craziness that characterized their 2000 and 2004 presidential campaigns, and return to the moderate liberalism that was so successful for Bill Clinton in 1992 and 1996. At that point, Republicans could find themselves locked out of the White House for a long time.

CHAPTER 2

THE END OF SERIOUS
POLICY ANALYSIS

O NE OF THE HALLMARKS OF GEORGE W. BUSH'S APPROACH TO
policy that is disturbing both to friends and foes alike is an apparent disdain for serious thought and research to develop his policy initiatives. Often they seem born from a kind of immaculate conception,
with no mother or father to claim parentage. As a consequence, Bush's
policy initiatives are frequently underdeveloped, leading to both substantive and political mistakes that could have been avoided, hurting his
policies and political fortunes at the same time.

THE POLICY PROCESS

TO UNDERSTAND HOW different the Bush Administration's policy
development process has been, one needs to know what historically has
been the case in both Republican and Democratic administrations.[1]

Generally speaking, policy initiatives percolate upward to the White
House from the departments. They are the ones that have to adminis-
ter the policies, know the issues more deeply, are in regular contact with

constituent organizations like interest groups and trade associations, have access to specialized data, employ many career staffers with long experience in their fields, and may have budgets for outside contractors who can fill in where there is a knowledge gap.

The White House, by contrast, has a very small policy staff, whose members tend to serve for just a year or two and turn over completely whenever there is a change of administration. It is really incapable of designing, researching, and implementing anything beyond the simplest initiatives. It must draw upon the broader resources of the departments to do anything remotely complex.

On issues with a budgetary component, the Office of Management and Budget will take the lead in assessing departmental initiatives. Since OMB has a career staff that serves from one administration to another, its institutional memory and experience make it well suited to tell whether an idea is worthwhile or just a rehash of some failed program from the past. And because it manages the budget as a whole, it is in a position to prioritize initiatives and avoid the myopia that individual departments may have.

I have been at many White House meetings where some allegedly new idea was under discussion. After all the political appointees in the room enthusiastically endorsed it, the career guy from OMB would finally speak. He would inform us that the same idea had been tried in the Truman Administration and didn't work, and that it came up again in the Ford Administration and didn't work then, either. And if the current administration insisted on moving forward yet again, it would discover that the chairman of the relevant Senate committee was unalterably opposed to it, and so on.[2]

OMB also has power because it decides what ultimately goes into the president's budget. Although the departments may try and go around OMB's priorities and lobby Congress directly, there is a limit to how much of this they can get away with. One way OMB keeps control is by requiring all administration officials to clear their congressional testimony before being presented on Capitol Hill. OMB officials review the testimony to ensure that it is consistent with the administration's program and have been known to cancel scheduled testimony when there is a conflict that cannot be resolved.

OMB also controls issuance of the Statement of Administration Policy or SAP, which is communicated to Congress before important votes, conveying the administration's official position on legislation. These statements are carefully worded to reflect the degree of the White House's support or opposition and may contain veto threats.

Issues without a budgetary focus usually go through the Office of Policy Development at the White House, where I served in 1987 and 1988. OPD often consists of various cabinet councils that would monitor broad issue areas, such as economic policy. At the request of a cabinet secretary wishing White House support for an initiative, an interagency working group might be established that would study an issue, seek input, and draft a report. This might lead to a cabinet meeting or a decision memo to the president, after which the initiative will either go forward and become an executive order or proposed legislation, or be sent back for further study.

One virtue of this process is that it allows the president to kill pet proposals from his cabinet secretaries without his fingerprints showing. He is always being buttonholed by one of them wanting his support for one thing or another. Setting up a working group to study the issue is one way the president can be responsive without making a commitment. If it turns out to be a bad idea, it can be derailed without the president being the bad guy.

Typically, if the administration chose to send a major initiative to Capitol Hill for legislative action, it would draft a detailed report on the proposal, with extensive analysis, data, and background material. Usually the Government Printing Office would publish these reports so that members of Congress and their staffs would be adequately informed about the arguments, options, and underlying rationale for a significant policy change. For example, when Ronald Reagan proposed the Tax Reform Act of 1986, the Treasury Department drafted a three-volume study of the subject.

OPD's main job was managing the process—scheduling meetings, controlling paper flow, and making sure that everyone's voice was heard. Its role was more that of an honest broker than an initiator or implementer of policy.

Bill Clinton made a key change in this process in 1993. He had campaigned on the idea that economic policy did not have sufficient stature within the White House. Too often, defense and foreign policy issues pushed aside domestic economic concerns, Clinton charged. Toward this end, he promised to create a new economic organization comparable to the National Security Council.

NATIONAL ECONOMIC COUNCIL

CLINTON'S CHARGE HAD some validity with regard to the George H. W. Bush White House.[3] As a Treasury Department official during that administration, I know too well how little he cared about economic policy. At one point Michael Boskin, chairman of the Council of Economic Advisers, had to threaten to resign just to get a face-to-face meeting with the president. Even when it was clear that the economy was the key issue of the 1992 campaign, Bush seemingly had to force himself to take any interest in the subject at all.[4]

The first President Bush paid a heavy price for his disinterest. Millions of Americans felt that he simply didn't care about what really mattered to them and that Bush much preferred spending his time on foreign policy. As a consequence, an overwhelming 63 percent of voters rejected him by voting for Clinton or Ross Perot in 1992, both of whom campaigned almost exclusively on economic policy.

True to his word, Clinton established a new White House organization, carved out of OPD, called the National Economic Council. More important, he persuaded New York banker Robert Rubin to come to Washington and head it up. Rubin proved to be very well suited to the task, which compensated for the innate flaws in the organization he headed.[5]

The basic problem is that economic policy is not at all comparable to defense and foreign policy in its nature. The NSC exists because there is an inherent conflict between the State Department and the Defense Department that requires mediation on a day-to-day basis. Moreover, national security issues often utilize classified information that demands special procedures and frequently involves extremely time-sensitive problems—things that must necessarily be acted upon immediately and require the president's personal attention.

By contrast, there are no intrinsic institutional conflicts among the economic agencies that require constant mediation. The information involved is almost never classified and decisions are rarely that time-sensitive. Consequently, there is simply no need for a specialized White House economic office that is structured like the NSC. Moreover, the White House has long had OMB and the Council of Economic Advisers (CEA) to deal with economic issues when they arose.

It is probably fair to say that most economists with an interest in public policy thought creation of the NEC was a mistake.[6] At a minimum, it would degrade the influence of the CEA and add another layer of bureaucracy to the economic policy process. It only worked as well as it did in Clinton's first term because of Rubin's exceptional managerial skills and the great respect everyone had for him. But when he left to become Treasury Secretary in 1995, there was a noticeable decline in the NEC's effectiveness.[7]

George W. Bush would have been well advised to abolish the NEC and go back to the pre-Clinton organizational structure. Unfortunately, he kept the NEC and placed his principal campaign economic adviser, Larry Lindsey, at its head. Lindsey was probably better suited to be chairman of the CEA. But the NEC came with an office in the West Wing of the White House, whereas the CEA was over in the less prestigious Old Executive Office Building. Columbia University economist R. Glenn Hubbard became CEA chairman.

Lindsey is a good economist, but in the hothouse atmosphere of the West Wing, where his office was just down the hall from Karl Rove and other White House bigwigs, he tended to get overly absorbed in day-to-day politics. As a consequence, the NEC drifted away from its central coordination function. From the earliest days of the Bush Administration, one heard about managerial problems at the NEC— memos and briefing books not being produced on time and things of that sort. The real problem, however, may have had less to do with Lindsey's lack of managerial skills than with inherent flaws in the nature of the NEC itself.

The NEC tried to be something it couldn't be—an originator of policy rather than just a coordinator. It also suffered by being a policy organization for a president who had little interest in the subject unless it advanced his political fortunes. This forced the NEC to become excessively political itself, with the result that policy analysis and development took a back seat.

John DiIulio

THE FIRST PUBLIC disclosure that the Bush White House's policy development process was broken came from John DiIulio, a respected University of Pennsylvania political science professor who was recruited to run the newly established Office of Faith-Based and Community Initiatives.

DiIulio quickly became disillusioned by the lack of focus on policy inside the White House. This was doubly discouraging to him because he strongly believed in Bush's plan to use faith-based organizations to deliver social services to the poor and disadvantaged, and because he was a trained social scientist who thought that ideas mattered. So when he discovered that they really didn't, he left the White House and went back to Philadelphia.

Ron Suskind, a Pulitzer Prize–winning journalist, tracked DiIulio down and interviewed him for an article about the Bush White House. Perhaps naïvely, DiIulio spilled his guts about the weaknesses and limitations of its policy development process, which appeared in an article by Suskind in the January 2003 issue of *Esquire*.[8]

DiIulio had detailed his concerns in a long memo to Suskind on October 24, 2002, that *Esquire* temporarily posted on its Web site after the White House attacked the veracity of Suskind's article.[9] In it, DiIulio complained that there was little "serious policy fiber" in the West Wing diet and that policy was often made by "on-the-fly" speechmaking. The Bush White House, he said, is "organized in ways to make it hard for policy-minded staff . . . to get much West Wing traction, or even get a non-trivial hearing.

"In eight months, I heard many, many staff discussions," DiIulio went on to say, "but not three meaningful, substantive policy discussions. There were no actual policy white papers on domestic issues."

The lack of substantive analysis and deliberation meant that the policy development process was dominated by those whose only knowledge and interest in a subject was purely political. "This gave rise to what you might call Mayberry Machiavellis—staff, senior and junior, who constantly talked and acted as if the height of political sophistication consisted in reducing every issue to its simplest, black-and-white terms for public consumption," DiIulio lamented.[10]

After the Suskind article appeared and his memo was posted on the Internet, DiIulio was deeply embarrassed and tried to recant his remarks about White House shortcomings in the policy arena.[11] But an unabashed Bush loyalist, former Bush speechwriter David Frum, soon confirmed them. In his book *The Right Man,* published in early 2003, Frum wrote that there was "a dearth of really high-powered brains" at the White House. "Conspicuous intelligence seemed actively unwelcome in the Bush White House," Frum added. There seemed to be "a bias toward the ordinary," he said.[12]

PAUL O'NEILL

ONE OF THE few people who probably could be considered a high-powered brain in the early days of the Bush Administration was Treasury Secretary Paul O'Neill. He had spent many years at OMB as a policy analyst early in his career, eventually rising to the number two position in the agency, and he knew very well how the policy process worked. O'Neill went on to become chief executive officer of International Paper and Alcoa and was widely considered one of the most competent business executives in the United States.[13]

O'Neill was recruited for the Treasury job by Vice President Dick Cheney, who knew him from the days when they both served in Gerald Ford's White House, where Cheney had been chief of staff. Unfortunately, O'Neill had little or no previous relationship with President Bush and it is clear that they never quite got on the same wavelength.

Having the president's trust can compensate for a lot of personal flaws in a Treasury secretary. As historian Arthur Schlesinger wrote of Henry Morgenthau, Franklin Roosevelt's secretary, "Morgenthau's inarticulateness, as well as the penchant for worry which so often darkened his face with apprehension, caused people to underrate him." But, "he chose good people, used them effectively, ran tight organizations, got results, and kept his mouth shut."

"Above all," Schlesinger continued, "his highest ambition was plainly not for himself. It was to serve Franklin Roosevelt."[14] As a consequence, Morgenthau was among the more influential Treasury secretaries despite proposing ideas that were at times misguided and on one occasion completely nuts—his plan to totally destroy Germany's industry at the end of the war and convert the nation into a pastoral state.[15]

One key source of friction between Bush and O'Neill was O'Neill's belief in the traditional policy development process. He was also frustrated by the lack of guidance from the president on precisely what he, O'Neill, was supposed to be doing. He later recounted his frustrations to journalist Suskind, who detailed them in his 2004 book *The Price of Loyalty*. In one passage, Suskind wrote:

> When a president doesn't offer explanation, even to his most senior aides, the problems are many. Bush often ascribed action to a general "I went on instinct" rationale, leaving O'Neill and others in the cabinet or the White House staff to ponder the intangibles that create "gut"—from some sweeping, unspoken notion of how the world works, to a one-size-fits-all principle, such as "I won't negotiate with myself," to a squabble with a family member over breakfast.
>
> Senior officials, guiding large ships in the fleet, were starting to feel they might *never* get to understand the way the President thought. After all his one-on-one meetings with Bush, and scores of group encounters, six months into the administration O'Neill realized that he didn't know the man's mind—something he could usually pick up in a good, long interview with a prospective hire.[16]

Lacking direction, O'Neill charted his own course. With some regularity, he was criticized for commenting publicly on the dollar, interest rates, taxes, Social Security, global warming, and a wide variety of other issues. As the *Washington Post* later commented, "During his rocky tenure as Treasury secretary, Mr. O'Neill proved to be a loose cannon, sometimes spooking financial markets with wild remarks, sometimes holding forth with extreme confidence on subjects, such as African development, about which he knew little."[17]

However, in many cases O'Neill simply became a lightning rod for the larger failure of the administration to chart or articulate a consistent economic policy. Since previous Treasury secretaries like James Baker and Bob Rubin had largely determined economic policy in their administrations, it was assumed that O'Neill could do the same. But the reality was that he could not. Unfortunately, no one told him.

In its November 5, 2001, issue, *National Review,* the most important conservative magazine in the United States, called for O'Neill to be fired, largely because the supply-side elements of the first tax bill had been so severely watered down.[18] The administration also seemed increasingly adrift on economic policy even before the World Trade Center and Pentagon attacks, it said. The reason, the magazine went on to say, is that its principal economic spokesman just wasn't up to the job and needed to go.

This was unfair to O'Neill. Critics didn't realize how little control he had over economic policy and how little direction he was getting from the president. As late as the middle of 2002, after working for Bush for eighteen months, O'Neill was still trying to get some guidance from him on the direction of economic policy. As he told Bush, "We went from the first tax cuts to 9/11 and we haven't really created an 'economic policy.' Tax cuts alone aren't an economic policy."[19]

Bush apparently didn't appreciate the criticism. Attacks on O'Neill by unnamed White House sources began appearing regularly in the press and there was growing speculation among pundits that he was on his way out.[20] And then one day he was out. On December 6, 2002, Vice President Cheney called O'Neill to tell him it was over.[21] After quickly composing a terse resignation letter, O'Neill returned to Pittsburgh and never looked back.

LARRY LINDSEY

INEXPLICABLY, LARRY LINDSEY was fired the same day as director of the NEC. Pairing the two departures this way inevitably led people to assume that they were let go for the same reasons. Whether this is true or not, neither deserved the public humiliation they were forced to endure. Lindsey had been with Bush since 1999 and was the architect of the tax plan that arguably won him the nomination and the election. He at least deserved better. Why Bush couldn't have just called him into the Oval Office and privately asked him to leave is a mystery. It sent a message to everyone that loyalty was a one-way street—absolute loyalty was demanded, but even Bush's most loyal lieutenants could be fired on a whim and publicly disgraced at the same time without so much as an explanation.[22]

I continue to believe that both O'Neill and Lindsey were victims of a system that places little value on substance and judges success or failure solely on the basis of short-term politics. The final straw for Lindsey, it was said, was when he publicly estimated that the cost of the Iraq war would be $100 billion per year.[23] At the time, the administration was lowballing the cost and Lindsey's estimate was mildly embarrassing.

It didn't matter to anyone that Lindsey had simply assumed that the war would probably cost about 1 percent of the gross domestic product because that is what wars of this type had cost in the past. It was a classic back-of-the-envelope calculation that economists do every day and is only designed to give a quick order of magnitude number in lieu of more detailed calculations. He never implied that the figure had come from the NSC or the Defense Department and made clear that it was his own estimation.

But rather than allow Lindsey to explain himself, he was thrown overboard for the sake of nothing, really. Everyone knew the war was going to be expensive and no one believed the administration's talk that the war could be fought on the cheap, anyway. It was a classic case of someone saying that the emperor was wearing no clothes. But in the end, Lindsey's estimate proved to be accurate.

After Lindsey's departure from the NEC, the White House recruited Wall Street banker Stephen Friedman to replace him. The thought seems to have been to get another Bob Rubin to run the organization and make it function more smoothly. By all accounts, Friedman did make the trains run on time, but not much else.[24] His profile was so low as to be invisible. This raised anew questions about precisely what the NEC was supposed to be doing. As columnist Robert Novak asked, "Why has Bush retained a superfluous economic position that fit his predecessor's needs?"[25]

Many observers thought that Friedman was only marking time until he could become Treasury secretary, as Rubin had done.[26] The lesson he apparently learned from Lindsey's sacking was to keep his mouth shut in public at all costs, simply nod "yes" at everything the president said, carry out his orders with dispatch, and make no effort whatsoever to influence policy.

By early 2005, Friedman realized that he was wasting his time at the White House, with neither influence nor prospects for a higher appointment, and he returned to Wall Street. His replacement was Indiana businessman Al Hubbard, who had worked for the elder Bush and known the younger Bush since their days together at Harvard Business School.[27] Although there were hopes that his long personal relationship with Bush would restore some stature to the NEC, this did not appear to happen. The organization continued to operate with no clear direction or function.

JOHN SNOW

O'NEILL'S REPLACEMENT WAS railroad executive John Snow, who had long been active in Republican circles. He had a Ph.D. in economics, good relations with Congress, and a genial personality. Like O'Neill, he was from an "old economy" industry and lacked Wall Street experience. Also, again like O'Neill, Snow had an unfortunate tendency to speak publicly about subjects such as the dollar when silence would have been the better course.

Snow seems to have learned the same lesson as Steve Friedman about his role, which was to sell the administration's initiatives but have no role in their development. Judging by his public schedule, Snow spent a good deal of his time, especially during the Social Security reform fight, giving speeches to high school students and other politically inconsequential groups.[28] His time would have been spent more effectively, in my opinion, using Treasury's highly skilled staff to address the many substantive questions raised about substituting personal accounts for Social Security's traditional benefits.

As chairman of the board of trustees of the Social Security trust fund, Snow should have been deeply involved in development of a Social Security reform proposal. Because of the secretary's position, the Treasury has long had staff people with deep knowledge of the Social Security system. And it has many analysts accustomed to dealing with finance who could have helped respond to technical questions about personal accounts, such as what rates of return could be expected, administrative costs, and others.

Unfortunately, it appears that this expertise was never called upon. The entire Social Security reform operation was run out of the White House, which had neither the depth of knowledge nor the resources to manage it effectively.

Although he was apparently doing exactly what he had been ordered to do, even if it was basically a waste of his time, Snow soon found himself in the same political wilderness that had ensnared O'Neill.[29] By the fall of 2004, it was widely reported that the White House was searching for a new Treasury secretary.[30] When questioned, a senior White House official denied that Snow was being pushed out. He could stay as long as he wanted, the official said, "provided it is not very long," the *Washington Post* quoted him as saying.[31]

Snow was ultimately retained only because Bush couldn't get who he wanted—perhaps because he didn't know who he wanted or perhaps because no one with the appropriate stature wanted to be treated the way O'Neill and Snow had been treated—as little more than errand boys.[32]

Unfortunately, the nature of the executive branch is such that if your boss, the secretary, is on the outs with the president, the entire department suffers. All the subcabinet officials find themselves in political Siberia as well. Thus, the public search for Snow's replacement tended to encourage the various undersecretaries and assistant secretaries at Treasury to leave for greener pastures.[33] It also made it increasingly difficult for the administration to recruit good quality replacements.

Many of the top jobs at Treasury remained vacant for months.[34] By the end of 2004, Treasury was being called a "neutered giant" because it had lost so much clout.[35]

During the 2004 election, Bush decided to make tax reform an issue, just as Ronald Reagan had done in 1984. But while Reagan had his own Treasury Department study the issue and make recommendations, Bush bypassed Treasury and promised to appoint a bipartisan commission to make a report. Not only did this waste a lot of time in reinventing the wheel, it contributed to a view that the administration never had any clear tax philosophy and had operated on a purely ad hoc basis all along. If its various tax initiatives had a unifying logic, then there would have been no need for a commission to tell Bush what his tax philosophy should be.

This downgrading of the second-ranking department in government did not serve Bush well.[36] The lack of senior-level staff and Snow's recruitment into full-time salesman for Social Security reform contributed to growing problems at Treasury in its core functions. For example, in early 2005 the Internal Revenue Service reported that the so-called tax gap had risen to over $300 billion—money that was owed to the federal government but uncollected, partly because the IRS lacked the resources to go after it.[37]

Treasury was also shown to be totally out of the loop when Deputy Secretary of Defense Paul Wolfowitz was named by Bush to be president of the World Bank. According to London's *Financial Times* newspaper, Bush had told Prime Minister Tony Blair before telling his own Treasury secretary about it. When Britain's Treasury officials called to discuss the appointment with their American counterparts, they knew nothing about it and were genuinely surprised.[38]

Of course, the president has the right to appoint whom he wishes to high-level positions.[39] But historically, the Treasury Department has taken the lead in recruiting a new World Bank president, since it oversees U.S. participation in the Bank and other international financial institutions like the International Monetary Fund on a day-to-day basis.

To have been completely bypassed on such an important decision is at least unusual and perhaps unprecedented.

Council of Economic Advisers

THE TREASURY WASN'T the only economic agency to suffer from Bush's disinterest in serious policy analysis. The CEA suffered as well. Established by the Employment Act of 1946, it has long attracted some of the finest economic minds in America as both members and staff. Among its chairmen were Arthur Burns and Alan Greenspan, both of whom went on to chair the Federal Reserve Board, and Joseph Stiglitz, who won the Nobel Prize in economics in 2001. James Tobin, another Nobel Prize–winning economist, served as a member of the Council. Lawrence Summers, who went on to become Treasury secretary and president of Harvard University, served on the staff during the Reagan Administration.[40]

Bush's initial choice for CEA chairman was R. Glenn Hubbard, a respected financial economist from Columbia University. Glenn and I worked together at the Treasury Department during the Bush 41 administration, where he was deputy assistant secretary for tax analysis and I was deputy assistant secretary for economic policy.

Hubbard's appointment was a smart one, but it was clear from the beginning that his main job was not to devise economic policies, but only to offer support for those Bush had already decided upon. Hubbard also learned the hard way that it was unwise to try and talk the president out of a decision he had already made, no matter how flawed it might be. On one occasion, I heard that he was rather strongly chastised by Bush for telling him that a decision he, Bush, had made was not good economic policy. Hubbard was told never to tell him that again.

Hubbard learned to live with Bush's style and ended up being quite effective, especially in the tax area. His previous experience at Treasury, where many of the same career staff people continued to work, proved invaluable. And although there were constant problems with the overlapping jurisdictions of the CEA and NEC, Hubbard and Lindsey were fundamentally in agreement on the general direction of economic policy.

The biggest problem the CEA had was that its substantive analysis of the issues didn't count for much in the Bush decision-making process. This was most apparent in the case of the steel tariffs, which were utterly unjustified either by economic theory or the facts of the case. Although the CEA made a strenuous effort to derail the tariffs, it was completely overwhelmed by the White House political people, with whom Bush ultimately sided.

After the terrorist attacks of September 11, 2001, the CEA was effectively downgraded by being physically moved out of the White House. In the name of security, the entire west wing of the Old Executive Office Building, where the CEA had long been located, was vacated. The CEA was moved to a commercial office building a block away; only the chairman retained an office in the OEOB.

Unfortunately, the loss of proximity led to a further loss of influence. Since the only influence the CEA has is in the power of its analysis, which is often offered informally in spontaneous meetings, its removal from the corridors of power was quite costly, both for the organization as a whole and for the maintenance of sound economic policy.[41]

Hubbard's political experience helped him cope with the institutional constraints. He was particularly skillful in shaping tax policy in the post-9/11 period. The bonus depreciation provision of the 2002 tax bill and the dividend relief in the 2003 tax bill owed much to Hubbard's thinking. But they resulted more from research he had done before joining the CEA than from what the CEA itself was able to do. For example, the cut in dividend taxes drew heavily upon a study of corporate taxes that Hubbard had drafted while at the Treasury Department ten years earlier.[42]

When Hubbard left the CEA in February 2003, its underlying lack of importance within the White House became more apparent. His replacement, respected Harvard economist N. Gregory Mankiw, found himself seriously disadvantaged in policy fights. He lacked both Hubbard's government experience and political skills, which had partially compensated for the CEA's institutional weakness. Consequently, the organization fell even further out of favor.

This in turn led to Mankiw being muzzled. Even though he could have aided Bush a great deal in the 2004 election—in which economic issues predominated, despite the war in Iraq—and helped refute many of John Kerry's attacks, Mankiw was kept on the bench. At the same time, the CEA was publicly criticized for fudging its economic forecast and withholding criticism of some Bush policies that it had to know were economically unsound, such as the Medicare drug bill.

The final indignity came when White House political staffers excised at least two chapters from 2005 Economic Report of the President on the eve of its release, after the report had already undergone extensive interagency review.[43] Such heavy-handed political interference with the Economic Report is unprecedented. Mankiw turned in his resignation a few days after the report was released and has refused to discuss the matter publicly.

Mankiw's replacement was monetary economist Ben Bernanke, who had been serving as a Bush appointee on the Federal Reserve Board after a long career at Princeton University. It was widely assumed that he was being groomed to replace Alan Greenspan as chairman of the Fed when Greenspan retired in 2006. However, there was no evidence that the CEA had risen in status, as Bush failed to appoint replacements for departing members Harvey Rosen and Kristin Forbes, leaving Bernanke alone on the Council throughout much of 2005.

When Bush finally got around to appointing replacements for Rosen and Forbes on September 21, 2005, he picked two very obscure economists, Katherine Baicker of UCLA and Matthew Slaughter of Dartmouth. Tellingly, neither is even a full professor, which suggests that economists of greater stature either weren't approached or turned down the opportunity to serve on the CEA because of its low status in the Bush White House.

POLICY VACUUM

SEVERAL THEMES HAD been evident in Bush's economic policy since the first days of the administration. First is a total subordination of analysis to short-term politics. As *Wall Street Journal* columnist Alan Murray put it just before the 2004 election, "For this administration, economic policy has been a direct extension of political strategy."[44]

Said economist Timothy Taylor, "Arguably, economic policy in the last four years has in some cases been based too much on short-term political concerns, rather than a mature consideration of long-term economic interests."[45]

Economist David Hale made a similar observation. "Economic policy," he said, "appears to be under the control of White House political advisers, not the traditional institutions of government."[46]

Second is a disregard for established economic agencies and total reliance on a small cadre of White House staffers, many with no substantive economic backgrounds, who regularly overrule those with experience and expertise on the issues under discussion. In a revealing comment from the inside, then–Deputy Commerce Secretary Samuel Bodman told a business audience on June 24, 2003, that policy was "totally stovepiped" and that administration appointees had very little big-picture policy information to guide them.[47]

Many analysts make the same criticism on the foreign policy side as well, which contributed to some of the problems in Iraq, they charge. Conservative columnist Max Boot fingered many of the same weaknesses in the White House national security operation previously detailed on the domestic side. After looking at various missteps in the war on terror, he said, "What's behind these failures? Every administration-watcher I've talked to, Republican or Democrat, points to a dysfunctional interagency process."[48]

A number of critics charged that the Bush Administration's flat-footed response to Hurricane Katrina late in August 2005 was another example. They charged that there was a lack of coordination between the military and relief agencies and between the federal government and state governments in Louisiana, Texas, and Mississippi. They also noted that the head of FEMA, the Federal Emergency Management Agency, was a political hack with no relevant expertise.[49]

Science policy is another area where critics complain of politicization and disregard for facts and established authorities.[50] Some of this simply involves legitimate debate over the science and policy related to global warming, stem cells, and missile defense.[51] But in light of the way Bush has treated his economic advisers, one cannot help harboring suspicions that the critics of Bush's science policy may have a point. Indeed, Bush's defenders don't really dispute the facts about politicization, but simply argue that what he is doing is no different than what past administrations have done.[52]

For this reason, much of the criticism one heard about the poor quality of Bush's economic team was often misdirected. Typical was the view of Jeffrey Birnbaum, Washington bureau chief for *Fortune* magazine. "With the economy wobbling and the stock market roiling," he wrote in 2002, "the President badly needs an A-team of economic advisors. Unfortunately . . . he doesn't have one. He barely has a C-team, when it's functioning at all."[53]

This theme continued well into 2005. As the *Wall Street Journal* put it in an editorial, "The Bush Administration hasn't always had the strongest or best coordinated team of economic advisers, to put it mildly."[54]

But people like Birnbaum were assuming that Bush's economic advisers were free to call their own shots and actually in control of their departments and agencies, as had been the case during the Clinton Administration and earlier. In fact, they had almost nothing to say about the substance of their responsibilities. They were only following orders handed down from the White House inner circle, acting mainly as salesmen who increasingly didn't believe in the product they were selling.

Bush's economists were also being used more for partisan political purposes than historically has been the case—cranking out numbers and spinning them in ways that would have been unthinkable in earlier administrations. As a consequence, the political capital of organizations like the Treasury Department and CEA has been deeply eroded, with analyses and pronouncements from these organizations no longer commanding the respect they once did.[55]

On the other hand, critics were right in the sense that there was a noticeable decline in the quality of Bush's policy advisers over time.[56] After the 2004 election, it was clear that the Bush Administration was having a more difficult time finding people who were willing to serve even in high-level positions. As the *Washington Post* reported, "The White House has found it harder to attract a top-flight team because some candidates are unwilling . . . to come to Washington to be White House cheerleaders."

The *Post* quoted one unnamed economist who had been considered for a position on the Council of Economic Advisers. Said the economist, "You can't be attracted to a job where you'd be out of the loop."[57] In the first half of 2005, more than half the senior positions at the Treasury Department were vacant in large part because the administration couldn't find qualified people willing to work there when the department seemingly had nothing to do.[58]

After the election, the White House tightened still further its already tight political control over the cabinet departments, forcing the secretaries to spend considerable time at the White House every week receiving direction from White House aides. Paul Light of the Brookings Institution saw this degree of White House oversight as unprecedented. "I find it absolutely shocking that they would have regular office hours at the White House," he said. "It confirms how little the domestic cabinet secretaries have to do with making policy."[59]

The White House also tightened its grip on personnel decisions, demanding even greater personal loyalty from every appointee, no matter how low-level. For example, newly appointed commerce secretary Carlos Gutierrez wasn't allowed to hire a single person in his department. As Robert Novak put it, "The Bush White House's icy hand does not discriminate between the mighty and the meek." He went on to say that the "dirty little secret" of the Bush Administration is its "chronic malfunctioning." More often than not, this was due to "bungled personnel decisions."[60] After Katrina, observers noted that there were a lot of Michael Browns in key positions—people running bureaus and agencies whose *only* qualifications appeared to be political loyalty.[61]

The danger, however, is that some crisis could come along, such as the stock market crashes of 1987 and 1989 or the Mexican debt crisis of the mid-1990s, that desperately requires top-level expertise. As the *New York Times* put it in a March 2005 editorial: "The clear lack of a deep bench from which to fill vacancies is cause for alarm, as is the extent to which our complex economic problems are beyond the ken of a mostly political, loyalist band of policy makers. That alarm, insistent though not yet overwhelming, would quickly reach deafening proportions if the United States were forced to respond to a sudden, destabilizing event like 9/11 without a credible Treasury team."[62]

HUBRIS

A RECURRING QUESTION among White House observers has been where exactly Bush gets his information and ideas. How does he come so quickly to major decisions without any apparent analysis or thought and stick to them with an absolute certainty that is almost religious in its intensity? As one of his former advisers, John L. Howard Jr., put it, "He uses a Sharpie pen. He's not a pencil with an eraser kind of guy."[63]

Journalist Ron Suskind looked deeply into the relationship between Bush's intense religious convictions and the total certainty he exhibits in his policies and decisions without ever really figuring it out. After all, many presidents have been deeply religious without being filled with the kind of hubris that Bush often exhibits. When Suskind asked a White House aide about this, the response was startling. You guys, the aide said, are "in what we call the reality-based community." Such people are defined, the aide went on, as those who "believe that solutions emerge from your judicious study of discernable reality."

Continuing, the aide told Suskind, "That's not the way the world really works anymore. We're an empire now, and when we act, we create our own reality. And while you're studying that reality—judiciously, as you will—we'll act again, creating other new realities, which you can study too, and that's how things will sort out. We're history's actors . . . and you, all of you, will be left to just study what we do."[64]

Other advisers have testified to Bush's lack of curiosity and unwillingness to study issues in depth before making decisions. Richard Clarke, one of his national security advisers, made this observation about Bush's modus operandi:

He doesn't reach out, typically, for a lot of experts. He has a very narrow, regulated, highly regimented set of channels to get advice. One of the first things we were told was, "Don't write a lot of briefing papers. And don't make the briefing papers very long." Because this president is not a reader. He likes oral briefings, and he likes them from the national security adviser, the White House chief of staff, and the Vice-President. He's not into big meetings. And he's not into big briefing books.[65]

At least with past presidents, there usually were back channels— kitchen cabinets—through which information and advice could be gotten to them. Sometimes these were even formalized. For example, Ronald Reagan had an economic policy advisory board of outside economists who would meet with him once or twice a year. But George W. Bush seemingly makes a point of having none of that. As he once told Brent Scowcroft, his father's national security adviser, "I have no outside advice. Anybody who says they're an outside adviser of this administration . . . is not telling the truth."[66]

One reason Bush often appears so unprepared for press conferences and even presidential debates is that he is unprepared. He would much rather discuss issues with those he knows already agree with him than suffer through a rigorous briefing that would prepare him to deal with contrary points of view or facts that don't support his decisions. Journalist Nick Lemann explains:

> In the early days of his Presidential campaign, Bush was introduced by his new circle of policy advisers to a Washington institution called a "murder board," in which a politician's aides fire hostile questions at him as a method of preparing for the rigors of public appearances. Bush resisted, and had to be talked into it. He prefers to assemble a group of friendly people from the conservative movement, who are profoundly grateful for being granted time in his presence, and to free-associate about the issues of the day—tuning up the instrument, as it were—while they listen. And, in trying to figure out his position on an issue, Bush . . . doesn't so much analyze as look for a hook—a phrase or a way of framing the issue that feels instinctively right to him. In his case, instinct usually takes him to a position where he is in charge and everyone else has to adjust.[67]

Perhaps when one has absolute faith in oneself, one feels no need to explain or justify one's actions. But even if that is the case and even if one is in fact correct in one's actions, one pays a price for an unwillingness to rationalize, explain, or meaningfully engage one's opponents on an intellectual level. Among themselves, conservatives worry that Bush has undermined support for conservative initiatives by focusing so much on raw political power at the expense of persuasion and engagement on the substance of issues. Ramesh Ponnuru, an editor at *National Review,* has voiced frustration with this aspect of the Bush Administration:

> So often, it appears more interested in getting its legislative agenda through sheer force—twisting enough arms to get the 218th vote in the House—than in persuading anyone that conservative (or conservative-ish) initiatives make sense. Overseas, it has been more interested in say-

ing that we are going to do what we are going to do than in getting people to agree that what we are doing is in the world's interests. The [Republican national] convention line-up suggests that the Republicans believe that the conservative message could never possibly appeal to the unconverted. It's a far cry from Reagan's approach. It reminds me of Rick Brookhiser's old line about the Republicans: In their hearts, they know they're wrong.[68]

The result is that Bush is failing to win any converts to the conservative cause and is interested only in expanding the Republican Party's partisan advantage, regardless of the consequences. It's a penny-wise/ pound-foolish strategy.

CHAPTER 3

Why the Bush Tax Cuts Didn't Deliver

Certainly, George W. Bush's most controversial domestic policy actions have been his significant cuts in federal taxes. This was quite an extraordinary political achievement, but one that accomplished relatively little economically. Far more could have been done to improve economic growth and reform the tax system if he had had a vision of what he was trying to do in the area of taxation. As a consequence, much revenue was sacrificed to achieve very little economic gain.

Taxes and the Economy

To understand Bush's tax program, it's important to know how economists generally have looked at tax policy in the postwar era. For most of that period, taxes were considered economically important only for their impact on disposable income. In other words, tax cuts or tax increases were just a way of putting dollars into peoples' pockets that they could spend on goods and services, or taking dollars out of their pockets to reduce their ability to spend.

This followed from the theories of John Maynard Keynes, an important British economist whose views dominated economic thinking from the 1930s through the 1970s. He thought that spending was the driving force in growth. Hence, if the economy was growing too slowly, the government's policy should be to pump it up by getting money out into the economy for people to spend via deficit spending. If inflation was a problem, then tax increases would reduce people's ability to spend and thereby get it under control.

Getting money into the economy could be done in any number of ways. For example, the government could just hire the unemployed and give them make-work jobs. Keynes himself once suggested burying money in deep mine shafts that were filled in. People would be employed in digging the money out.[1] No governments ever took him up on this suggestion, but many have done something similar: building roads and bridges that there was no real need for.[2] Keynes called this pyramid-building.

Although tax cuts are also a way of getting money into the economy, they were considered deficient by the Keynesians for two reasons. First, most taxes are paid by the relatively well-to-do, who would likely save most of a tax cut rather than spend it. Second, those who would be most likely to spend any increase in their after-tax income were too poor to pay any taxes, meaning that a tax cut would do nothing for them. In 2004, for example, no one with an income below $40,000 paid any federal income taxes in the aggregate, according to the Joint Committee on Taxation, and those with incomes above $200,000 paid 48.8 percent of the total.[3] Thus tax cuts were viewed as an inherently inefficient way of stimulating spending.

Interestingly, the president most influenced by Keynesian thinking, John F. Kennedy, went totally against Keynesian theory when he proposed a big tax cut in 1963. Although he justified his tax cut on Keynesian grounds, it was a very non-Keynesian proposal, because its central element was an across-the-board cut in income tax rates, including a reduction in the top rate from 91 percent to 70 percent.

"It is a paradoxical truth that tax rates are too high today and revenues are too low, and the soundest way to raise the revenues in the long run is to cut the rates now," Kennedy said in his Economic Club of New York speech on December 14, 1962.[4]

When the impact of the Kennedy tax cut became a political issue in the late 1970s, further analyses were undertaken. DRI and Wharton Econometric Forecasting Associates were contracted by two congressional committees to study the impact of the Kennedy tax cut.[5] After reviewing these studies, the Congressional Budget Office drew the following conclusion:

> The effect of the 1964 tax cut on the federal deficit has been a matter of controversy. . . . The direct effect of the tax cut was to reduce revenues by some $12 billion (annual rate) after the initial buildup. The increase in output and later in prices produced by the tax cut, according to the models, recaptured $3 to $9 billion of this revenue at the end of two years. The result was a net increase in the federal deficit of only about 25 to 75 percent of the full $12 billion.[6]

Thus, while the Kennedy tax cut may not have paid for itself entirely, there is overwhelming evidence that the federal government did not lose nearly as much revenue as expected, owing to its expansionary effect on the economy.[7]

Some of Kennedy's advisers, especially John Kenneth Galbraith, Kennedy's tutor at Harvard, preferred to see a big increase in government spending to stimulate the economy. He was also afraid that Republicans would like tax cutting too much.[8] To this day, no one really knows why Kennedy chose this particular approach to economic stimulus. Nevertheless, the tax cut's passage in 1964—rammed through Congress by Lyndon Johnson after Kennedy's assassination—was widely viewed as a victory for Keynesian economics. Indeed, Keynes even appeared on the cover of *Time* magazine on December 31, 1965, some twenty years after his death.

As a consequence of the preoccupation with spending as the driving force in the economy, there was little interest in the structure of taxation by economists. Since all that really mattered was how much taxes were as a share of income, it didn't really matter how taxes were raised. In theory, a 100 percent tax rate with a 90 percent rebate was economically equivalent to a flat 10 percent tax rate.

TAX REFORM

THEREFORE, MOST ACADEMIC discussion of taxation related to administration and fairness. The principal goal of tax reformers was to get rid of "loopholes" that allowed the wealthy to avoid paying their "fair share." In 1969 and 1976, Congress passed major tax reform bills—signed in each case by Republican presidents—that were largely designed to get rid of "tax expenditures," a term coined by Treasury tax expert Stanley Surrey to describe all deviations from an ideal tax system.[9]

This "ideal" tax system would theoretically tax all income comprehensively. Capital gains would be taxed the same as wages and there would be no special incentives for saving or investment, such as Individual Retirement Accounts. Carried to its logical extreme, however, a comprehensive income tax would require homeowners to pay taxes on the rent that they pay to themselves and other forms of "income" that would appear bizarre to most people.[10]

In the mid-1970s, this notion of tax reform was pushed aside by concerns about how to raise economic growth, reduce unemployment, and tame inflation. It seemed to many politicians and economists that increasing the rate of capital formation by providing tax incentives for saving and investment would be helpful. There were also growing concerns that inflation was raising the tax burden, thereby reducing the incentive to work. It was common to hear stories about workers refusing overtime for fear that they would get pushed up into a higher tax bracket and thus lose money on the deal. Of course, this couldn't happen unless tax rates went above 100 percent. Nevertheless, the fact that people often said such things shows that they were well aware of what economists called "bracket creep."

This led to the development of what came to be called "supply-side economics." According to this philosophy, the Keynesians had it all wrong. It's not spending that drives the economy, but production. And production occurs only when people and businesses have an incentive to produce. Hence, the rate of return on productive economic activity—work, saving, and investment—was the key to growth. Taxes had a major effect on the profitability of such activity and thus were critical to growth.

Ronald Reagan adopted this philosophy and made it the cornerstone of his economic policy. Toward this end, he strongly favored tax reduction, especially what economists call the marginal rate of taxation—the tax that applies to the last dollar earned. In 1980, this rate went as high as 70 percent at the federal level. Reagan proposed cutting this to 50 percent and reducing lower rates as well. He achieved this goal in 1981, and in 1986 was able to bring about a further reduction in the top rate to just 28 percent.

In 1988, Reagan was succeeded by his vice president, George H. W. Bush. Although he ran as if he would in effect fulfill Reagan's third term, Bush did not really share Reagan's tax vision, despite having pledged not to raise taxes in his acceptance speech at the Republican convention. In the 1990 budget agreement, Bush accepted a Democratic demand for higher taxes as part of the deal and the top rate was raised to 31 percent. This was widely viewed by conservatives as a betrayal of his convention pledge—"Read my lips: no new taxes," he said—and it undoubtedly contributed to his defeat in 1992.[11]

Development of the Bush Plan

When George W. Bush decided to run for the presidency in 1999, he clearly understood that he was carrying some baggage in the tax area, owing to his father's apostasy. He told Bob Bartley of the *Wall Street Journal* that breaking the tax pledge was his father's biggest political mistake. It destabilized the Republican base, he said, and allowed Pat Buchanan's insurgent presidential campaign to gain ground in 1992 as well as contributed to support for Ross Perot in the general election.[12]

Moreover, the younger Bush knew that he would have a tough fight for the Republican nomination from wealthy publisher Steve Forbes, who had come out of nowhere to challenge Bob Dole for the nomination in 1996 largely by campaigning on a big tax cut and the flat tax. These would be the foundation of Forbes' campaign for the nomination in 2000 as well.

For both of these reasons, therefore, Bush knew that he would have to make a significant tax cut a major part of his campaign platform. It would inoculate him against his father's mistake and undercut support for Forbes. Toward this end, Bush put together a group of economists led by Larry Lindsey to draft a tax cut for him.[13]

Lindsey and a few other economists worked throughout the summer of 1999 on a tax plan, meeting with Bush periodically to review options. It was unveiled on December 1 and its key element was a reduction in the top income tax rate from 39.6 percent (where it had been raised from 31 percent by Bill Clinton in 1993) to 33 percent, and the bottom rate from 15 percent to 10 percent. Other rates were also reduced. The rate cuts would be phased in over a period of years.

The plan also contained a number of gimmicky elements, including a new tax deduction for two-earner couples, allowing those who do not itemize to deduct charitable contributions anyway, doubling the child credit to $1,000, and increasing contribution limits on education savings accounts from $500 to $5,000. Subsequently, Bush also proposed new Individual Development Accounts, a refundable tax credit for health insurance, and a tax credit for financial institutions that matched savings by those with low incomes.

Yet another tax gimmick was a Bush proposal to allow teachers a deduction of up to $400 per year to buy unreimbursed school supplies.

"Teaching is noble work," Paul Gigot of the *Wall Street Journal* commented, "but is it $400-a-year more deserving than, say, policing or firefighting?" Gigot said that the idea deserved public ridicule and showed that Bush was little different from Al Gore in his willingness to "promise anything to win."[14]

Although the tax rate reductions were unobjectionable to Reaganites and supply-siders, most wanted something bolder. They had hoped at least to get the top rate back down to 31 percent, where it had been before Bill Clinton took office. "Compared to my flat tax plan, Bush's plan is a Mini-Me tax cut," Steve Forbes declared.[15] The right-wing *Manchester Union Leader* called Bush's plan "a slightly-enlarged Xerox copy of the namby-pamby plan passed by Congress earlier this year—a credit here, a deduction there, a couple of percentage points to go around."[16] Columnist Robert Novak complained that Bush had missed the boat on tax reform.[17]

It's important to keep in mind that the economy was booming at the time Bush announced his tax plan, growing at better than 4 percent per year. The unemployment rate was low and the stock market was skyrocketing.[18] In other words, there was no need for economic stimulus. Lindsey explained that the tax cut would be an insurance policy to make sure that growth continued.[19]

Another goal of the Bush plan was, simply, to take money away from the government. Rapid growth plus congressional gridlock—Bill Clinton blocked Republican tax and spending plans while Republican control of Congress blocked Clinton's—had led to the emergence of budget surpluses in 1998 and large surpluses were projected well into the future. Indeed, there was serious talk about literally paying off the national debt.

Although many conservatives liked the idea of paying off the debt, Bush's advisers were more concerned that surpluses would lead to new spending programs. By cutting taxes, this would take those funds away from the politicians and allow taxpayers to spend their own money. This was less of a tax policy than a political philosophy. And as a political platform, it proved successful, helping Bush win both the Republican nomination and the election in 2000.

Selling the Tax Cut in 2001

Presidents-elect normally rethink their campaign proposals after the election. Things that might have been said purely for political effect may be abandoned and others rethought in light of changed circumstances. For example, once in office, Bill Clinton quickly dropped his plan for a middle-class tax cut and instead turned to tax increases and deficit reduction.[20]

Also, presidents-elect now have access to government experts and data to more fully develop and refine their proposals. Interaction with these experts is usually done by transition teams, often made up of those who will be appointed to key positions in various departments and agencies. Sometimes deeper analysis than is possible on the campaign trail forces plans to be reevaluated or pushed aside.

George W. Bush was denied a normal transition period by the long recount after the 2000 election. He couldn't even start making appointments for top positions because there was no way of doing FBI background checks. Consequently, when the election was finally decided in December, Bush was well behind in his preparations for taking office on January 20.

Perhaps if he had had a normal transition period, Bush may have rethought his tax plan in light of current economic conditions. The stock market had peaked in March 2000, and by December it was generally recognized that the economy was in a slowdown, with many economists, including Larry Lindsey, forecasting a recession.[21] Yet rather than reconsider either the size or shape of his tax cut—which, remember, was devised to keep an economic boom going—Bush chose simply to stick with his original plan.

Although the plan didn't change, the rhetoric definitely did. President Bush and his advisers now talked primarily about the virtue of putting dollars into people's pockets and getting people to spend more, just like the old Keynesians did. And with projections of slow growth causing the budget surplus to evaporate by the day, they also stopped talking about the need to keep money away from greedy politicians. Anyway, those greedy politicians were now all Republicans, who controlled the White House and both houses of Congress simultaneously for the first time since 1954.

This basic change—away from supply-side economics and toward Keynesian economics—was immediately apparent to those on the political left, if not necessarily among Bush's supporters. "This weird revival of Keynesianism says a lot about the rickety intellectual basis for a large tax cut," wrote Sebastian Mallaby of the *Washington Post*.[22] Liberal columnist E. J. Dionne opined, "Bush wants a supply-side tax cut without making a supply-side case."[23] Said Princeton University economist Uwe Reinhardt, "Judging by their own words, President Bush and his advisers have all reverted to Keynesianism."[24]

It soon became obvious to Congress, if not the White House, that changed circumstances required a major change in the tax cut. In particular, there was widespread support for something that would put money into the economy fast. The idea of a quickie tax rebate became extremely popular on both sides of the political aisle.[25]

BUSH SUPPORTS A TAX REBATE

AS IS SO often the case in Washington, policymakers approach situations as if they were unique and ideas as if they had never been tried before. Thus the experience of the 1975 tax rebate was completely ignored in the rush to enact another rebate in 2001.

The first rebate bill was signed into law on March 29, 1975, and equaled 10 percent of a taxpayer's 1974 tax bill, with a minimum of $100 per taxpayer and a maximum of $200.[26] In theory, taxpayers were to take the checks and immediately go out and buy stuff, which would encourage more production, raise employment, and stimulate economic growth. This was the epitome of Keynesian thinking.

However, even by Keynesian standards, the 1975 rebate proved to be a total bust. Studies by economists Alan Blinder, Franco Modigliani (winner of the Nobel Prize in economics in 1985), and Charles Steindel prove conclusively that most of the rebate was saved or used to pay down debt rather than spent. In short, it provided no Keynesian stimulus to spending and thus no increase in economic growth.[27] Although the higher saving may have been helpful, it was completely canceled out by the increase in the budget deficit to pay for the rebate. In other words, the government's negative saving offset the higher private saving, leaving nothing additional left over for new investment.

Nevertheless, once the idea of a rebate took hold in 2001, there was no stopping it and Bush fully embraced it, signing it into law on June 7. *Wall Street Journal* editor Bob Bartley said that Bush was invoking the ghost of Keynes.[28] Steve Forbes called the rebate "crazy."[29] At least Treasury Secretary Paul O'Neill, a senior official in the Office of Management and Budget in 1975, understood that the rebate was an addition to the Bush tax cut and not a substitute for it.

"Some suggest we send a rebate to the taxpayers now, and stop there," O'Neill said. "That's not good enough. I was here when we tried that in 1975, and it just didn't work. If we want to change consumption patterns, we need to make permanent changes in people's tax burdens."[30]

In the end, Congress enacted the rebate as an advance on the tax rate reduction, which lowered the bottom tax rate from 15 percent to 10 percent. Since even the richest taxpayers paid some taxes at the 15 percent rate, everyone with a positive tax liability would pay lower taxes in 2001, which would be reflected on the returns they filed the following year. This is where the rebate came from.

Despite his misgivings, O'Neill threw his considerable managerial skills into getting the rebate checks out as soon as possible. The first checks, totaling $300 to $600 per taxpayer, went out the week of July 23 and continued through September 24. In total, $35.5 billion was distributed.[31]

Polls and press reports immediately made clear that this was going to be a replay of 1975. Large retailers like Sears were so doubtful of any increase in sales resulting from the rebate that they didn't even bother aiming their advertising at it.[32] A Gallup poll taken during the second week in July found that just 17 percent of respondents expected to spend their rebate. The rest would save it or use it to pay bills, which is the same thing economically.[33] Other polls by Bloomberg and the University of Michigan confirmed these results.[34]

Of course, people may tell pollsters one thing and then do another. However, subsequent economic research concluded, just as studies of the 1975 rebate had done, that it was a very ineffective tool of economic stimulus. Little of the money was spent, most was saved, and the impact on economic growth was minimal.[35]

FINAL TAX BILL

ALTHOUGH IT WAS lousy economics, the addition of the rebate to the 2001 tax bill unquestionably aided its final passage. Unfortunately, it and other add-ons to the original Bush proposal ballooned its cost, forcing a scale-back of some important provisions, which undermined their effectiveness.

The final bill cut the top rate from 39.6 percent to 35 percent, rather than 33 percent as Bush had proposed. Moreover, this rate cut was phased in very slowly. The top rate would fall by just one point to 38.6 percent from 2001 to 2003, by another point in 2004 and 2005, and not reach 35 percent until 2006.

Many economists argued against this tax policy. The cut in the top rate arguably was the most economically powerful element of the Bush plan. Harvard economist Martin Feldstein argued that it would have cost virtually nothing in terms of lost revenue to make the rate cut effective immediately or even to go further and cut the top rate to 28 percent, where it had been from 1987 to 1992.

"Cutting the top personal income tax rate to 28 percent from 33 percent would cut total revenue by very little," Feldstein explained.

"Even if changes in taxpayer behavior are ignored, the estimated cost of the tax plan would increase by only about five percent. The behavioral responses of taxpayers to the lower marginal tax rates would offset two-thirds of that estimated additional revenue loss."[36]

Subsequent analysis showed that the phase-in of the rate cuts was economically damaging, because taxpayers pushed income into the future when it would be taxed less. The result was actually to slow economic growth from what would have been the case had Congress enacted no tax cut at all. A 2004 paper by economists Christopher House and Matthew Shapiro, both of the University of Michigan, concluded that "the slow recovery from the 2001 recession may have been, in part, attributable to declines in labor supply owing to the phased-in nature of the income tax reductions."[37]

Although no conservative opposed the 2001 tax bill, few cheered it, feeling that it had too many tax gimmicks in it and too little in the way of tax rate reductions. Said Tom Donlan of *Barron's:* "All we ever wanted, all we ever need is lower tax rates for all taxpayers; instead the President gives us a witch's brew."[38]

Alan Reynolds of the Cato Institute spoke for most supply-siders when he said, "The primary objective of the $1.35 trillion cut passed Memorial Day weekend seems to have been to maximize revenue loss rather than to minimize tax distortions and tax disincentives."[39]

Former House Ways and Means Committee chairman Bill Archer, Republican of Texas, complained that all the new tax gimmicks would make fundamental tax reform harder to accomplish in the future.[40] Adding new special provisions to the tax code created new constituencies for the status quo, he said, making it harder to put together a coalition that would support wiping the slate clean and getting rid of all special provisions.

Even those who were inclined to be more charitable had to admit that the expiration of the entire tax cut in 2010 undermined much of its economic value. The reason for this was that congressional Republicans needed to use a technical budget procedure known as "reconciliation" to get the tax cut enacted over a potential Democratic filibuster. But under Senate rules, permanent changes in law could not be made using this procedure. Hence, nothing in the tax bill could be in effect for more than ten years.

Theoretically, therefore, the top rate would go back to 39.6 percent on January 1, 2011. All the other rate cuts and tax changes would also expire and go back to their pre-2001 levels. This was especially bizarre in the case of the estate tax, which was scheduled to disappear in 2010 and then reappear, phoenixlike, in 2011. This led some estate planners to worry about what might happen to wealthy individuals on life-support in late 2010—a few weeks of additional life could mean a significantly higher tax bill.

TAX CREDIT MANIA

DESPITE HAVING JUST enacted one of the largest tax cuts in American history, and with tax rebates still in the mail, the reaction in Congress to the terrorist attacks of September 11, 2001, was to propose still more rebates.

In October, the House of Representatives passed a bill abolishing the Corporate Alternative Minimum Tax and giving businesses a retroactive rebate for past payments under that tax.[41] In effect, America's biggest corporations would get $25 billion in rebate checks, just as individual taxpayers had gotten earlier. Ford Motor Company would have gotten one for $2.3 billion and IBM one for $1.4 billion. I identified the source of this absurd policy in the theory underlying the individual rebates in a *Wall Street Journal* article.

"The AMT rebate plan is the logical extension of making tax rebates to individuals the centerpiece of the Bush administration's earlier tax legislation," I wrote. "The idea is that putting dollars into peoples' pockets will cause them to spend, thereby stimulating growth. By the same logic, putting dollars into corporate coffers presumably will cause businesses to invest."[42]

Harvard economist Robert Barro echoed these sentiments. Writing in *BusinessWeek,* he said, "One thing we surely do not need is more rebates, which were never a net economic stimulus."[43]

Unfortunately, the rebate concept was consistent with the drift of Republican tax thinking since 1994. Up until that time, Republicans had understood that changes in marginal tax rates were the key to changing economic behavior. Hence, things like raising the personal exemption were consistent with the idea of reducing marginal rates—if taxable income is reduced, then this will tend to lower the tax rate on the last taxable dollar.

But in the early 1990s, Republicans lost sight of the importance of thinking at the margin. They stopped talking about raising personal exemptions and instead adopted the idea of giving people a tax credit just for having children. A tax credit differs from a tax exemption in that it subtracts directly from one's tax liability, whereas an exemption or deduction only reduces taxable income. Thus, a tax credit saves everyone the same dollar amount of taxes, while the tax saving from a deduction or exemption will depend on one's tax bracket.[44]

As best as I can tell, this fundamental change in tax philosophy was done for no other reason than simple math. It was easier to tell people exactly what their tax saving would be with a tax credit than with a higher exemption.[45] But the result was to blur the distinction between taxing and spending. What difference is there, really, between a $500 tax credit and a $500 per taxpayer spending program? The answer is that there is little difference at all conceptually.

Moreover, there is literally no difference between a tax credit and a spending program in some cases because credits have become refundable, meaning that one can get a tax refund from the government even if one pays no income taxes. This is why the Earned Income Tax Credit has become the largest federal welfare program.[46] And there is growing pressure to make the child credit refundable as well. This has encouraged liberals to simply convert their own welfare proposals into refundable tax credits and label them as "tax cuts."[47]

As Shawn Macomber of the conservative *American Spectator* magazine put it, "Conservative eagerness to surrender when debate over family tax credits comes up has only emboldened the opposition to push harder."[48]

Thus, by adopting tax credits as a key part of their tax policy, Republicans became more like Democrats. Not too many years earlier, Republicans had understood the difference. When Jimmy Carter proposed converting the personal exemption into a tax credit in 1978, it was universally opposed on the Republican side. "The idea of converting exemptions into credits is bad tax policy," the *Wall Street Journal* editorialized at the time.[49] In September 2001, it made the same argument.

"Tax credits have nothing to do with 'fiscal stimulus,'" the *Journal* said. "They are social, not economic, policy. If this sort of tax policy spurred economic growth, the Bush tax rebate would already have done the trick. It was based on the same logic: that taxpayers will spend any tax windfall and consumer spending will spur the economy."[50]

When Republicans put forward yet another special tax gimmick to help tsunami victims in early 2005, Andrew Ferguson, a speechwriter for George H. W. Bush, concluded that Reaganism in the Republican Party was "deader than the Dodo."[51]

POST-9/11 TAX POLICY

THE HOUSE PROPOSAL for a business rebate died in the Senate. But Congress did allow businesses to deduct or depreciate new investments in capital equipment more rapidly. Since lagging business investment was a leading cause of slow economic growth, it was hoped that this would encourage firms to move up investment plans and stimulate growth and employment.

Although the so-called bonus depreciation was hailed by all supply-siders as a move in the right direction, once again they were disappointed by the way the White House sold it. It was basically Keynesian economics on the business side—getting businesses to spend.

The Bush Administration would have been on stronger ground, economically, if it had argued that increased depreciation allowances were a move toward fundamental tax reform. Supply-siders, especially the late economist Norman Ture, have long argued that no business can really be said to have a profit until it has recovered all its costs of production, including investments in capital equipment. Hence, businesses should be allowed to write off immediately or "expense" capital equipment, just as they have always been allowed to deduct wages and raw materials.[52]

Economist Vernon L. Smith, winner of the Nobel Prize in economics in 2002, argues that expensing would also improve the fairness and simplicity of the tax code. Businesses would no longer have to differentiate between capital expenses and operating expenses, keep extensive records on the dates that equipment was put into service and taken out of service, or worry about precisely what depreciation schedule applies to each asset.[53]

The second major Bush tax cut, with the bonus depreciation provision, was signed into law on March 9, 2002. But almost immediately there were calls for yet another tax cut. Writing in the conservative *Weekly Standard* magazine on April 8, economist Steve Moore said that the tax cuts already enacted had done virtually nothing to stimulate growth. Tax policy changes, he said, "had little to do with the nation's improved economic performance."[54]

This proved to be the opening shot of yet another tax-cutting effort, which gathered steam during the summer. Treasury Secretary Paul O'Neill suggested an economic conference where a coherent, coordinated economic policy could be developed. Bush agreed and in August convened an economic summit in Waco, near his home in Crawford, Texas, and invited a variety of economists and business leaders to explain to him why the economy was still lagging despite two major rounds of tax cuts.

The speaker who appeared most to impress Bush was stockbroker Charles Schwab, who argued that the double taxation of dividends was retarding investment. This suggestion dovetailed with what some of Bush's own advisers were thinking and led to the third major tax cut of the Bush presidency.

Taxing Dividends

Although the theory that a cut in dividend taxes would boost the stock market was somewhat dubious—as was the idea that a boost in the stock market would stimulate economic growth—the idea of eliminating the double taxation of dividends was well grounded in principle.[55] Unfortunately, inept White House political strategy almost seized defeat from the jaws of victory.

Since at least the 1930s, most economists have recognized that the corporate income tax is essentially a double tax that raises the cost of capital and has other undesirable economic effects. When income is earned by a corporation it is taxed and then the same income is taxed again when paid out to its owners, the shareholders, in the form of dividends. In theory, corporations should be taxed no differently than sole proprietorships or partnerships, where income is taxed only once.[56]

William Vickrey, winner of the Nobel Prize in economics in 1996, spoke for most economists when he called for abolition of the corporate income tax in his presidential address to the American Economic Association. It "inflicts a double whammy on the economy," he said, that ultimately hurts workers most because it reduces investment, which lowers productivity and, eventually, wages.[57]

Over the years, a long line of Republicans and Democrats, liberals and conservatives, have called for abolition of the corporate income tax in order to eliminate double taxation.[58] In 1976, Jimmy Carter campaigned on the idea of taxing income only once.[59] The following year, the New York Times even ran an editorial entitled "Abolish the Corporate Income Tax."[60]

In the 1980s, Ronald Reagan talked often about how all taxes were ultimately paid by individuals. Corporations merely collected the taxes and did not bear any tax burden themselves.[61] In 1992, George H. W. Bush's Treasury Department issued an extensive report on integrating the corporate and individual income taxes into a single tax system.[62]

Treasury Secretary Paul O'Neill had been thinking about how to get rid of the corporate income tax long before Bush's Waco conference. In an interview with the *Financial Times* in May 2001, he called it "an abomination" and said that Bush was "intrigued" with doing something about it.[63] Moreover, the chairman of Bush's Council of Economic Advisers, R. Glenn Hubbard, had actually written the 1992 Treasury report and was probably the leading academic authority on the economics of the corporate income tax.[64]

Consequently, the ground was already well plowed when Schwab made his suggestion for abolishing the corporate double tax by allowing individuals to receive dividends tax-free. This proposal formed the basis of a new tax proposal put forward in January 2003 for Bush's fiscal year 2004 budget.

However, Congress was starting to become concerned about the budget, which had gone from substantial surplus to large deficit in just two years. This made it impossible to enact full elimination of taxes on dividends, as Bush had proposed.

At this point the White House adopted a strategy that even its supporters found difficult to comprehend. It insisted on making dividends fully tax-free even if only for a single year, in hopes that it could extend the provision in later years. Should such a measure have passed, however, its economic impact would have been virtually nil, since corporations are not going to increase their investment based on a tax provision without any degree of permanence.

Bill Thomas, chairman of the House Ways and Means Committee, proposed an alternative, in which both the capital gains tax and the tax on dividends would fall to just 15 percent, from a maximum of 20 percent and 38.6 percent, respectively. This modest scale-back could be enacted for five years under the budget cap, whereas the president's proposal could be done for only three years, eventually cut back to just one year after its cost was revised upward.

Nevertheless, the White House fought the Thomas plan. Conservative economist Kevin Hassett of the American Enterprise Institute called this "bizarre" since Thomas's plan would have had just as positive an economic impact as the original Bush proposal.[65] Cato's Alan Reynolds said Bush's all-or-nothing approach showed a failure of leadership.[66]

In the end Bush caved and supported the Thomas plan. It was signed into law on May 28, 2003. But the fact that there was any tax cut at all owed far more to Representative Thomas's leadership than to Bush's.

First Term Wrap

TAXES PLAYED A surprisingly small part in the 2004 presidential campaign. John Kerry's plans were not very bold, and although he was critical of Bush's tax cuts, he resisted calling for their repeal. Bush's principal initiative was to call for a tax reform commission. This puzzled many conservatives because it implied that Bush had no vision of tax reform himself, otherwise he would simply have asked the Treasury Department to draft such a plan, as Ronald Reagan had done in 1984.

Indeed, a lack of vision proved to be the hallmark of Bush's first-term tax policy. There was a lot of effort and much was accomplished, but it ultimately added up to very little economically. Much revenue was sacrificed to achieve not very much in terms of improving the tax code or stimulating economic growth. Although the tax cuts undoubtedly raised the growth rate a bit, their impact was far less than that of the Federal Reserve, which cut interest rates sharply. Even if taxes had not been cut at all, the normal working of the business cycle would have led to an upturn in growth.

In retrospect, if Bush had had a vision of tax reform, much more could have been accomplished with the revenue that was available. He could have gone a long way toward implementing a flat rate tax system, for example.[67] Instead, we ended up with a tax code that was much more complicated and more riddled with gimmicks and loopholes than it was before Bush took office. If Congress ever does seriously take up tax reform, much of what Bush accomplished will have to be reversed.

In 2005, just before his tax reform commission was due to report, Bush signed into law a grab bag of energy tax gimmicks—I mean incentives—designed to encourage production and conservation. The Joint Committee on Taxation's report on these tax provisions ran to 139 pages, suggesting at a minimum that simplification was not among the bill's accomplishments. Every one of them would have to be repealed under any vision of fundamental tax reform, liberal or conservative. It was an inauspicious start to the debate on tax reform that Bush hoped to have in 2006.

CHAPTER 4

THE WORST LEGISLATION
IN HISTORY?

AT 3:01 A.M. ON SATURDAY, NOVEMBER 22, 2003, SPEAKER OF the House pro tempore Doc Hastings, Republican of Washington, gaveled to an end debate on S. 877, the Medicare Prescription Drug, Improvement, and Modernization Act of 2003, and ordered the House of Representatives to vote on final passage of this landmark legislation. Pursuant to standard practice and Rule XX of the House of Representatives, he said this would be a fifteen-minute vote. Almost three hours later, members of the House were still voting.

A few weeks earlier, on October 29, forty-one members of the House Republican Study Committee had written to the House Republican leadership insisting that the final Medicare drug bill be made available for at least three days prior to any vote, so that members could study the provisions.[1] This was not done. The conference report was filed at 1:17 A.M. on November 21 and House debate began that same day, culminating in a vote the following morning.

The congressmen signing the RSC letter did not explicitly promise to vote against the drug bill if their concerns were disregarded. However, their principal demand was so minimal—they just wanted to know exactly what they were voting for—that the leadership's decision to bring the bill up for an immediate vote could not be interpreted as anything but utter disrespect for forty-one members of the Republican caucus, not to mention the legislative process.

Needless to say, hardly any member of the House was actually able to read the conference report, which was not even printed and ran to hundreds of pages of indecipherable legalese, before casting their votes. Even many of those supporting the legislation felt that such undue haste was inappropriate for a measure that was expected to cost $400 billion over the next ten years.

With virtually united opposition from Democrats, the White House and Republican leaders in the House found themselves in a jam. The bill was losing by a vote of 216 to 218 when time was up. So the vote was kept open while arms were twisted to get the last couple of votes needed for passage. The record indicates that in the end, Congressmen Ernest Istook (R-OK), Trent Franks (R-AZ), Butch Otter (R-ID), Jim Marshall (D-GA), Calvin Dooley (D-CA), and David Scott (D-GA) changed their votes from "nay" to "yea."

When the vote finally ended at 5:53 A.M., the count was 220 in favor and 215 against the drug bill. (Jeff Miller, Republican of Florida, and John Culberson, Republican of Texas, switched their votes from "yea" to "nay" at the last minute, suggesting that they would have voted favorably if their votes were really needed for passage.)[2] During the whole time the vote was ongoing, C-SPAN's cameras, which are controlled by the House leadership and normally pan from side to side of the House chamber, were trained exclusively on the Democratic side, so that viewers could not see the furious arm-twisting on the Republican side.[3]

To their everlasting discredit, twenty-five signers of the RSC letter caved in and voted for the drug bill, even though their concerns were completely ignored. The roll of the ignoble (all Republicans) includes John Kline (MN), Michael Burgess (TX), Randy Neugebauer (TX), Virgil Goode (VA), Trent Franks (AZ), Joe Pitts (PA), Roscoe Bartlett

(MD), Johnny Isakson (GA), Dave Weldon (FL), Donald Manzullo (IL), Ernest Istook (OK), Sue Myrick (NC), Phil Crane (IL), Pete Hoekstra (MI), Kevin Brady (TX), Mac Thornberry (TX), Tim Murphy (PA), John Carter (TX), Devin Nunes (CA), Mark Souder (IN), Mark Kennedy (MN), Chris Chocola (IN), Steve King (IA), John Boozman (AR), and Randy Forbes (VA).

Congressman Otter tried to justify his vote switch on the grounds that failure of the bill under consideration would have led to passage of an even more costly one.[4] This is absurd. Since Republicans controlled the House of Representatives, the leadership would simply have pulled the bill off the floor in the event of defeat.

Subsequently, it was discovered just how much pressure had been brought to bear on recalcitrant Republicans. Rep. Nick Smith (R-MI), who was retiring from the House in 2004, reported that explicit offers of financial support and endorsements were made for his son Brad, who hoped to succeed him in Congress, if Smith would only support the drug bill. Smith stuck to his no-vote and his son was defeated.

Because Smith went public with his experience, the House Ethics Committee was obliged to investigate what appeared to be a blatant case of bribery—money in return for a congressional vote. House Majority Leader Tom DeLay (R-TX) was fingered as the one who made the offer and he was "admonished" for doing so in a September 30, 2004, report from the committee.[5] This slap on the wrist, however, did not in any way diminish DeLay's power.

I was personally stunned by the heavy-handed effort to get the drug bill passed. Throughout the summer of 2003, the White House signaled that Bush would sign *any* bill, no matter what was in it.[6] This position seemed so irresponsible, I assumed that Bush was playing a game of trying to have it both ways—appearing to be for the drug bill while all along knowing that it was probably impossible for the House and Senate to reconcile their differences on the legislation. So the realization that the White House was serious all along came to me as a disturbing revelation.

COSTS ARE COVERED UP

JUST HOW SERIOUS the administration had been became apparent after the drug bill was safely signed into law, when it became known that it had covered up internal estimates of the cost of the legislation, which was limited to $400 billion by the congressional budget resolution. Any amount higher than this would have been subject to a point of order that at least would have delayed the legislation and more than likely derailed it altogether.

Throughout most of American history, when Congress needed an estimate of the cost of a new program, it was provided by the administration. But in the early 1970s, Congress decided that it could not trust the numbers coming out of Richard Nixon's Office of Management and Budget, and so it established the Congressional Budget Office to "crunch" its own numbers, which are official for legislative purposes.

Normally the CBO works closely with its administration counterparts so that their estimates are not far off from one another. If they differ, CBO tries to make clear how and why. This transparency helps avoid mistakes and gives Congress the best available information on which to base its decisions.

But the CBO is a relatively small organization and is often vitally dependent on raw data from agencies such as the Census Bureau, Social Security Administration, and others to be able to estimate the budgetary effects of programs. And because of the highly technical nature of budgetary analysis, especially for new programs that may have unknown effects on people's behavior, CBO must work closely with the administration, which may have much more staff and deeper resources to draw upon.

In the case of the drug bill, the key administration analyst was Richard Foster, chief actuary for the Centers for Medicare & Medicaid Services (CMS). During the summer of 2003, as Congress was debating the drug bill, he concluded that CBO's estimate of the cost of the legislation was too low. CBO had put the net budgetary cost at $394.3 billion between 2004 and 2013, but Foster had come to the conclusion that the real number would be much higher.

Before explaining the significance of this, it is important to understand how artificial both CBO's and Foster's estimates were. That is because the new drug benefit would not actually take effect until 2006—two years into the estimation period—and then be phased in over a period of years. Thus, CBO had spending going from virtually nothing in 2004 and 2005 to $27.6 billion in 2006, $40.2 billion in 2007, and rising to $65.1 billion in 2013, the last year estimated. In other words, spending would be more than twice as great in the second five years of the program as in the first five years: $122.1 billion versus $272.2 billion.

And, of course, it was extremely artificial that the cost of the drug bill was estimated for only ten years in the first place. As a program designed to be a permanent addition to Medicare, its cost should have been calculated in perpetuity. An estimate by two respected economists, well before the final vote, concluded that the unfunded liability of the Bush Administration's original proposal was $6 trillion and that the Senate version would have had an unfunded liability of $12 trillion.[7]

Consequently, it was laughable when, in early 2005, the ten-year cost of the drug benefit suddenly escalated to almost $800 billion, causing much wailing among members of Congress who were shocked, shocked, to discover that this law cost more than they thought.[8] The bulk of the CBO reestimate, however, consisted of simply changing its ten-year forecast window from 2004–2013 to 2006–2015, thus dropping two low-cost years at the front end, in which total spending for the drug benefit was just $2.5 billion, and adding two high-cost years at the back end, in which spending would be $112.7 billion and $126.7 billion, respectively.[9]

But it was critical to passage of the drug bill in 2003 that it not be one penny greater than $400 billion over the 2004–2013 period. If there were even serious doubts about this estimate, it probably would have made it impossible to get those last couple of votes necessary to pass the legislation in the House. Therefore, it was essential that any hint of doubt about the $400 billion estimate be buried until after the bill was signed into law.

The problem was that Foster had concluded well before the final vote that the true cost of the drug benefit would actually be $534 billion over the initial ten years—a third higher than CBO was estimating. There was little doubt within the administration that release of Foster's estimate would kill the drug bill. As the *Wall Street Journal* observed, "It is undeniable that the Medicare bill wouldn't have passed in its current form had $540 billion been the accepted cost fiction."[10]

Foster was a career employee of the Department of Health & Human Services who probably couldn't have been fired from the government. But he could have been removed as chief actuary, demoted, transferred, and otherwise punished if he ran afoul of his political boss, Tom Scully, CMS administrator.

In any event, Scully threatened Foster with being fired should he disclose any information to Congress that the drug bill would cost more than $400 billion before it was signed into law. Sadly, Foster caved in to the pressure, kept his mouth shut, and allowed a massively expensive piece of legislation to pass Congress under false pretenses.

TRUE COSTS COME OUT TOO LATE

BUT AS IS SO often the case in Washington, the truth did eventually out, disclosed by reporter Amy Goldstein in the *Washington Post* on January 31, 2004—almost six weeks after the drug benefit had been signed into law by President Bush. She reported that the $534 billion estimate, which eventually appeared in the president's budget, was widely known among those who negotiated the final provisions of the legislation.[11] Even the CBO was eventually forced to admit that its original estimate was off and that the original ten-year forecast should have been $557.7 billion.[12]

It has never been clear precisely who is lying here—administration sources, like Health & Human Services Secretary Tommy Thompson, who claimed that up-to-date estimates were given to congressional leaders (at least on the Republican side; Democrats plausibly claim they were always kept in the dark), or the congressional leaders who kept this information secret lest it derail the legislation.[13]

Eventually, the HHS inspector general concluded that Scully had withheld information requested by Congress, but that no laws were violated.[14] Were he still a government employee at that point, he would have been liable for disciplinary action. But by the time the IG investigation was completed, Scully was back in the private sector. As a *Los Angeles Times* editorial observed, this made him "a convenient fall guy."[15]

With the buck stopping with Scully, the investigation into what the White House knew about the true cost of the drug bill before its enactment ground to a halt. For this, Scully's career as a lobbyist has no doubt been rewarded at 1600 Pennsylvania Avenue. Unfortunately, taxpayers and retirees will long pay the price for this ill-considered legislation, from which they might have been spared had the truth not been covered up at a critical moment in time.

Robert Moffit of the Heritage Foundation spoke for most conservatives on this disgraceful episode. "There's no excuse for what the administration did," he said. "The people who were hurt the most were congressional Republicans who put their faith in estimates that turned out to be wrong."[16]

The clearest indication of precisely how costly the drug bill actually was came on March 23, 2004, when the Medicare trustees issued their annual report, as required by law. It contained estimates by Medicare's actuaries, headed by Foster, which cannot be edited by political appointees. They showed that over the first seventy-five years of the drug program—now known as Medicare Part D—the cost would be $10.8 trillion in present value terms, with taxpayers footing the bill for $8.1 trillion of that.[17]

What this meant is that there would have to be a fund of $8.1 trillion, outside the government in a mutual fund earning private returns, to pay the future costs of the program for seventy-five years over and above the modest premiums that recipients pay. Without that, future benefit cuts and/or tax increases are inevitable.

But even this massive figure is only part of the story. In the 2004 Medicare trustees report, the actuaries presented for the first time cost estimates in perpetuity. This is important information because much of the cost of the drug program actually comes more than seventy-five years in the future. The actuaries estimated that this cost, again in present value terms, was $21.9 trillion, of which $16.6 trillion was unfunded. That is, taxpayers will have to pay $16.6 trillion out of their income taxes in the future to pay for the drug benefit.

In 2005, the Medicare trustees upped their estimate of the long-term cost of the drug benefit to $18.2 trillion. It's hard to put such a number into a context that people can understand—they can barely comprehend billions, let alone trillions. But according to the actuaries, $18.2 trillion in present value terms is equivalent to 1.9 percent of the gross domestic product forever. In 2005, this would have come to $232 billion—more than all the corporate income taxes collected by the federal government and 26 percent of all personal income taxes. In other words, the individual income tax would have to rise by 26 percent immediately and forever just to pay for the drug program.

Interestingly, the Social Security actuaries estimated in 2005 that the unfunded obligation for that program in perpetuity was just $11.1 trillion (present value).[18] This means that if the drug program were repealed, then Social Security could be funded forever without having to raise taxes or cut benefits, and the federal government would still be able to cut $7.1 trillion off its long-term indebtedness. It's too bad that some Democrat didn't propose this as an alternative to President Bush's Social Security reform legislation.

What is really scary is that all estimates of health care spending have erred on the low side. This is especially the case for new programs, where actuaries have little experience or data to guide them. Thus, if one looks at the first report of the Medicare trustees in 1966, it estimated spending for that program (hospital insurance only) at $8.8 billion in 1990 (as far out as the estimate went). It actually was $67 billion—7.6 times greater than estimated.[19]

It is doubtful that the nation can even afford the cost of the drug benefit as it is. If it turns out to be low by a factor of seven or eight over the next twenty-five years, then it is clear that the program is grossly unsustainable. This is even more obviously the case when one looks at the projected increases for the rest of Medicare, Parts A and B, which pay for hospitalization and doctor's visits, respectively. According to the 2005 estimate by the actuaries, the unfunded liability (present value in perpetuity) for Part A was $24.1 trillion and another $25.8 trillion for Part B, for a grand total of $68.1 trillion for the entire Medicare program, equivalent to 7.1 percent of GDP forever—about the same as the entire individual income tax.

Thus, in theory, we could abolish Medicare along with the individual income tax and the national balance sheet would be unchanged. Of course, that is not going to happen. But it helps put into perspective the cost Americans are paying for the Medicare program. In effect, every dollar of federal income taxes we pay goes to finance just one thing: Medicare.

REPUBLICANS SELL THEIR SOULS

ONCE UPON A time in the not-too-distant past, Republicans were deeply skeptical about so-called entitlement programs like Medicare. These are programs for which no annual appropriation is necessary. Spending is automatic for everyone and everything that meets specified criteria.[20] In the case of Medicare, the principal criterion is simply being at least sixty-five years old. Historically, Republicans have felt that such programs—virtually free of budgetary control—were the epitome of bad policy. Ronald Reagan's Office of Management and Budget director

David Stockman articulated this position well during an appearance on the ABC News program *Issues and Answers* on March 22, 1981.

Said Stockman: "I don't believe that there is any entitlement, any basic right to legal services or any other kinds of services, and the idea that's been established over the last ten years that almost every service that someone might need in life ought to be provided, financed by the government as a matter of basic right, is wrong. We challenge that. We reject that notion."

Although Stockman later got into trouble for some things he said to a reporter that almost cost him his job, this was not one of them. On this occasion, he was reflecting a widely held view within the Republican Party on the evil of entitlements.

Fast forward twenty-two years and we see a very different philosophy within the Republican Party. Instead of fighting entitlements, the party now embraces them.

It would be one thing if this flip-flop were based on some careful analysis of elderly medical care, which concluded that expanded drug availability might reduce unnecessary hospitalization. Indeed, it would be possible to make such a case. Columbia University economist Frank Lichtenberg, for example, has done considerable research showing that drug innovation can save money by reducing the demand for other forms of medical care.[21]

However, this was not the situation. It is quite clear that Republican support for this massively expensive new entitlement program was based on one thing and one thing only: votes. The elderly wanted subsidies to pay for the rapidly rising cost of prescription drugs, they are a very large and growing part of the population who vote in the highest percentages of any age group, and Republicans wanted their support.[22] Therefore, they threw all budgetary restraint aside (along with their principles) and simply gave the elderly what they wanted in order to buy their votes.

Lichtenberg, by the way, opposed the legislation as devised solely to meet a political need, with no economic rationale whatsoever. He told

Daniel Altman of the *New York Times,* "This just seems like a creature of political expediency or compromise. It's not plausible to me that there's really an economic logic to the political policy that's being proposed."[23]

It is revealing that on the eve of the final congressional vote, former House Speaker Newt Gingrich, Republican of Georgia, who had led the charge in cutting Medicare in 1995 after Republicans took control of Congress, urged his fellow Republicans to vote for the drug bill in a *Wall Street Journal* op-ed. His core argument was simple politics: Vote for the drug bill or go back to being in the minority. "Obstructionist conservatives can always find reasons to vote no," he said, "but that path leads right back into the minority and it would be a minority status they would deserve."[24]

Objective political professionals were less sure that the drug bill was really in the GOP's interest. Charlie Cook, one of the best, wrote in July 2003, "For all this talk about prescription drugs being a breakthrough issue for the GOP, I think it just as easily could become a liability they really don't need given everything else that is going on." Cook thought that by not giving seniors the more generous bill pushed by Democrats, they were bound to be disappointed by the smaller version written by Republicans. Eventually there would be a backlash and Republicans would be worse off politically than if they had done nothing.[25]

Business Week's Howard Gleckman warned that seniors were anticipating drug benefits as generous as those offered by corporate pension plans, which typically covered 70 percent of drug costs. With the new Medicare drug benefit picking up only about a third, disappointment was baked into the cake. When the program finally takes effect in 2006, there is guaranteed to be widespread complaints from seniors, even from those who previously had no drug coverage at all, when it doesn't meet their expectations.[26]

Instead of listening to Newt on this occasion, Republicans would have been a lot better off listening to, of all people, Sen. Ted Kennedy of Massachusetts, the principal liberal in the Democratic Party for forty years. In the summer of 2003 he bucked his own party's leaders, who were adamantly opposed to the Republican bill on the grounds that it was not generous enough, and endorsed it.[27] Said Kennedy on CNN's *Inside Politics* on June 18, the drug bill was "just a down payment." When it was passed, "We're going to come back again and again and again and fight to make sure that we have a good program."

In the Middle East, they call this the camel's nose under the tent. Unless you act immediately, pretty soon the whole camel is inside the tent.

Political Backlash

The irony is that Republicans appear to have bought themselves very little additional support among the elderly for the multitrillion-dollar largesse they bestowed upon them. Every poll taken in the wake of the drug bill's passage showed a high level of dissatisfaction among the elderly. The titles on the releases by various polling organizations well summarize their findings:

ABC News/*Washington Post:* "Muted Reception Greets Medicare Reform Bill" (December 8, 2003).

Gallup: "Medicare Changes Fall Short with Seniors" (January 27, 2004).

Kaiser Family Foundation: "Survey Finds People with Medicare More Negative Than Positive Toward New Drug Law" (August 10, 2004).

Contributing to the political letdown from the drug legislation were reports that drug prices were rising so rapidly that the new subsidy was barely going to cover the ongoing increase, thus doing nothing to improve the affordability of prescription drugs.[28] According to a May 2004 AARP study, the 197 most commonly used name-brand drugs had risen in price by 27.6 percent over the previous four years, compared with a general price level increase of just 10.4 percent.[29]

Commenting on the study, Ron Pollock of Families USA said, "It's the functional equivalent of going to a used car salesman and being told you're getting a great deal because you got a $3,000 discount. Only before you came, he raised the price of the car by $4,000."[30]

The GOP's political error became apparent almost immediately. In a February 2004 *Washington Post* story, reporters Amy Goldstein and Helen Dewar found that discontent was so strong in Congress that the drug bill would fail if the vote were taken again. They quoted Sen. Lindsey Graham, Republican of South Carolina, as saying, "There is buyers' remorse among many who voted for it."

Goldstein and Dewar found Democrats already gloating. Said Congressman Rahm Emanuel, Chicago Democrat and former Clinton White House operative, "Republicans thought they were going to get a big political bang. They've got a dud. Unless they turn perceptions around, they've got an anchor around their neck."[31]

Among political conservatives, there was universal disgust at the administration's actions in ramming a bad bill through Congress and covering up its true cost. *National Review* editor Rich Lowry reflected a widely held view on the right in his February 2, 2004, column:

> The Medicare revision—up 30 percent in just two months—is just a taste of the entitlement cost explosion to come as retiring boomers begin to fatten themselves on all the benefits of the Geriatric State. Instead of trimming back and reforming retirement benefits, the administration and Congress added to them last year. Ronald Reagan used to say that calling Congress drunken sailors was unfair to drunken sailors. It still is. Drunken sailors might spend freely, but at least it's their own money and at least they don't live in fear of elderly voters complaining that they aren't getting enough free drinks.[32]

Conservative columnist Robert Novak wrote in his newsletter in March 2004, "The Medicare drug prescription bill, crafted by the White House and the congressional Republican leadership, now is shaping up as a political disaster with Bush accused of falsifying its massive price tag. Designed to give short-term political pleasure at the cost of long-term pain, there is now also short-term pain apparent."[33]

By summer, most political observers agreed that the drug benefit was a failure politically, giving no boost whatsoever to George Bush or congressional Republicans. "The measure is a bust on the hustings," wrote *Business Week*'s Howard Gleckman.[34] Novak reported in a column that this view was even shared by senior White House officials, who privately admitted that "last year's prescription drug bill was a disaster substantively and politically."[35]

Although Bush went on to best John Kerry in the November presidential election and his party kept control of the House and Senate, even increasing their numbers, there is no indication that the drug bill provided any political benefit. As columnist Harold Meyerson observed, "There's no evidence to suggest that Bush's Medicare reform . . . yielded him any votes at all."[36]

More than likely, Republicans would have done just as well electorally if they had passed a much more targeted bill with a much lower cost or simply done nothing. It would not have been hard to make the case that Medicare's costs were already out of control and that a new unfunded drug benefit was unaffordable. It would have had the added virtue of being true.

BIG CORPORATIONS ARE BIG WINNERS

NO SENSIBLE PERSON would argue that Medicare's policy of paying virtually unlimited sums for hospital care while paying nothing for prescription drugs made any sense. And no one denied that some seniors needed help paying for prescription drugs. But many already had perfectly good prescription drug coverage from their employers. Yet they, too, ended up being covered by the Medicare drug benefit.

I puzzled for a long time about why Republicans would write a bill that provided benefits even for those who had no need for them. They were making it more expensive without improving health care in any way at all.

The answer became clear when the *New York Times* reported that the drug program would reimburse corporations for the drug benefits they were already providing to their retirees.[37] The federal government would send huge checks to some of the largest corporations in the United States for costs that they were already contractually obligated to pay. The final legislation provided a 28 percent tax-free subsidy that is expected to average $660 per retiree per year.

The numbers are huge. After passage of the legislation, the *Wall Street Journal* reported that General Motors anticipated receiving $4 billion to cover its prescription drug costs. Other big recipients included Verizon ($1.3 billion), BellSouth ($572 million), Delphi ($500 million), U.S. Steel ($450 million), American Airlines ($415 million), John Deere ($400 million), United Airlines ($280 million), and Alcoa ($190 million).[38]

Other companies planned to drop their drug coverage and let the federal program take it over.[39] Either way, the effect is to substantially raise corporate profits. *BusinessWeek* estimates the aggregate profit increase at $8 billion per year—$6.5 billion for the subsidy itself and another $1.5 billion because the subsidy is tax-free.[40] And under existing accounting rules, future savings can be added to the bottom line immediately.[41]

Oddly, this aspect of the drug bill has been almost entirely ignored even on the political left. Instead, they have concentrated their criticism on the pharmaceutical companies. The added drug demand will fatten their profits, they say, and the federal government will have no power to control them, because the drug bill prohibits using the government's buying power to negotiate lower prices.

This may be true in the short run. But in the longer run, it is inevitable that price controls will be imposed on drugs. Realistically, it will be the only way that exploding costs can be controlled quickly. Indeed, some new cancer drugs now cost $100,000 for a single course of treatment.[42] There is no way that taxpayers will be able to afford this expense. That is why virtually every other industrialized country substantially controls the prices of most prescription drugs.[43] It is also the reason why Canada sells the same drugs available here for lower prices.[44]

The problem is that price controls eventually dry up the supply of new drugs—just as rent controls in New York City led to a decline in new apartment building.[45] Unfortunately, it takes a long time for this effect to become apparent because there is a large existing stock of drugs and housing. It will be very hard to know in the future what drugs might have been discovered if price controls had not been imposed. Someday people are going to die because price controls prevented new drug developments that would have saved them.[46]

Despite having made the nation's public finances vastly worse by ramming the drug benefit through Congress, President Bush nevertheless launched a major effort to reform Social Security as his first order of business after being reelected. Oddly, no one laughed as he said over and over again that Social Security reform was necessary to avoid national bankruptcy. Yet as we have seen, Social Security's unfunded liability is 60 percent less than just that of the drug program and only 16 percent that of the Medicare program as a whole.

In early 2005, a few Republicans in Congress suggested that it might be prudent to reopen the drug bill, before substantial spending for it began, which would doom any future effort to cut benefits. Even though he was no longer running for office, Mr. Bush reacted with uncharacteristic venom at the suggestion. At the swearing-in ceremony for new HHS secretary Michael Leavitt, Bush said, "I signed Medicare reform proudly and any attempt to limit the choices of our seniors and to take away their prescription drug coverage under Medicare will meet my veto."[47]

Keep in mind that up until this point, Mr. Bush had not vetoed a single bill. This may explain why Mr. Bush had so much difficulty getting political traction on his Social Security proposal. He simply had no credibility as someone who cares one whit about whether the nation can afford all the entitlement promises it has made. Therefore, he was forced to fall back on arguments for reform that were less compelling to the American people. Thus, one cost of the drug bill may be that his effort to privatize Social Security—a worthy goal—will fail to become law.

In September 2005, there was some effort among the dwindling band of true conservatives in Congress to at least delay implementation of the drug benefit to pay for Hurricane Katrina. Some even suggested repeal. Said Sen. John McCain (R-AZ), "I'm saying cancel it. It was a bad idea to start with."[48] White House aides rejected the suggestion.

Worst Legislation in History

FOR THESE REASONS, I believe that the Medicare drug bill may well be the worst piece of legislation ever enacted. That it was enacted by a president and Congress controlled by my party is a source of great distress to me. It will cost vast sums the nation cannot afford, even if its initial budgetary projections prove to be accurate, which is highly doubtful. It will inevitably lead to higher taxes and price controls that will reduce the supply of new lifesaving drugs.[49] And all of this will be done without even giving my party any long-term political benefit—after supporting the drug bill, the AARP immediately turned around and launched an intensive attack on Bush's Social Security reform.

Said former House Majority Leader Dick Armey (R-TX), "The recent expansion in Medicare to include prescription drugs provides an example of how policies that expand government are ultimately harmful to Republicans."[50]

Sadly, there is no place to turn. Democrats opposed the legislation only because they thought it wasn't expensive enough. This left many elderly believing they could have done better if only those miserly Republicans hadn't been so cheap. It is doubtful that anything less than 100 percent reimbursement for all drugs for the elderly would have satisfied them.

In the future, it will be a simple matter for Democrats to run against every problem that develops in the drug program and continue to promise seniors a better deal no matter how much it costs. Moreover, if costs do explode—as seems inevitable—Democrats will be in a position to excoriate Republicans for anything they do to rein them in. For this reason, smart liberals like columnist Bob Kuttner concluded that passage of any drug bill was fundamentally in the Democrats' political interest.[51]

On the other hand, if Democrats had still been in control of Congress and the White House, they would have had less incentive to pander to the elderly. Because many of the elderly suspected them of secretly wanting to destroy Medicare, Republicans had to pay a premium to buy the AARP's support. Democrats might have been able to cut a better deal, demanding some sacrifice by the elderly in return for the new benefit. And because they have credibility as the party of Medicare, they might have gotten it, thus giving us a less expensive bill in the end.

CHAPTER 5

THE WORST RECORD ON TRADE SINCE HOOVER?

HERBERT HOOVER IS RIGHTLY REVILED FOR HAVING THE WORST record on international trade of any president. The Smoot-Hawley Tariff, which Hoover signed into law in 1929 after passage by a Republican Congress, was a significant factor in triggering and deepening the Great Depression.[1] Since then, all presidents except George W. Bush have made free trade a cornerstone of their international economic policy. While his rhetoric on the subject is little different from theirs, Bush's actions have been far more protectionist.

Historically, the Republican Party was the party of tariffs and protection. From Abraham Lincoln down to Hoover, a high tariff on imported manufactured goods was the foundation of Republican trade policy. The Democrats, on the other hand, as the party of the workingman, were the party of free trade. They understood that tariffs raised the prices of goods, fattened the profits of businessmen, and acted like a tax on the poor. A stem-winding expression of this popularly held Democratic view was made by Congressman (later Speaker of the House) Sam Rayburn of Texas in a 1913 speech:

The system of protective tariff built up under the Republican misrule has worked to make the rich richer and the poor poorer. The protective tariff has been justly called the mother of trusts. It takes from the pockets of those least able to pay and puts into the pockets of those most able to pay. The two great parties in the long past took distinct positions upon the tariff question—the Democratic Party of the masses on the one side and the Republican Party of the classes on the other side; the Democratic position being that the only reason on earth for the levy of a tariff tax at all is for the purpose of raising money to defray the expenses of the government, and that whatever protection came to industry from this tax was only incidental and arising out of the system, and no reason for the tax.[2]

But after the disaster of Smoot-Hawley, which led to a collapse of world trade and sowed the seeds of World War II, a bipartisan consensus emerged that protectionism needed to be resisted at all costs. It was too easy for it to get out of control, leading to tit-for-tat retaliation by other countries that could explode into a trade war or even a shooting war.

POSTWAR CONSENSUS

AMONG FRANKLIN D. ROOSEVELT's first acts in office was to reverse Smoot-Hawley.[3] He later insisted that the institutionalization of free trade be a key element of postwar planning, which led to creation of the General Agreement on Tariffs and Trade.[4] Harry Truman made adoption of free trade a requirement for nations to receive Marshall Plan aid, which probably did more to revive the economies of Europe than the aid itself.[5] Dwight Eisenhower supported creation of the Organisation for Economic Co-operation and Development to help maintain free trade among the major industrialized countries.

John F. Kennedy recognized that free trade was in the United States' interest even if done unilaterally, but would be better still if we could persuade other countries to lower trade barriers at the same time. This also made free trade easier to sell politically, since it looked as if we were getting something in return for giving something to foreigners by opening our market to them. And Kennedy understood that trade is not static, that there is a tendency toward protectionism unless countered by active efforts to expand free trade.

Consequently, Kennedy initiated a round of multilateral trade negotiations, concluded under Lyndon Johnson, which eventually led to a reduction in world tariff levels by about a third. Under Richard Nixon, another round of trade negotiations began, known as the Tokyo Round, which Jimmy Carter pushed through an increasingly protectionist Democratic Congress in 1979.

By the 1980s, the parties had largely reversed their historical positions on trade. The Democrats, especially in Congress, had come to view protection in terms of protecting jobs for working people rather than as a tax on them. And with American businesses becoming increasingly multinational, Republicans now saw free trade and access to foreign markets as being central to their constituency.

Ronald Reagan spent much of his presidency fighting off congressional efforts to stem imports of foreign autos and electronics. But he was also determined to spread free trade as well, and not just fight back against encroaching protectionism. Toward this end, he initiated talks with Canada and Mexico on establishing a North American free trade zone, and inaugurated another multilateral trade negotiation known as the Uruguay Round.

George H. W. Bush pushed forward negotiations on both the Uruguay Round and the North American Free Trade Agreement, known as NAFTA. Although he was unable to conclude either agreement, Ross Perot and Pat Buchanan nevertheless pilloried him in 1992 for allowing foreigners to steal our markets and our jobs, contributing to economic malaise, they said.

Although Bill Clinton ended up benefiting from these attacks on

President Bush, he refused to give in to the temptation to become a protectionist himself. On the contrary, to his great credit, he stuck to the free trade policy of his postwar predecessors, concluded the Uruguay Round, and rammed NAFTA through Congress despite strong resistance from his own party. Indeed, it is doubtful that any president other than Clinton could have gotten NAFTA enacted under the circumstances.

GEORGE W. BUSH

GEORGE W. BUSH came into office hoping to follow in the footsteps of earlier presidents and expand world trade by further breaking down barriers, which increasingly have taken the form of subsidies that distort prices and create an unlevel playing field. His first U.S. trade representative, Bob Zoellick, was widely known for his commitment to open trade and free markets and was anxious to start a new round of trade negotiations.

But before negotiations can begin, it is necessary for Congress to give the president negotiating authority, sometimes called fast-track authority. Of course, the president could negotiate whatever he wants and then submit it to Congress for approval. But without negotiating authority in advance, such an effort would likely succumb to inevitable amendments and filibusters. Thus, the main purpose of negotiating authority is for Congress to bind itself to granting an up-or-down vote on the package at the end of the process.

In 2001, Congress was not in the mood to grant negotiating authority. Democrats were mostly against anything that would either expand trade—and threaten American jobs, in their opinion—or help Bush, whose election was considered illegitimate by many. But Republican control of Congress was very thin, and with the economy in recession many Republicans were extremely skittish about casting a vote to promote trade and possibly threaten domestic jobs.

Those Republicans in steel-producing districts in Pennsylvania,

Ohio, and West Virginia were especially fearful of electoral retaliation. They demanded that Bush do something to help the steel industry as the price for their vote on trade-negotiating authority.

In June 2001, Bush initiated an investigation by the U.S. International Trade Commission into whether the steel industry was being injured by imports. It was virtually preordained that it would find that imports were indeed injuring the domestic steel industry, because of the low legal threshold for such a determination, and the ITC did indeed find injury in December. Under the law, President Bush had until March to decide what specific actions he would take to protect the steel industry.

At the same time, Republicans from agricultural areas were complaining about low farm prices and demanding more subsidies, even though Bush had promised to move toward a more market-based system during the 2000 campaign.

Bush's actions on the agriculture bill were important for trade because the whole point of the new round of trade negotiations, known as the Doha Round, was supposed to be about removing subsidies for agriculture, which cost taxpayers in the industrialized countries dearly while making it impossible for farmers in the developing world to compete. Thus such subsidies end up impoverishing both those in the rich countries and poor countries alike.

Unfortunately, Bush made exactly the wrong decision in both cases, thereby destroying all hope of accomplishing anything meaningful in the Doha Round, even if he got fast-track authority from Congress.

STEEL

HISTORICALLY, ECONOMISTS HAVE identified only one legitimate justification for trade protection—for what are called "infant" industries, those that are just getting started and competing against well-established rivals. This was Alexander Hamilton's view in his famous "Report on

Manufactures" submitted to Congress on December 5, 1791.[6] It was later endorsed by the great economists John Stuart Mill and C. F. Bastable as the one exception to the general rule of free trade.[7]

So it is ironic that the industry that has most sought and received protection over the years is not a new one like electronics or computers or software, but the quintessential old industry: steel. It is always just on the verge of being competitive, it has said over and over and over again, and only needs a little breathing space to invest and modernize. Then the tariffs and quotas can be relaxed.

But that day never comes. Since 1969, the U.S. steel industry has been the recipient of continuous protection in one form or another. In a 2000 study for the American Institute for International Steel, which represents steel importers, economists William Barringer and Kenneth Pierce estimated that up until that point U.S. consumers had paid between $90 billion and $151 billion (in constant 1999 dollars) more for products made with steel, such as autos and appliances, than they would have paid without the protection.[8]

Many academic studies have concluded that protection of the steel industry has done nothing whatsoever to improve its competitiveness. The higher prices simply raise industry profits or reduce its losses. Indeed, studies show that protection actually reduces the incentive to innovate, as companies and unions find a higher return in lobbying politicians for protection and handouts than from investing in new technology.[9]

Although steel is obviously not an infant industry, even many of those who usually support free trade have made an exception for steel on national security grounds. We need adequate domestic manufacturing capability to build ships and tanks in the event of war, they say.

In fact, the Defense Department's need for steel is far less than is commonly thought. Today's weaponry depends much more on high-tech composite materials than on ordinary steel. According to an October 2001 Commerce Department study, no weapons system is dependent on imported steel, there will be more than sufficient domestic capacity for all DoD needs for the foreseeable future, and there are far cheaper ways of ensuring its needs than through trade protection. For example, DoD could stockpile steel for emergencies or build its own steel plants.[10]

Shortly after the ITC found that the U.S. steel industry was being injured by imports, economists Joseph Francois and Laura Baughman estimated that adoption of its recommendations would lead to a loss of eight jobs in steel-consuming businesses for every job saved among steel producers. The cost to American consumers would be about $450,000 per job saved.[11]

BUSH PLAYS POLITICS

IN LATE 2001, the Doha Round of multilateral trade negotiations officially started. But well into 2002, the U.S. could not meaningfully participate because Congress had yet to pass fast-track authority. The two hangups still were steel and agriculture.

On March 5, Bush sought to assuage those concerned about steel by imposing a 30 percent tariff on steel imports. In an amazing example of doublespeak, Trade Representative Zoellick explained that this was a major step toward free trade. He said that the tariffs would compensate for government subsidies often given to foreign steel producers. Most observers, however, saw Bush's action as nothing but cynical politics—buying a few votes in politically important swing states.

"This policy reflects the triumph of the Bush political advisers who trumpet their admiration for President William McKinley, that paragon of Republican protectionism—compassionate conservatism for government-addicted corporations," conservative columnist George Will wrote. "Bush's steel policy is what results when intelligent people take up intellectual slumming—abandoning of proven free-trade principles—for the pleasure of political opportunism."[12]

Zoellick later admitted that domestic politics were primarily behind the steel decision. At a meeting in São Paulo, he said, "We are committed to moving forward with free trade, but, like Brazil, we have to manage support for free trade at home."[13]

The Europeans and Japanese immediately drew up lists of U.S. goods that would be subjected to retaliatory tariffs. On a trip to Beijing in April, hoping to open the Chinese market to more U.S. exports, Zoellick found them unresponsive. Why should they open their market, they asked, when the U.S. was in the process of closing its market? As Peter Wonacott of the *Wall Street Journal* reported, "The steel dispute has cast the U.S. in the awkward role of defending protectionist practices even as it preaches free trade to those criticized for their closed markets."[14]

The *Wall Street Journal* worried that Bush's abandonment of principle on trade was weakening his ability to influence other countries on a variety of issues. "The policy mattered less than the abandonment of principle," it editorialized. "It signaled to the world that Mr. Bush was not the president he had seemed after September 11; his moral and strategic clarity could be compromised for a price."[15]

By summer, a wide variety of steel-using businesses were complaining about being caught in a cost-squeeze. Their raw material cost had risen by 30 percent, but they were unable to raise their own prices to compensate. This was especially the case for businesses facing international competition, since finished goods made with steel were not subjected to the tariffs. This put U.S. manufacturers at a competitive disadvantage in both the domestic market and foreign markets.

Even those in Congress who had supported the president's decision started having second thoughts. Rep. Donald Manzullo, Republican of Illinois and chairman of the House Committee on Small Business, complained about the law of unintended consequences. Many small businesses, he said, were bearing the brunt of the cost of aiding a few large steel producers.[16]

Still, Bush achieved one thing from his steel policy—it probably did get him the last couple of votes he needed in the House to get trade promotion authority, so that the U.S. could finally participate meaningfully in the ongoing Doha Round of negotiations. On July 27, 2002, 215 House members voted for the conference report on the trade bill, while 212 voted against it.

STEEL ENDGAME

BY JANUARY 2003, data showed that the steel tariffs had cost far more jobs in steel-using businesses than could possibly have been saved among producers. According to economists Francois and Baughman, 200,000 jobs had been lost among users, and there were only 187,500 total jobs in the entire steel industry. They found that substantial numbers of manufacturers had been forced to outsource—move their production outside the U.S. to escape the tariffs.[17] It is unlikely that these jobs would ever return.

In the words of management guru Peter Drucker, "Bush's tariff action thus only accelerated the long-term decline of the traditional Midwestern steel producers and the jobs they generate."[18]

In May 2003, the World Trade Organization ruled that the steel tariffs were illegal under world trade law. After a U.S. appeal was rejected in September, the European Union prepared to impose retaliatory tariffs on U.S. goods.

In a follow-up study in September, the ITC concluded that the steel protection policy had been a net loss for the country. It calculated that on balance the nation was worse off to the tune of $42 million.[19] However, as economist Gary Clyde Hufbauer noted, this figure greatly underestimated the negative economic effect because the ITC saw the increased tariff revenue for the government as a plus for the economy, which is ridiculous.[20]

In any case, the ITC found that workers were worse off by almost $400 million, while steel-consuming businesses lost about $600 million as a result of the steel tariffs. If one also views the $650 million in tariff revenue as a negative for the economy as a whole, then the actual loss comes to $1.6 billion, offset by a modest $300 million increase in profits for steel producers.

Even the larger calculation yields an economic cost that is quite trivial in an $11 trillion economy. Nevertheless, it is revealing that the steel tariffs had an unambiguously negative impact on the economy.

In December 2003, Bush finally bowed to reality and lifted the tariffs. But he continued to pay a heavy price in the Doha trade talks, as other countries repeatedly rejected U.S. entreaties to lower their barriers to U.S. goods. As the *Wall Street Journal* put it, "When the world's main economic power indulges in protectionism, everyone else figures it's safe to do the same."[21]

London's *Financial Times* newspaper seconded the *Journal*'s point. Said the *Times*: "More than any single action by the Bush administration, the steel tariffs sowed doubts around the world about whether the U.S. can do what it is asking of other countries—make politically difficult decisions at home to advance the prospects of free trade abroad."[22]

AGRICULTURE SUBSIDIES

CONTRIBUTING TO THE failure of Doha was President Bush's ill-timed decision to raise agriculture subsidies on the eve of the trade talks. He also picked a bad time to start a trade war with Canada over lumber.

Congress traditionally does a farm bill every five years. The 1996 bill went a long way toward creating a free market in agriculture, eliminating a number of subsidies and regulations. However, when a new bill was written in 2001, it was very much a return to the old, discredited subsidy approach. The final bill, signed into law by Bush in May 2002, raised spending by almost $90 billion above previous law and was estimated by the Congressional Budget Office to cost $470 billion over five years—almost $100 billion per year.

Although Bush had promised to move toward a more market-oriented agriculture policy during the 2000 campaign, he made no effort to implement such a policy as the farm bill moved through Congress. Writing in the conservative *Weekly Standard* magazine, Fred Barnes commented that the legislation showed that "the era in which big government was over is over."[23]

The importance of the new agriculture subsidies went well beyond the budgetary cost or the impact on farmers. It basically doomed the world trade talks, which were primarily about reducing farm subsidies worldwide, especially in Europe, where farmers are even more politically powerful than they are here. When pushing for the new trade round, the United States had enthusiastically endorsed this goal, believing that it would increase U.S. exports.

But the only hope there was of achieving any meaningful reduction in agricultural subsidies was by appealing to the basic principle that subsidies are wrong—they are costly, inefficient, and a poorly targeted way of helping farmers, with much of the money going to people who are already well-to-do. By working together with the few other countries that consistently support free trade, like Australia, it might have been possible to shame the Europeans into making some kind of deal. But once Bush signed a massive increase in U.S. subsidies right at the start of the trade talks, he lost all credibility on the issue and it became a foregone conclusion that no agreement would be reached on the central topic of the negotiations.

It also didn't help that the Bush Administration was simultaneously alienating Canada, another of the small band of free traders, by slapping a 29 percent tariff on Canadian lumber in March 2002. Not only did this raise the cost of homebuilding in the U.S., but it led Canada to retaliate by putting a 71 percent tariff on U.S. tomato exports. [24]

Sadly, another consequence of failing to curb agricultural subsidies is to further impoverish farmers in the less developed countries. By forcing down prices for agricultural products, they drive many poor farmers out of business, making them dependent on food aid from the West.[25]

CHINA SCAPEGOAT

IN 2003, THE Bush Administration increasingly turned toward scape-goating China for American economic and trade woes. It was a rare week when Commerce Secretary Don Evans didn't issue some blistering attack on the Chinese for dumping their goods here, manipulating their exchange rate, or some other unfair action to give them a trade advantage.

On November 18, the Bush Administration announced a decision to impose new trade restrictions on imports of Chinese textiles. A petition from four textile industry groups, led by South Carolina Republican textile magnate Roger Milliken, initiated the new trade restrictions. It alleged that Chinese imports "threatened to impede the orderly development of trade and caused market disruption in the U.S." No proof was offered to support this allegation. The mere fact that imports of Chinese textiles had risen in recent years, which is all the petition demonstrated, is legally insufficient to prove market disruption. The claim was simply asserted and should have been dismissed out of hand.

The totally political nature of the textiles decision was widely understood. "In steel as well as textiles," the *New York Times* reported, "President Bush has been willing to compromise his often-stated goal of promoting global free trade with the more political goal of stemming the loss of manufacturing jobs."[26]

To show just how absurd the situation was, one of the new restrictions applied to brassieres. Yet there is no domestic manufacturer of this product. Some components are produced in the United States, but all are exported to low-wage countries in Latin America for manufacture. This is done solely because of a law requiring a degree of domestic content in order to avoid trade barriers when the final product is imported. In other words, it is entirely an artificial arrangement. The reality is that

100 percent of brassieres are imported, so there really is no domestic industry to protect.

Furthermore, there is no evidence that China has a protected market, which might justify some sort of action. Although China runs a large trade surplus with the United States, it runs a deficit with the rest of the world.[27] Moreover, the International Monetary Fund rejected the idea that China was artificially holding its currency down to stimulate exports and hinder imports. "There is no clear evidence that the renminbi is substantially undervalued at this juncture," it concluded in a November 18 report.[28]

The day after the U.S. textiles decision, China canceled a trade mission to the United States that probably would have led to billions of dollars in orders for American goods. In previous weeks China had signaled a desire to increase its imports of planes from Boeing, jet engines from General Electric, and a variety of agricultural products as well as chemical and telecommunications equipment. Such purchases likely would have been greater than the value of the goods that were now restricted, creating vastly more jobs—and better-paying ones—than those protected in the textiles industry.[29]

OUTSOURCING

IN 2003, THE issue of "outsourcing" hit the headlines. Newspapers and popular magazines were filled with stories about U.S. high-tech companies that were hiring foreign companies, especially in India, for jobs like software programming. These jobs were thought to be safe from layoffs, and so the threat of Indian programmers suddenly created fear among a highly educated group of workers who thought their jobs were safe.

To economists, however, nothing new was really going on. It was simply a case of international trade expanding to include services. Dropping prices for telecommunications and computers made it increasingly easy to purchase services from places like India for a fraction of the domestic cost.[30]

In the annual Economic Report of the President issued in February 2004, the president's Council of Economic Advisers weighed in on the outsourcing debate, stating a view that would be considered unobjectionable in any university economics class. As the CEA wrote:

> One facet of increased services trade is the increased use of *offshore outsourcing* in which a company relocates labor-intensive service industry functions to another country. For example, a U.S. firm might use a call-center in India to handle customer service–related questions. The principal novelty of outsourcing services is the means by which foreign purchases are delivered. Whereas imported goods might arrive by ship, outsourced services are often delivered using telephone lines or the Internet. The basic economic forces behind the transactions are the same, however. When a good or service is produced more cheaply abroad, it makes more sense to import it than to make or provide it domestically.[31]

Advance copies of the Economic Report circulate throughout the administration well before its release, and extensive editorial changes are often made. So this passage had been seen by any number of politically astute officials long before the report was published. None apparently saw it as anything other than a simple restatement of economic conventional wisdom.

CEA chairman Greg Mankiw even emphasized the point about outsourcing at the press conference announcing the new Economic Report. "Outsourcing is just a new way of doing international trade," he said.[32]

Consequently, Mankiw was very much taken aback when a firestorm erupted over his outsourcing comments, which seemed to endorse the idea of moving American jobs abroad at a time when unemployment was the principal domestic economic problem. Especially painful was the attack by Speaker of the House Dennis Hastert, Republican of Illinois. "An economy suffers when jobs disappear," the speaker deadpanned. Soon, a number of politicians from both parties were calling on President Bush to sack Mankiw.

Mankiw quickly apologized to Representative Hastert for his "lack of clarity." But even many liberals and Democrats came to his defense. "Mr. Mankiw is right," a *Washington Post* editorial declared.[33] Janet Yellen, Robert Reich, Laura Tyson, and other top Clinton Administration economic officials conceded that Mankiw was well within the economic mainstream.[34]

"The White House has been quick to betray sound free-trade policies to suit its political interests," the *New York Times* commented, "so there was an element of comeuppance in watching it take a beating. But someone should point out that Mr. Mankiw was right."[35]

Sadly, rather than stand by his principal economic adviser, President Bush effectively threw him overboard. Although he didn't fire Mankiw, he kept him at arm's length for the rest of the year and refused to back him up. He was basically muzzled and returned to Cambridge soon after the election.

Free Trade Agreements

AFTER THE DE FACTO collapse of the Doha Round—due almost entirely to U.S. missteps on steel and agriculture—the Bush Administration turned toward free trade agreements with individual countries or small groups of countries. Economists are dubious about the value of such agreements, which in this case were often less about free trade than pursuing new avenues for U.S. protectionism.

Before 2001, the U.S. had free trade agreements only with Israel, and with Canada and Mexico through NAFTA. In 2001, Bush signed an agreement with Jordan. In 2002, he initiated talks with Australia, Chile, Singapore, and five Central American countries (Costa Rica, El Salvador, Guatemala, Honduras, and Nicaragua). In 2003, the negotiations with Singapore and Chile were successfully concluded and new talks began with Morocco, Bahrain, four Andean nations (Colombia, Peru, Ecuador, and Bolivia), and five nations in Southern Africa (Botswana, Lesotho, Namibia, South Africa, and Swaziland). In 2004, talks with the Central American countries (to which the Dominican Republic was added) and Australia were completed.

Although the amount of activity involved in pursuing FTAs was certainly impressive, economists had serious doubts about them. "Nearly all scholars of international economics today are fiercely skeptical, even hostile, to such agreements," said economists Jagdish Bhagwati and Arvind Panagariya, both of Columbia University.[36]

Key reasons for this hostility are that bilateral agreements divert attention and resources away from multilateral agreements, which are vastly preferable. FTAs may divert trade flows rather than increase them and may lead trade blocs to impose restrictions on trade with those outside the bloc, thus raising the overall level of protection. Supporters of FTAs on the other hand mostly argue that they are better than nothing and may provide building blocks upon which broader trade agreements can be developed. No one believes that FTAs are optimal trade policy.[37]

Nevertheless, FTAs have become almost the sole Bush Administration effort to open trade. Yet even while doing so, it has often used such agreements to pursue protectionist objectives. An especially egregious example of this is when the Bush Administration nearly scuttled the free trade agreement with Australia in order to maintain protection for the sugar industry, despite universal condemnation for the sugar program, which adds some $2 billion per year to consumer costs mainly to enrich a few Florida producers.[38]

According to the *Financial Times,* George W. Bush personally made the decision to exclude Australian sugar from the FTA.[39] This became the first such agreement ever negotiated to exclude an individual product from its provisions. Although agreeing to these harsh terms caused Australian prime minister John Howard, one of Bush's strongest allies in the war on terror, considerable political difficulties at home, Bush apparently believed that protecting his Florida political contributors was more important.

Free traders were dismayed by the Australian sugar episode, fearing that it would send a bad message to others. The *New York Times* spoke for many. "The agreement sends a chilling message to the rest of the world," it said. "Even when dealing with an allied nation with similar living standards, the administration . . . has opted to continue coddling the sugar lobby, rather than dropping the most indefensible form of protectionism. This will only embolden those around the world who argue that globalization is a rigged game."[40]

In early 2005, the Bush Administration put enormous pressure on Congress to approve the Central American Free Trade Agreement, known as CAFTA. Although the economic benefits from this agreement were quite modest, the administration had little choice but to press hard for its passage in order to salvage some semblance of a trade agenda. However, the price for passage was very high, with Republicans demanding restrictions on Chinese imports as the price for their vote.[41] Consequently there was very little likelihood that passage of the agreement would lead to a net reduction in trade barriers.

CAFTA also proved costly to taxpayers, because the administration was forced to agree to many new pork barrel projects in order to buy the last couple of votes—necessary because CAFTA passed the House by just a 217 to 215 vote on July 28, 2005. Free traders worry that this will encourage members of Congress to demand even more payoffs for future votes. "The price was very high for such a small agreement," lamented economist Gary Clyde Hufbauer. "Each time you do this, you have more claimants, and Doha could generate a record number of claimants that would make its passage all the tougher."[42]

DUMPING?

THE BUSH ADMINISTRATION'S excuse for much of the new trade protection that has occurred on its watch is that it was mandated by law. That is, laws in effect before it took office to protect domestic producers against "dumping" require the imposition of tariffs and give the president no latitude in enforcing them. This is true to some extent. However, in many cases the Bush Administration has simply used the antidumping statutes as backdoor protectionism that could have been resisted, if it had chosen to do so.[43]

The term "dumping" is often used loosely to mean selling foreign products at below cost, possibly because they are subsidized by a foreign government.[44] However, legally, dumping exists simply when a product is sold in the U.S. for less than it is sold for in other markets. There need not be any evidence that the product is being sold below cost or that there is any subsidy involved.

Although dumping is assumed to be unfair when it involves international trade, there are many reasons why a business might sell products at seemingly unprofitable prices that are commonly accepted as reasonable in the domestic market. For example, when introducing a new product against established competition, a business may need to sell at a loss in order to gain a foothold in the market. It may need to dispose of inadvertent overstocks or it may hope to make a profit through ancillary sales—think of Barbie dolls that are sold cheaply because the real profit is in the clothes.

There are also technical problems with measuring dumping that often overstate its incidence. For example, exchange rates may distort market prices, allowing a product to sell below cost in a foreign currency even when it is selling for the same price at home. In other cases, U.S. businesses simply use antidumping petitions as a competitive tool in order to prevent foreign competitors from reducing prices and undercutting their profits and market share. Even when foreign firms are confident of winning a dumping case, they may not want to go through the effort to defend themselves and so back off.[45] Also, the method by which government agencies calculate dumping tends to exaggerate its occurrence because it ignores cases where foreign products are sold at higher prices in the U.S.—a practice known as "zeroing."[46]

Nevertheless, the idea that there is something inherently unfair or unjust about dumping has been deeply entrenched in U.S. law for more than one hundred years. However, the law was rarely enforced until the 1970s. At that time the law was broadened to allow tariffs even in cases where there was no dumping even alleged, but merely the existence of injury to a domestic industry resulting from imports. Tariffs could also be imposed as retaliation for a foreign country's restrictions on U.S. exports. These cases tend to get lumped together with actual dumping cases in the popular media.

Much of the Bush Administration's protectionism has taken place under the cloak of antidumping, which makes it seem as if tariffs result simply from the enforcement of long-standing law rather than as a matter of policy. But many of these antidumping investigations are in fact instigated by the Commerce Department as a matter of policy and are basically rigged to guarantee that dumping will be found.

Almost all of the tariffs imposed on Chinese furniture, Vietnamese shrimp, and other goods have taken place under the guise of antidumping when they are really policy actions.[47] As a consequence, other countries increasingly are using their own antidumping laws against American goods.[48]

ASSESSMENT

BUSH'S OVERT PROTECTIONISM may not be that great quantitatively. Nevertheless, he may be the most protectionist president since Hoover. The main reason is that all of Hoover's successors except Bush understood the fragility of free trade and the dangers of playing politics with it. They also understood that there is an inherent drift toward protectionism that needs to be vigorously resisted and offset by aggressive trade-opening measures. Bush has gone in the opposite direction, repeatedly using protectionism to buy short-term political support and sabotaging multilateral trade negotiations.

Bush has also repeatedly treated the World Trade Organization with contempt. He has taken actions that he knew would be ruled illegal, such as the steel tariffs, and made little effort to redress illegal elements of U.S. law, such as the Foreign Sales Corporation and the Byrd Amendment. The former was a tax provision that the WTO ruled to be a de facto subsidy. It was finally repealed in 2004 with the White House and Treasury Department doing virtually nothing to aid the effort. The Byrd Amendment is a law enacted in 2000 that allows some antidumping duties to be paid directly to private businesses, which the WTO has also ruled to be illegal. According to the GAO, half the benefits of this legislation went to just five companies.[49] Again, the Bush Administration made no effort to fix the problem and bring the U.S. into compliance with international law.[50]

And Bush has failed to appoint strong free traders to the International Trade Commission, which has become more of an accomplice to protection than a defender against it, as it was intended to be.[51] As a result, the small and declining number of free traders in Congress has been forced to do most of the heavy lifting.

While Bush has initiated some trade-opening agreements on a bilateral basis, economists are generally skeptical of the value of such measures. Even their supporters recognize that they are modest at best and no substitute for multilateral action.

Consequently, free trade is probably in its weakest position since the 1920s. The ultimate consequence of Bush's abandonment of principle may not come on his watch. But the danger of protectionism is growing and could lead to future actions that will lower the standard of living of all Americans.[52]

CHAPTER 6

IS ENRON A METAPHOR FOR BUSH'S ECONOMIC POLICY?

T HE 2002 COLLAPSE OF ENRON, THE GIANT ENERGY TRADING company, may in some ways be a metaphor for the Bush Administration's economic policy. Enron borrowed heavily, paid little in taxes, and made big profits in ways that were known to be contrary to sound business practices. But as long as the profits kept rolling in, there was an army of financial analysts, auditors, journalists, and politicians—including people like economist Paul Krugman, who received $50,000 as an Enron adviser—prepared to testify that Enron had found the Midas touch.[1] Those who had the temerity to suggest that something was fundamentally amiss were dismissed as worrywarts and killjoys.

So, too, the Bush Administration's economic policy has been built largely on a massive increase in the public debt—both on-budget and off-budget. As Vice President Cheney told Treasury Secretary Paul O'Neill, "Deficits don't matter."[2] At the same time, interest rates fell even as the economy grew and the Federal Reserve tightened monetary policy. Thus, the administration seemed to have its cake and eat it, too.

But if we know anything about economics, it is that unsustainable trends don't continue. Sooner or later the underlying imbalances will be corrected—perhaps with a bang, perhaps with a whimper, but corrected in any event. Just as circumstances eventually caught up to Enron and all its enablers, so, too, I fear that the basic unsoundness of Bush's economic policy is going to catch up with us.

Business and Government

In *The Wealth of Nations*, Adam Smith wrote that the interests of businessmen and the public were almost always in conflict. The former want to limit competition while the latter benefit from an increase in it. "To narrow competition," Smith said, "can only serve to enable the dealers, by raising their profits above what they naturally would be, to levy, for their own benefit, an absurd tax upon the rest of their fellow citizens."[3]

Consequently, businessmen are always looking for ways to reduce competition. Sometimes they will even do so by conspiring. "People of the same trade seldom meet together, even for merriment and diversion, but the conversation ends in a conspiracy against the public, or in some contrivance to raise prices," Smith observed.[4]

Such conspiracies are far less dangerous to consumers, however, than government-sanctioned restraints on competition. Without government enforcement, private cartels always fall apart after a time. But when government imposes trade protection and other limitations on competition, it can go on indefinitely. For this reason, governments should be extremely wary of enacting such policies, especially when urged by businesses to do so.

Said Smith, "The proposal of any new law or regulation of commerce which comes from this order, ought always to be listened to with great precaution, and ought never to be adopted till after having been long and carefully examined, not only with the most scrupulous, but with the most suspicious attention. It comes from an order of men, whose interest is never exactly the same with that of the public, who generally have an interest to deceive and even to oppress the public, and who accordingly have, upon many occasions, both deceived and oppressed it."[5]

This explains why many government regulations, which businessmen are presumed to hate, were actually imposed at their behest. Regulation is like an overhead cost that is more easily borne by existing businesses and large ones. It inhibits competition by preventing new entrants into an industry and the growth of small firms, thereby raising profits for large, established companies.[6] In other cases, businesses may lobby for regulations they know they can meet, but which their competitors may have difficulty meeting because of particular circumstances. Or they may desire to create or maintain regulations upon which they make money, such as companies in the business of making, say, pollution control equipment.[7] For example:

- After a federal regulation on pool slides drove all its competitors out of business, the Aquaslide 'N' Dive Corporation heavily lobbied the Consumer Product Safety Commission to retain the regulation when the commission decided it was no longer justified.[8]
- California cement producers lobbied to protect the endangered brown pelican in order to prevent construction of a new terminal in Redwood City for the importation of foreign cement.[9]
- Package delivery companies UPS and FedEx are normally fierce competitors, but when threatened by entry of Deutsche Post into the U.S. market they immediately joined forces to get the Department of Transportation to bar it from doing business here.[10]
- Telecommunications companies frequently use government regulations to prevent potential competitors from getting into the business.[11] Currently they are fighting companies that offer phone services over the Internet.
- Liquor wholesalers are fighting efforts to allow consumers to buy wine over the Internet—for no other reason except to maintain their legal monopoly on wine distribution and prevent consumers

from having more choice at lower cost. State agencies regulating interstate liquor sales are generally considered to be obsolete and are just leftover remnants of Prohibition.[12]

There is also evidence that over time, regulatory agencies become "captured" by those they regulate. So even if they were established with the purpose of penalizing an industry, eventually they become its partner. That is because companies lobby heavily to get regulators appointed who will be friendly to them, and because those appointed to regulatory commissions often come from the industry they regulate or plan to work in it after they leave office. The best examples are things like the Civil Aeronautics Board, which prevented new airlines from coming into existence for fifty years, thus ensuring guaranteed profits for those airlines that were in existence when the CAB was created.[13]

In the end, most regulation is imposed with the consent of the regulated. As Nobel Prize–winning economist George Stigler once put it, "As a rule, regulation is acquired by the industry and is designed and operated primarily for its benefit."[14]

Genuine supporters of free markets, such as economist Milton Friedman and the late Bill Simon, secretary of the Treasury from 1974 to 1977, denounce just as strongly government policies that subsidize businesses as those that unfairly penalize them. As Simon once wrote:

Throughout the last century the attachment of businessmen to free enterprise has weakened dramatically as they discovered they could demand—and receive—short-range advantages from the state. To a tragic degree, coercive regulation has been invited by businessmen who were unwilling to face honest competition in the free market with its great risks and penalties, as well as its rewards, and by businessmen who have run to the government in search of regulatory favors, protective tariffs, and subsidies, as well as those monopolistic powers which only the state can grant. . . . During my tenure at Treasury I watched with incredulity as businessmen ran to the government in every crisis, whining for handouts or protection from the very competition that has made this system so productive.[15]

Unfortunately, Simon's attitude is more often the exception than the rule among Republicans, who have a chronic inability to differentiate between free market policies and those that are pro-business. They simply are assumed to be the same thing. But nothing could be further from the truth. In reality, the last thing most businessmen want is a truly free market, which would force them to compete and erode their profits. What they really want are subsidies, monopolies, and protection. As *Wall Street Journal* columnist Alan Murray recently put it, "Capitalists, for the most part, don't much care for capitalism. Their goal is to make money. And if they can make it without messy competition, so much the better."[16]

The failure to recognize this fact has often led Republicans to enact bad policies that are seen as pro-business in a mistaken belief that they are supporting the free market, when actually they may be doing exactly the opposite.

THE REGULATORY PRESIDENT

GEORGE W. BUSH appears to have come into office with a genuine desire to implement meaningful deregulation—the kind that would level the playing field, lift unjustified burdens from law-abiding businesses, and not just be a means by which the federal government bestowed gifts on favored constituencies.[17] Free market advocates applauded the White House for appointing John D. Graham, a respected Harvard public policy professor, as head of the regulatory review unit at the Office of Management and Budget, and George Mason University law professor Tim Muris to head the Federal Trade Commission.[18]

Free marketeers celebrated Bush's renunciation of the Kyoto Treaty on global warming shortly after he took office in 2001.[19] And they cheered when all of the "midnight regulations" imposed in the last days of the Clinton Administration were frozen.[20] In Bush's first year, OMB sent back to the regulatory agencies for further review more rules than were blocked during the entire eight years of the Clinton Administration.

Unfortunately, this proved to be a temporary regulatory respite. "After that initial rally, however, principle appeared to give way to politics, and the final disposition of many Clinton midnight regulations, including the Environmental Protection Administration's controversial arsenic standards, proved little different from the Clinton version," George Mason University economist Susan Dudley lamented.[21]

In 2002, there was growing political pressure on the White House from Congress and the public to tighten regulation of corporations to prevent the recurrence of financial scandals like those of Enron and WorldCom, and increase health and safety regulations as well.[22] With the political winds blowing in favor of more, not less, regulation, the Bush Administration noticeably shifted its regulatory policy. John Graham signaled this new attitude in an interview with the *Wall Street Journal* in March 2002.

Said Graham, "There's no allergy to regulation" in the Bush Administration. "It's unquestionable" that there would be growth in environmental, safety, and social regulation. "Social regulation is in many ways a response to the acknowledged limits of capitalism," Graham argued. The Bush Administration was not opposed to regulation per se, he said, but only wanted to make sure that it was "more efficient, effective and responsive to public need."[23]

There also were signs that Bush was backsliding on Kyoto. A government report endorsed the science underlying global warming.[24] And the World Trade Center attacks brought forth a host of new regulations relating to immigration, airline safety, and the like. OMB's regulatory office even bragged about having issued forty-one significant new regulations in this area in its annual report to Congress. That report also estimated the total cost of government regulation at $620 billion per year—approximately equal to total federal domestic spending.[25]

By 2003, the upward trend in federal regulation was unmistakable. The number of federal workers engaged in regulation jumped to 241,782 that year from 184,782 in 2002, and 175,087 in Clinton's last year. Regulatory spending by the federal government jumped by 27 percent to $40.5 billion from $31.8 billion just a year earlier. Interestingly, although Enron was driving a tougher approach to economic regulation, neither the staffing nor the budgets of the economic regulatory agencies showed much of an increase. The vast bulk of the increase was for social regulation.[26]

At the same time, the Bush Administration began lowballing estimates of the cost of government regulation, which fell to at most $44 billion—a massive reduction from the previous year that clearly was not the result of any decline whatsoever in the actual burden of regulation.[27] This may possibly be a case of improved methodology that more accurately reflects the true cost of regulation. But that is highly unlikely because academic research has tended to raise estimates of regulatory costs as methodology has improved. For example, a 2001 study commissioned by the Small Business Administration put the gross cost of federal regulation at $843 billion in 2000—equivalent to more than $8,000 per American.[28] An updated version of that study upped the cost to $1.1 trillion in 2004—$10,172 for every American household.[29]

Analysts also noted that OMB circulated a forty-eight-page memo to federal agencies in September 2003, called Circular A-4, on how to calculate the costs and benefits of regulations, which made it easier to justify such regulations.[30] Economist Susan Dudley noted that the Bush requirements were now considerably less demanding than those of the Clinton Administration. She pointed out that the threshold for justifying regulation was lowered by not insisting on a finding of "market failure" first, and allowing agencies to consider "other possible justifications," such as promoting privacy or freedom, although no examples of regulations of this type were offered. Dudley concluded that the circular was "inconsistent" with an administration committed to restoring limited government.[31]

By the end of 2003, the Bush Administration was proudly promoting its imposition of new regulations banning the diet supplement Ephedra and protecting consumers from "mad cow" disease. It also celebrated a "get tough" policy toward corporate wrongdoers. As the *New York Times* observed, "The man who drew cheers in 2000 by promising to roll back government interference with the private markets has, in recent months, gladly signed legislation to restrict telemarketing and e-mail spam and boasts at fund-raisers that he will lock up executives who abuse the public trust in their companies." James Gattuso of the conservative Heritage Foundation complained that he had not heard the word "deregulation" out of the administration in two years. "This stuff about the antiregulation president is a Howard Dean myth," he said.[32]

Roots of Enron

Unquestionably the biggest boost to reregulation by the Bush Administration was the Enron scandal—by which I mean not just the problems involving that particular company, but those involving a host of others as well, such as Global Crossing and WorldCom, that were involved in various cases of actual wrongdoing, unethical behavior, and changing mores about proper corporate conduct in the post–stock market boom era. Their sins were different, but they all got lumped together in the minds of the public and Congress. This led to broad-brush efforts to fix those problems, which often penalized the innocent along with the guilty. The reality, which was seldom stated, was that these corporate scandals involved a confluence of circumstances—sort of a perfect storm—that would have fixed itself in the absence of government meddling. But the pressure to "do something" was too great, and it was easier to hand down the sentence first and worry about the verdict later.

In some ways the sorts of corporate scandals of the early 2000s are inherent in the nature of the modern corporation, because ownership and control are divided between two different groups of people—managers control corporate assets that are owned by a diverse group of shareholders, few of whom have either the incentive or ability to monitor the day-to-day activities of the managers. Shareholders depend vitally on corporate boards, to whom management is theoretically responsible, to look out for their interests. But managers are often able to manipulate boards for their own interests, by appointing their cronies to them and denying boards essential information, leaving shareholders vulnerable to misappropriation of corporate wealth that rightfully belongs to them. As long ago as 1776, Adam Smith identified this as a problem that could easily lead to scandal.

Said Smith, "The managers of such companies . . . being the managers rather of other people's money than of their own, it cannot well be expected that they should watch over it with the same anxious vigilance with which the partners in a private co-partnery frequently watch over their own. Like the stewards of a rich man, they are apt to consider attention to small matters as not for their master's honor, and very easily give themselves a dispensation from having it. Negligence and profusion, therefore, must always prevail, more or less, in the management of the affairs of such a company."[33]

In the early 1930s, Adolf Berle and Gardiner Means wrote a highly influential book, *The Modern Corporation and Private Property,* in which they argued that this disconnect between ownership and control of corporate assets undermined the idea that capitalism was self-regulating through Smith's "invisible hand."[34] It required government oversight, they said, to ensure that shareholders were protected and that managers did not abuse their power. This thinking was critical to establishment of the Securities and Exchange Commission and many laws and other institutions designed to compensate for the imbalances in information and incentives faced by managers and shareholders.[35] But in the end, management retained the upper hand.

In the 1980s, shareholders temporarily gained an advantage when the so-called junk bond, a type of speculative bond that was not considered investment-grade, was developed and helped finance leveraged buyouts and hostile corporate takeovers.[36] Previously, shareholders wishing to discipline corporate managers really had only the option of a proxy fight, which was extremely expensive and usually unsuccessful. But junk bonds made it much easier to raise even billions of dollars of capital that could be used to finance corporate takeovers that could release shareholder value frequently held hostage to self-indulgent managers. For example, managers often used corporate profits to finance ill-advised expansions into lines of business that did nothing to enhance shareholder value, but created comfortable little empires for well-connected managers.[37]

Unfortunately, public revulsion against hostile takeovers, which were often thought to cause job losses as companies streamlined operations to boost profits, led to their demise, culminating in the conviction of junk bond king Michael Milken for violations of securities laws in 1990, for which he served twenty-two months in federal prison. To this day, I have never been able to figure out exactly what he did wrong except make too much money, too fast, too publicly.[38] Instead of settling with prosecutors in a plea bargain, I wish he had used a trial to vigorously defend himself.

In any event, the end of the hostile takeover era reestablished the primacy of managers and put shareholders back into a subordinate position.[39] Enron is a perfect example. In this case, managers were engaged in investments involving offshore partnerships, self-dealing, derivatives, and shenanigans that the board either didn't know about or fully understand. But Enron's managers could not have pulled off their mischief unless they had powerful enablers.

The most important enablers were Arthur Andersen, Enron's public accountant, which signed off on its questionable books, and the financial analysts who overlooked or avoided looking too closely at its shady practices because they worked for investment banks hopeful of gaining highly profitable banking business from Enron.[40] In the end, they all suffered for their sins. Enron and Arthur Andersen went out of business and reforms were put in place that helped insulate the "buy" side of investment banks from the "sell" side, which reduced the pressure on analysts to fudge their forecast but also cut their income considerably. For a while some analysts like Merrill Lynch's Henry Blodget were the equivalent of rock stars in the investment community.[41]

Eventually the market would have sorted things out.[42] The fact that bad accountants and conflicted analysts were able to be successful for a while was more a consequence of the stock market bubble than a failure of capitalism. Unfortunately, it is in the nature of bubbles that they breed conditions that allow the unscrupulous to rise to the top for a time. As long ago as 1873, the great economist Walter Bagehot observed that bubbles were a prime breeding ground for fraud:

> The good times . . . of high price almost always engender much fraud. All people are most credulous when they are most happy; and when much money has just been made, when some people are really making it, when most people think they are making it, there is a happy opportunity for ingenious mendacity.[43]

This is an important reason why bubbles are such a problem. When they inevitably burst, they encourage a loss of faith in capitalism itself, as was the case in the 1930s, and the imposition of unnecessary and burdensome restrictions that ultimately cost much more in terms of economic dynamism and growth than the bubbles they were designed to prevent. As University of Illinois law professor Larry Ribstein recently explained:

> A boom encourages unwarranted trust in markets, leading to the speculative frenzy of a bubble and then to the inevitable bust. The bust, in turn, leads first to the disclosure of fraud and then to the mirror image of the bubble—a kind of speculative frenzy in regulation. A political context combining long-standing interest group pressures with panic and populism virtually ensures against a careful balancing of the costs and benefits of regulation. Regulators are more likely to react to past

market mistakes than to prevent future mistakes. Even worse, post-bust regulators are likely to ignore the benefits of market flexibility and, therefore, to impede the risk-taking and innovation that will bring the next boom.[44]

In the words of Stephen Bainbridge, a securities law professor at UCLA, "Corporate scandals are always good news for big government types. . . . There is nothing a politician or regulator wants more than to persuade angry investors he or she is 'doing something' and being 'aggressive' in rooting out corporate fraud."[45]

Sarbanes-Oxley

A PRIME EXAMPLE of regulatory overkill is the Sarbanes-Oxley Act (sometimes abbreviated as SOX), enacted by Congress in 2002 in the wake of the Enron scandal.[46] When a political crisis like this hits, Congress usually reacts by reaching out and grabbing every legislative idea that appears relevant that may have been kicking around for years, throws them together in a vast cut-and-paste operation, and enacts it with little, if anything, in the way of hearings, analysis, or thought. "It's hard to argue logic in a feeding frenzy," Sen. Phil Gramm (R-TX) said of the rush to enact Sarbanes-Oxley.[47] Congressman Oxley later admitted, "It was difficult to legislate responsibly in that type of hothouse atmosphere."[48]

Experienced legislators know that such opportunities present themselves from time to time and have learned to take advantage of them to enact legislation that would never see the light of day under normal circumstances. Sarbanes-Oxley is no exception. As Yale University law professor Roberta Romano recently explained, "Many of the substantive corporate governance provisions in SOX are not in fact regulatory innovations devised by Congress to cope with deficiencies in the business environment in which Enron and WorldCom failed. Rather, they may more accurately be characterized as recycled ideas advocated for quite some time by corporate governance entrepreneurs. . . . The failure of Enron, then, provided the occasion for implementation of corporate governance initiatives that were already in the policy soup."[49]

Although there are many provisions in Sarbanes-Oxley, the key ones require independent audit committees, restrict companies from buying consulting services from the same accounting firms that do their audits, prohibit corporate loans to officers, and require executives to personally certify financial statements. But in a fundamental sense, these provisions were even more substantive than they appear, because the legislation significantly preempted an area of law, corporate governance, which historically has always been the province of the states. Leo Strine of the Court of Chancery in Delaware, where most large U.S. corporations are based, has blasted Sarbanes-Oxley for unnecessarily intruding in state affairs, calling the legislation a "strange brew" of "dubious value."[50] In short, Sarbanes-Oxley represents one of the most important diminutions of federalism in many years.

The first thing that was apparent from Sarbanes-Oxley was that the costs of auditing and financial reporting increased sharply. Although the costs increased most for large public companies in absolute dollar terms, in a relative sense the burden was greatest for small and medium-sized companies. Initial indications were that costs directly associated with remaining public had increased by 100 percent, encouraging a number of companies to consider going private in order to avoid such costs.[51]

More important, many corporate executives found themselves so consumed by red tape and paperwork that they had little time for real management. Scott McNealy, CEO of Sun Microsystems, likened the impact of Sarbanes-Oxley to throwing "buckets of sand into the gears of the market economy."[52]

Further adding to the burden of Sarbanes-Oxley was the appointment of William Donaldson as chairman of the Securities and Exchange Commission in January 2003, who threw himself aggressively into enforcement of the legislation, to the consternation of other Republican members of the commission.[53] It was another case in which the White House seemed more interested in appointing people who looked good on paper, without giving sufficient consideration to whether they were philosophically compatible.

As corporations learned more about their new responsibilities under Sarbanes-Oxley, the costs of compliance jumped. A May 2004 report by Foley & Lardner, a Chicago law firm, found that the cost of being public had risen by $1.6 million per year for all companies with less than $1 billion in annual revenue. Increases were relatively larger for smaller firms. Executives complained that their compliance costs were becoming increasingly unpredictable.[54] An August 2004 survey by Financial Executives International, a trade group, found an increase in estimated costs of 62 percent over the previous year. Typical additional costs for a large public corporation jumped from $1,930,000 per year to $3,140,000.[55] However, some firms reported extraordinary costs associated with Sarbanes-Oxley. General Electric said it was spending $30 million.[56] And Hank Greenberg, chairman of AIG, the big insurance company, said it was costing his company an astonishing $300 million per year to comply.[57]

There were growing reports of public companies going private to avoid Sarbanes-Oxley requirements, and private companies contemplating going public that were abandoning such plans. Money managers moved to set up funds to finance buyouts.[58] There were also reports of foreign companies delisting from U.S. stock exchanges in order to avoid being burdened by U.S. regulations that applied to them as well as domestic companies. There was a sharp drop in new listings by foreign companies.[59] And there were even reports that Sarbanes-Oxley was encouraging outsourcing of jobs to India, as businesses sought ways of reducing their compliance costs.[60]

Perhaps most distressing were reports that Sarbanes-Oxley was inhibiting new business formations, investment, entrepreneurship, risk-taking, and job creation.[61] Said columnist David Ignatius of the *Washington Post,* "Hoping to restore investor confidence, Congress passed the Sarbanes-Oxley bill, which required corporate chief executives, in effect, to take personal responsibility for what their underlings were doing in complicated financial transactions. That sounds great in principle, but in practice it has added to the wariness of CEOs, and probably reduced the job-creating dynamism of the economy."[62]

There was one area, however, where Sarbanes-Oxley unquestionably created jobs: among accountants. Two University of Illinois accounting professors calculated that public companies had spent 120 million hours by 2004 complying with just Section 404 of the legislation. The Big Four accounting firms spent another 12 million hours, for a total of 132 million hours—equivalent to 66,000 people working on nothing else for a year. The professors calculated the dollar cost of this work at between $10 billion and $13 billion, but concluded that these costs were doing almost nothing to correct the sorts of problems that led to the Enron collapse. On the contrary, Sarbanes-Oxley may be sowing the seeds of future problems by creating a false sense of security, they said.[63]

Even British prime minister Tony Blair noted the "delicious irony" of Sarbanes-Oxley creating jobs and profits for those with major responsibility for the problems the legislation was designed to fix. Said Blair in a May 26, 2005, speech, "Sarbanes-Oxley has provided a bonanza for accountants and auditors, the very professions thought to be at fault in the original scandals."[64]

There were rising complaints in 2005 about lost productivity by executives due to Sarbanes-Oxley, growing difficulty by companies in attracting qualified directors, and increasing numbers of companies considering going private, selling out, or merging with other companies as a consequence.[65] Surveys of the cost of complying with Sarbanes-Oxley continued to rise. Financial Executives International estimated the cost at $4,360,000 per company, up 39 percent over the previous year.[66] An estimate by Foley & Lardner put the annual cost at $14.3 million for every company with sales over $1 billion. A common estimate was that Sarbanes-Oxley cost $1 million per $1 billion of revenue in the aggregate.[67]

As large as these numbers are, however, they pale in comparison to the impact on corporate value resulting from Sarbanes-Oxley. University of Rochester economist Ivy Xiying Zhang looked carefully at the impact of the legislation on stock prices and concluded that it cost $1 trillion in lost capitalization.[68] This may help explain why the stock market was unable to mount a sustained upward trend despite good economic news in 2005.

In April 2005, columnist Robert Novak reported that Bush Administration officials were alarmed by the growing cost of Sarbanes-Oxley, which they saw as impeding economic growth, but not enough to do anything about it.[69] Congressman Oxley admitted that there were serious problems with his legislation, but said that the Republican-controlled Congress was not going to revisit the issue.[70]

Free Market or Pro-Business?

Liberals tried to portray Enron's collapse as resulting from deregulation and a cozy relationship with the Bush Administration, which supposedly looked the other way at its wrongdoing because of large campaign contributions.[71] The truth was that George W. Bush had no love for Ken Lay, Enron's chairman, because Lay had backed Bush's opponent, Ann Richards, in the Texas governor's race.[72] Moreover, the Bush Administration rebuffed Enron's requests for aid. It was, in fact, the Clinton Administration that was most receptive to Enron, aiding it with numerous loans and loan guarantees from the Export-Import Bank, Overseas Private Investment Corporation, and World Bank.[73] And although Enron did push for deregulation when it thought it would profit, it was not shy about opposing deregulation when it was benefiting from the existing regulatory environment.[74]

In short, Enron was simply doing what most large businesses do—appealing to free markets when it was in its interest do so and throwing the free market overboard in a heartbeat when it would profit from subsidies, regulation, or other government aid. And like most big businesses, Enron was bipartisan in its pursuit of favors. Ironically, although Bush was hit for Enron's collapse, he was largely blameless. If there is any blame to assess, Clinton deserves more of it, since Enron's problems largely developed on his watch, with the collapse coming shortly after Bush came into office, before he was in a position to do much of anything one way or another.

Nevertheless, the perception that Bush is more of a pro-business than a free market kind of guy is correct. He seldom misses an opportunity to subsidize or bail out big businesses that are in trouble, even if he didn't do so in Enron's case.

A good example is Bush's decision to give the airline industry billions of dollars in government aid in the wake of the World Trade Center and Pentagon attacks. Critics pointed out that the enabling legislation was passed with unseemly haste—just days after the attacks—and that there was a lack of consideration to any alternatives. The size of the aid package was so large, former labor secretary Robert Reich noted, that it exceeded the market capitalization of the six largest airlines.[75] It also brought forth predictable—and equally unjustified—requests for government aid from a long list of other industries.[76]

Not surprisingly, the prospect of government aid immediately foreclosed other options the airlines may have had for coping with the impact of 9/11. For example, banks that had been considering making loans to United Airlines immediately took them off the table when the prospect of a government guarantee arose. And workers, who had just signed a big new contract, were spared from making any contribution to United's recovery.[77] Four years later the bailout program was still in effect and there was no evidence that the airline industry had returned to health. Some analysts blamed the former for the latter, because the subsidies short-circuited an industry restructuring.[78]

Another area where Bush Administration subsidies may have created more problems than they cured is terrorism insurance. In the wake of 9/11, it was clear that the insurance industry was unprepared to deal with potential terrorist targets, with the result that insurance could not be obtained for many construction projects, forcing them to shut down. But this was a temporary problem that would have sorted itself out if allowed to do so. The insurance industry must always cope with new risks and has developed products and procedures for dealing with risks far greater than those of 9/11. There is insurance for hurricanes, floods, and earthquakes that involve far more widespread and costly damage. In the absence of government intervention, the insurance industry would have rebounded just as it had many times in the past.[79]

Ironically, federal terrorism insurance ended up hurting the insurance industry by foreclosing the development of new policies that would have been more profitable than those mandated by the government.[80] Nor is there any evidence that the availability of terrorism insurance has aided commercial property development, since most developers perceive the risk of terrorism to be so low that it's not worth insuring against.[81] In the absence of federal preemption, the insurance industry would have had more incentive to develop policies and products that the market would have found more attractive.

The fact that Bush has tended to look first to subsidies for business before considering other options is evidence of a pro-business attitude rather than a free market philosophy such as Ronald Reagan had. At the same time, the Bush Administration resists doing things that would genuinely help businesses grow the economy, such as enacting meaningful deregulation, preferring instead to give aid in some other way to compensate for the regulations. But this sort of approach only increases economic distortions and ultimately reduces growth. As my old boss, Sen. Roger Jepsen (R–IA), used to put it, putting one's hand on a block of ice doesn't compensate for having the other one on a lighted stove.

During the 2004 election, Bush was criticized by conservatives for failing to make the political case for deregulation. James Gattuso and former Reagan attorney general Ed Meese, both of the Heritage Foundation, criticized Bush for imposing 100 economically significant new regulations each year of his presidency, compared to 90 per year during the Clinton Administration and just 70 per year under Reagan.[82] A 2005 report by the Competitive Enterprise Institute warned that Bush had put into the pipeline a vast increase in government regulation that was going to impact heavily on the economy in coming years.[83]

The White House pushed to increase its control over government regulatory agencies in Bush's second term.[84] However, the goal was not deregulation, but pro-business regulation, which is not at all the same thing.[85] Rather than lift the yoke of government off their backs, businesses "emerged as the leading advocate for government action," the *Wall Street Journal*'s Alan Murray noted.[86] For example, in many areas the Bush Administration and Republicans in Congress were pushing to pre-empt tough state regulation with more lax federal regulation of banking and insurance, even if it meant throwing federalism out the window.[87]

The Bush White House and congressional Republicans also paid lip service to their pledge to avoid unfunded mandates on the states—a key element of the Contract with America in 1994. According to the National Conference of State Legislatures, states spent $29 billion in 2004 complying with federal mandates, including several enacted during the Bush Administration.[88]

Historically, the Republican Party has been the party of business. "After all, the chief business of the American people is business" is Calvin Coolidge's often misquoted phrase.[89] But during the Reagan era, Republicans differentiated between small businesses and entrepreneurs, who just wanted the burden of government lifted from their backs, and big businesses that, more often than not, were looking for a government handout—trade protection, subsidies, and regulations to stifle their competitors. George W. Bush is a throwback to the pre-Reagan era, incapable of telling the difference between being pro-business and being for the free market.[90]

In the words of Columbia University historian Alan Brinkley, "Since 1932, we have not had a president who has been more closely allied with business and more sympathetic to large and powerful corporations."[91]

CHAPTER 7

ON THE BUDGET,
CLINTON WAS BETTER

IT'S NOT UNCOMMON FOR PERCEPTIONS OF PRESIDENTS TO CHANGE after they leave office. As the next chapter discusses, opinions about Richard Nixon are much different today than when he left office, with many liberals who hated him at the time now viewing his domestic policies in a much more favorable light. Something similar is under way with regard to Bill Clinton. Many conservatives who thought he was the devil incarnate when he was in the White House are now inclined to look upon his domestic policies more favorably.

The key reason for this reassessment has been the extremely poor record of George W. Bush on the budget from the point of view of conservatives. In light of Bush's big-spending ways, Clinton now looks almost like another Calvin Coolidge. As a friend once noted about disco music, it seemed so bad at the time because it was being compared to the golden age of rock and roll that had come before it. But by comparison to the awful music that came afterward, disco sounds pretty good today. So too with conservatives and Clinton. Compared to Ronald Reagan, he was awful. Compared to George W. Bush, he looks a lot better.

CLINTON'S CAMPAIGN

BILL CLINTON CERTAINLY did not come into office in 1993 as a fiscal conservative, even though he tried to campaign like one in 1992. He made noises about reducing the deficit, to be sure, but that was just politics. Ross Perot was hammering George H. W. Bush mercilessly on the deficit and Clinton went along for the ride. Clinton put out a plan to balance the budget, but it was mostly smoke and mirrors. It worked as well as it did politically only because Bush was so monumentally incompetent about dealing with the attack on his record and resisted putting forward any kind of hopeful vision for the future.

I was at the Treasury Department at the time and was extraordinarily frustrated that Perot and Clinton had both published books detailing their economic plans that were widely available in every bookstore in the U.S. Where, I kept asking, was the Bush book? Eventually the campaign produced a document outlining Bush's second-term agenda, but it was so poorly distributed that I never was able to land a copy of it for myself and had to make a photocopy of the only one I could find in the department.[1]

Some years afterward, I mentioned this to Andrew Ferguson, who had been a White House speechwriter at the time. He told me that he and Bob Zoellick, then deputy chief of staff in the White House, had actually written the Bush "book" over a long weekend, well after Perot's and Clinton's books had been published by commercial publishers. But rather than follow their lead, the Bush people printed the document themselves, and many senior administration officials never got copies.

So what happened to those that were printed? I asked. Somewhat sheepishly, Ferguson told me that a truck pulled up to the White House after the election and unloaded thousands upon thousands of the Bush books that were printed and never read. That incident always seemed like a good metaphor for the 1992 Bush campaign—too little, too late at every turn. Even Bill Clinton was baffled by Bush's political ineptness. He called the lack of a Bush economic plan "an act of economic insanity and an act of political insanity."[2]

In politics, something always beats nothing—and a plan with numbers will always beat one without any. So Clinton's proposal was politically astute, even if it lacked substance. In his book, he laid out a laundry list of specific proposals that would reduce the deficit—he even carried the numbers out to two decimal places, which was like an inside joke to economists, who laugh at such faux precision. Clinton said he would cut spending by $145 billion over four years and raise taxes by $150 billion, for $295 billion of gross deficit reduction.[3]

Analysts quickly noted that three-fourths of these presumed deficit savings would immediately be consumed by $220 billion of new spending that Clinton also proposed in the same book. And as they looked more deeply at the specifics, they found that he had greatly exaggerated his deficit savings while seriously underestimating the cost of his new spending.[4] *Washington Post* columnist Robert Samuelson said much of Clinton's plan was "patently dishonest."[5] Rich Thomas of *Newsweek* called the Clinton program "economic fantasy."[6] Morgan Stanley economist Stephen Roach accused Clinton of using "make believe numbers."[7]

As the campaign came down to the wire and it looked as if Clinton might win, financial markets started to get a bit nervous. They were particularly concerned about the combination of a Democratic president and a Democratic Congress—the first time that would have existed since the Carter Administration, whose economic mismanagement was a very bad memory, especially for those in the bond market. As markets began to slide, the financial press was filled with foreboding. The credit markets column in the *Wall Street Journal* on October 21 reflected a typical view:

> The bond market sell-off accelerated yesterday after the final presidential debate as more investors bet that Arkansas Gov. Bill Clinton will win the presidential election and step up spending to jumpstart the

economy. . . . Bond traders and money managers said that investors were reacting to fears that a Democrat in the White House will mean increased spending, a larger budget deficit and increased inflation, which would be bad news for fixed-income investments. Said Hugh Lamie, executive vice president at M. D. Sass Investors Services Inc.: "It looks like a Democratic Congress and president with a proclivity toward fiscal and monetary stimulus will have their feet on the gas pedal."[8]

By contrast, if there was some indication that Bush might pull it out, markets rallied. When the bond market rose on October 28, analysts credited this factor. "The late finish was powered by the results of a new Cable News Network poll which showed that the presidential race had narrowed. . . . Traders saw the Democrat's lead . . . evaporating," the *New York Times* reported.[9]

CLINTON IN OFFICE

IN THE END, George H. W. Bush lost in large part because the Republican base was dispirited by the abandonment of his tax pledge and unwillingness to even express regret over this action.[10] The reason seems to have been an inexplicable loyalty to Dick Darman, his budget director and architect of the 1990 budget deal. Even after Darman's disloyalty to Bush was put on full display in a four-part *Washington Post* series in early October, Bush said that he still had "full confidence" in him.[11]

The loyalty wasn't even reciprocated. When a plan was floated for Bush to ask for the resignations of all his economic officials, as a way of demonstrating to voters that his second term would turn over a new leaf, Darman alone refused to go along and the idea was dropped. At the Treasury Department, senior officials stopped referring to Darman by name and just called him "that asshole." Similar opinions were held on

Capitol Hill. Steve Bell, Republican staff director of the Senate Budget Committee, even called a reporter and said, "Remember how I told you that Darman is a no good, lying SOB and I said it was off-the-record? Well, it's on the record now."[12]

The spark to this outrage was the *Post* series written by Bob Woodward, which portrayed Darman as plotting to overthrow the tax pledge as soon as it was made. One way he did this was by making the pledge so strict that it was impossible for it not to be broken at some point. He did this at his confirmation hearing to be OMB director, when he said that the pledge would be in effect "forever." He also said that the pledge applied broadly to any revenue-raising measure, including fees or a tax rise that might be offset by other tax cuts, such as was done in the 1986 Tax Reform Act. He called this the "duck test"—if it looks like a duck, walks like a duck, etc., then it's probably a duck—or in this case, a tax increase and a violation of the pledge.[13] Since it was inevitable that some revenue-raising measure was bound to be put forward by the administration at some point, Darman apparently hoped that this would open the door to wholesale abandonment of the pledge, which he saw as standing in the way of a budget deal that would balance the budget.

Woodward had obtained intimate access to Bush Administration officials by saying that he was going to use the material in a book that wouldn't appear until after the election. Tellingly, he never actually promised any of his sources that he wouldn't use the material before that. They just assumed it. When it looked like Bush was going to lose, however, Woodward decided to cut his losses and put the material out, even if it meant effectively double-crossing all his sources, who thought they would be long gone from government by the time the book came out.[14]

He may have burned his bridges with the Bush crowd, but after Election Day Woodward didn't care, because his series bought him access to the Clinton people, who now viewed him as one of their own. Consequently, Woodward was given a bird's-eye view from the inside as Clinton was forced to accept the necessity of deficit reduction and sacrifice his planned expansion of government investments in health, education, and training as well as the middle-class tax cut he had campaigned on.

As Woodward recounts the debate, Clinton wanted to have a bold liberal agenda, but was talked out of it mainly by Bob Rubin, the former head of Goldman Sachs who had come to Washington to head the National Economic Council. Although Clinton went ahead and asked Congress for a stimulus package of spending to help put people back to work, he didn't fight for it very hard and it died in the Senate, where Republicans were united in opposition—not so much because they opposed the plan in principle, but because they wanted to send Clinton an early message that he would have to deal with them if he wanted to get legislation passed.[15]

Defeat of the stimulus plan strengthened the hand of those Clinton advisers who wanted to make deficit reduction the prime initiative. These included OMB Director Leon Panetta and Treasury Secretary Lloyd Bentsen, as well as Rubin. Rubin knew that markets were wary that the Clinton Administration would be a replay of Carter's and that this fear needed to be nipped in the bud or else markets would be fighting Clinton for the next four years. He also thought that the Federal Reserve would keep interest rates high to counteract the perceived inflationary effects of the budget deficit, so that deficit reduction was essential to Fed easing and bringing interest rates down, which would be a much more powerful stimulus to growth than more spending.

Eventually, after much resistance, Clinton bought into the need for deficit reduction. He finally conceded that the success of his program depended on the Federal Reserve and "a bunch of fucking bond traders."[16] This led him to propose a significant deficit reduction package, including an increase in the top income tax rate to 39.6 percent from 31 percent, and ram it through a very reluctant Democratic Congress and united Republican opposition. It is also why it took so long for Clinton to come up with a health plan, because the principal sticking point was how to pay for it. When the health plan eventually was scrapped, it was in large part because it was widely viewed as a massive tax increase.[17]

The Economics of Gridlock

ELECTION OF A Republican Congress in November 1994 for the first time since 1952 put an end to any expansive spending plans Clinton may still have had. The resulting gridlock meant that government spending effectively was on autopilot for the next six years—Congress wouldn't fund Clinton's plans and he vetoed those of the Republicans in Congress. All of Clinton's thirty-eight vetoes came after Republicans took control of Congress and half of those were either authorizations for spending or appropriations bills.[18] Following is Clinton's explanation for vetoing H.R. 4733, the Energy and Water Appropriations Act of 2000:

> The bill provides nearly $700 million for over 300 unrequested projects, including nearly 80 unrequested projects totaling more than $300 million for the Department of Energy; nearly 240 unrequested projects totaling over $300 million for the Corps of Engineers and more than 10 unrequested projects totaling in excess of $10 million for the Bureau of Reclamation. For example, more than 80 unrequested Corps of Engineers construction projects included in the bill would have a long-term cost of nearly $2.7 billion. These unrequested projects and earmarks come at the expense of other initiatives important to taxpaying Americans.[19]

This era of benign neglect meant that as defense spending fell, following the end of the Cold War and the first Iraq war, the money didn't automatically flow into increased social spending, as had been the case following the Vietnam War. Defense spending fell by 1.4 percent of GDP between 1993 and 2000, and domestic discretionary spending fell from 3.8 percent to 3.3 percent. Even spending on entitlements fell for temporary demographic reasons, from 10.2 percent of GDP to 9.8 percent. Finally, interest on the debt fell, largely because of falling interest rates, from 3 percent of GDP to 2.3 percent. The result was an overall decline in spending of 3 percent of GDP, from 21.4 percent to 18.4 percent, the lowest level since 1966, before the Great Society geared up.

On the revenue side, individual income taxes rose by 2.5 percent of GDP, mainly as the result of rising incomes that pushed people up into higher tax brackets and higher capital gains taxes from the booming stock market. Corporate income taxes and payroll taxes added another 0.8 percent, for a total revenue increase of 3.3 percent of GDP. In all, lower spending and higher revenues constituted a fiscal turnaround of 6.3 percent of GDP, which explains how a deficit of 3.9 percent of GDP in 1993 became a budget surplus of 2.4 percent by 2000.

Clinton economists later tried to paint this fiscal turnaround as a conscious policy objective rather than the mostly unintended result of political gridlock. They even argued that they had discovered a new paradigm—deficit reduction was now seen as being stimulative, the exact opposite of Keynesian economics.[20] Nevertheless, it was a remarkable accomplishment, especially considering that Clinton was often under attack from the left wing of his party for having basically adopted Dwight Eisenhower's economic policy.[21] Even his own Council of Economic Advisers chairman, Nobel Prize–winning economist Joseph Stiglitz, was among the critics.[22] So was Clinton's former secretary of labor, Robert Reich.[23] It took more fortitude than Republicans usually credited him with for Clinton to stand up against his own people and instinctive populism.

This is especially true regarding welfare reform, Clinton's greatest achievement in terms of conservative finance. For decades conservatives had argued that welfare was fostering a culture of dependency that was bad for everyone involved—taxpayers and poor people alike.[24] When Clinton first said he wanted to "end welfare as we know it" during the 1992 campaign, it was widely viewed by conservatives as a transparently phony effort to appear more conservative and take the edge off his liberal image.

But to his credit, Clinton was sincere. Although he vetoed welfare reform twice, he signed it in 1996.[25] It set strict limits on how long people could stay on welfare and required recipients to work. Many liberals predicted dire consequences, especially if the nation went into another recession, but by all accounts the reform was a smashing success. Welfare recipients who were thought to be unemployable did indeed find jobs once forced to do so, and kept them through the 2001 recession.[26] It was really a triumph of conservative policy and Clinton deserves a lot of credit for supporting the effort and not killing it, as he easily could have done with a simple veto.

Perhaps the most remarkable thing about welfare reform is that it represents the only time in American history that an entitlement program has been repealed. Historically, they have been viewed as virtually impossible to cut and the principal cause of expanding government. Yet, the legal right to welfare was eliminated and its status as an entitlement abolished. That a Democratic president signed such historic legislation must be viewed as the domestic equivalent of Nixon going to China.

I think Clinton meant it when, in his 1996 State of the Union Address, he said, "The era of big government is over." How else to explain that civilian employment in the executive branch fell by 237,000 workers between 1992 and 2000?[27] That's an impressive performance that any conservative Republican would love to take credit for. Clinton even presided over one of the most significant reductions in government regulation in history.[28] All of Al Gore's efforts to reinvent government apparently had some impact after all. Of course, the motive was not to get government off the backs of the people, but rather to make it more responsive to their needs, thus improving the image of government and of liberalism. Former CEA chairman Stiglitz explained this strategy:

> The Clinton administration abhorred the wastefulness of many federal programs and the inefficiency of many regulations—and we actually tried to do something about the problem, partly because we believed that unless we could convince voters that the money they paid to government was well used and regulations were well directed, we would lose their support. While Reagan and Bush had railed against the gov-

ernment, public sector employment actually increased during their presidencies. During the Clinton years, the percentage of the national workforce employed by the federal government contracted to levels not seen since the New Deal, a remarkable achievement given the new tasks which the government had undertaken in the intervening seventy years (including Social Security, Medicare, and other programs that touched the lives of every American family). Yet we initiated these reductions, not in order to tear down government, but to reaffirm its role—not just in national defense and homeland security, but in promoting technology and education, providing infrastructure, and enhancing security of all kinds, including health and economic security. By showing that government could be efficient and innovative, we hoped that there would be renewed support for government, and for those endeavors which lie within the responsibility of government.[29]

The Bush Reversal

For these reasons, growing numbers of conservatives now view Clinton as having governed as one of them—at least on economic policy. Conservative *Los Angeles Times* columnist Max Boot has called him the most conservative Democrat in the White House since Grover Cleveland—which is saying a lot, since Cleveland was more conservative on economics than most Republican presidents.[30] "Clinton had better economic policies than most American presidents, fiscal policy included," says free market economist Tyler Cowen of George Mason University.[31]

Barron's columnist Jim McTague had this to say in 2004: "Clinton's presidency is not to be belittled. . . . Arguably, he was the most fiscally responsible, business-friendly president since World War II. He's more an heir to Ronald Reagan than is the current occupant of the White House."[32] And I myself wrote this in the *New York Times*: "Conservatives should rethink the Clinton presidency. At least on economic policy, there is much to praise and little to criticize."[33]

Much of this reassessment of the Clinton record has come about because of the extremely poor budgetary performance of his successor—the disco effect, perhaps. George W. Bush has turned out to be one of the most free-spending presidents on record, even after discounting the effects of the Iraq war and post-9/11 homeland security requirements. Apparently, there is no pork barrel program so egregiously unjustified that he won't sign it into law. Amazingly, he is the first president since John Quincy Adams to serve a full term without vetoing anything.[34]

Early on, Bush signaled that he was not an antigovernment kind of guy and had no qualms about increasing spending if he thought it would buy him the support of some politically important constituency. One of his first actions in office was to bribe the so-called soccer moms with a vast increase in education spending, despite a paucity of evidence relating educational attainment with school spending.[35] The fig leaf for conservatives was increased testing to ensure performance. But conservative education expert Chester Finn saw little payoff. "It's Potemkin reform, a façade underwritten by billions in new spending," he said.[36]

Congress quickly figured out that Bush could easily be rolled on spending.[37] Although he often threatened to veto legislation, he always backed down, usually without receiving anything more than cosmetic concessions in return. Michael Franc of the Heritage Foundation called the veto "an empty threat" in the Bush Administration. Marshall Wittmann of the conservative Hudson Institute said there was "more bark than bite" in Bush's veto threats.[38] This only emboldened Congress, despite Republican control, to lard on ever more pork, confident that any veto threat was unlikely to be carried out. In my opinion, just one veto by Bush early in his administration probably would have saved many billions of dollars of wasteful spending, because future veto threats would have been credible.

According to Citizens Against Government Waste, a watchdog group, there has been more pork barrel spending during the Bush years than at any time in American history. By their calculations, the Clinton years were fairly typical, with the amount of identifiable pork barrel spending varying between $10 billion in 1995 and $17.7 billion in 2000. The number of projects went from a low of 958 in 1996 to a high of 4,326 in 2000. But the Bush years are in a class by themselves. Both the amount of money and the number of pork barrel projects have risen every year, from $18.5 billion and 6,333 projects in 2001 to $27.3 billion and an amazing 13,999 projects in 2005.[39]

Further hindering White House efforts to restrain spending has been Bush's own proclivity for "big projects." In the words of journalist Fred Barnes, whose reporting often reflects the Bush White House viewpoint, "For Bush, achieving these is more important than balancing the budget. By definition, that makes him a big government conservative willing to embrace deficit spending for the sake of large, critical government programs."[40]

Among those big projects was a proposal in 2002 to sharply increase foreign aid. The motive is not entirely clear, since Bush himself noted that "poverty doesn't cause terrorism."[41] It garnered him praise on the editorial pages of liberal newspapers and in liberal foreign policy journals, but not much else.[42] Two years later, when the Asian tsunami hit, the United States was still criticized as being "stingy" by a United Nations official. Although he quickly took it back after a sharp retort from Secretary of State Colin Powell, there is no question that the United States is and always will be viewed as stingy by liberals and the aid community.[43] As a *New York Times* editorial put it, "Are We Stingy? Yes."[44] Although the United States contributed more to tsunami relief than any other country, there is no evidence that it garnered anything except resentment because there wasn't more.[45]

The Bush approach to foreign aid marks a sharp contrast to Reagan's. One of Reagan's first actions was to commission a Treasury Department study of the multilateral development banks, which found them to be almost a complete waste of money.[46] When Reagan spoke before the first joint meeting during his administration of the World Bank and the International Monetary Fund, he made it clear that what developing countries needed wasn't foreign aid, but economic free-dom.[47] There is now a virtual consensus among economists that for-eign aid doesn't work except in very rare circumstances, and more often than not simply contributes to corruption and state mismanagement of the economy.[48] Nevertheless, George W. Bush continued to press for still more foreign aid, while at the same time denying many developing countries what they really wanted: access to our market. Even after promising to aid tsunami victims in any way possible, he wouldn't allow India and Thailand to export their shrimp to the United States.[49]

Government Grows

By 2003 most conservatives and libertarians were disgusted by Bush's free-spending ways. "He's the biggest-spending president we've had in a generation," charged Steve Moore of the conservative Club for Growth. "His fiscal record is appalling," said Ed Crane of the libertar-ian Cato Institute.[50]

In August, Cato's Veronique de Rugy and Tad DeHaven compared spending in the first three years of the Bush and Reagan Administra-tions. During this period, real outlays rose by 6.8 percent under Reagan, but more than twice that, 15.6 percent, under Bush. On domestic discretionary programs, Reagan cut them by 13.5 percent while Bush increased spending by 20.8 percent. Looking at the cabinet depart-ments, Reagan cut spending in nine of fourteen of them, but Bush cut spending in only two, Transportation and Treasury. Perhaps most telling were the differences in the Department of Education's budget, which Reagan cut by 21.8 percent but Bush increased by a whopping 60.8 percent.[51]

In September, the Brookings Institution released a study showing that there were more than 1 million additional people on the federal government's payroll in 2002 than there had been in 1999. While the number of civil service employees was down, there were 727,000 additional people working for federal contractors and another 333,000 working on government grants. Even accounting for jobs that may have been added late in the Clinton Administration and those involving homeland security, there was still a healthy increase in government employment resulting from Bush's policies, the study found.[52]

The end of the fiscal year in September 2003 brought forth a number of analyses noting the sharp rise in spending under unified Republican rule despite the party's past promises to control spending if only those free-spending Democrats weren't in control.[53] The year brought "an extraordinary expansion of government power and spending that showed Republicans were willing to deep-six their party's traditional commitment to fiscal conservatism and limited government," wrote Janet Hook in the *Los Angeles Times*.[54] As the *Wall Street Journal* observed:

> The final tallies show that overall spending grew by almost 9 percent for the 2003 fiscal year ending September 30, and by 21 percent over the past two years. This is before that $400 billion (yeah, right) Medicare prescription drug benefit and this year's energy and omnibus spending bills. If Bill Clinton had tolerated this, Republicans would be shouting from the rooftops. . . . This is astonishing when you recall that only a few years ago "revolutionary" Republicans were proposing to eliminate actual federal programs. Instead, the GOP is now slowly restoring or adding to programs that it once took the political heat for killing or shrinking.[55]

Analysts correctly noted that the fundamental cause of the explosion of spending was the end of gridlock, which had held it in check during the 1994–2000 period. "Now, Republicans go along with Bush's spending initiatives, while he accedes to theirs," Fred Barnes observed.[56] Writing in the *New York Post,* columnist John Podhoretz suggested that the Democratic candidate in 2008 might be successful by attacking Republican budgetary profligacy and promising to bring back gridlock.[57]

In 2004, conservatives fretted that Bush's first term had seen the largest real increase in domestic discretionary spending in postwar history.[58] The *Wall Street Journal* published the following comparison:[59]

President	Fiscal Years	Avg. Annual % Increase
Lyndon Johnson	1965–1969	4.3
Richard Nixon	1970–1975	6.8
Gerald Ford	1976–1977	8.0
Jimmy Carter	1978–1981	2.0
Ronald Reagan	1982–1989	−1.3
George H. W. Bush	1990–1993	4.0
Bill Clinton	1994–2001	2.5
George W. Bush	2002–2004	8.2

Journal columnist George Melloan thought that Democrats had a great issue to use against Bush and the Republicans, but would probably be too stupid to take advantage of it. To the extent that they criticized them on spending, it was always for not spending enough.[60]

The White House responded by showing that its proposed spending increases had been quite modest. But this was just statistical legerdemain because it ignored supplemental appropriation requests.[61] Normally appropriations are made before a fiscal year begins. Supplementals are theoretically for unanticipated additional spending in the current fiscal year after it has already begun. However, the Bush Administration often intentionally left items out of its regular budgets that were not at all unanticipated, such as for the Iraq operation, so that they could be funded through supplementals, thus maintaining the fiction that its budget requests were modest.[62]

I recall being invited to a White House briefing where a political appointee from the Office of Management and Budget tried to sell this snow job to some conservative economists and being astonished at both the idiocy of the effort and its brazenness. Either way, I was pretty insulted that they thought we would fall for this BS.

As budget expert Stan Collender has pointed out, the Bush Administration had a habit of putting out inaccurate budget numbers. The deficit in its 2004 budget appears to have been deliberately overestimated just so that a lower figure could be reported right before the election, thus giving the illusion of budgetary improvement. The following year, the deficit projected in January 2005 was also significantly higher than estimated in the midsession budget review in July. This led Collender to conclude that budget numbers produced by the Bush Administration "should not be taken seriously."[63]

Lacking effective criticism during the presidential campaign from John Kerry for excessive spending, Bush promised still more spending to buy votes wherever possible. Battleground states like Missouri were especially blessed with boatloads of new federal grants from one end of the state to the other.[64] Although Bush continued to talk about cutting the deficit in half, analysts had trouble squaring this promise with all the others he had made involving tax cuts and other proposals. The numbers simply didn't add up.[65]

Bush also continued to indulge in his proclivity for "big projects" by proposing a manned mission to Mars in 2004. Gregg Easterbrook of the Brookings Institution pointed out that fully funding such a mission would ultimately cost at least $600 billion, with no reason to believe that anything worthwhile would be discovered. The whole idea was "hopelessly unrealistic," he said.[66] Former White House budget director Charles Schultze agreed, calling the Bush plan "grandiose" and a "losing investment" that would displace more valuable scientific missions now being conducted by unmanned vehicles.[67]

Conservative columnist Andrew Ferguson lamented that Bush's laundry list of new programs in his acceptance speech at the Republican National Convention effectively marked "the death of American conservatism."[68] Former Republican congressman Joe Scarborough attacked Bush for only paying "lip service" to smaller government and a balanced budget.[69] Only the monumental ineptness of John Kerry in running to his party's left and failing to give conservatives any reason at all to support him kept many from deserting Bush as they had deserted his father. Even so, it was not uncommon for conservatives to say that the return of gridlock was a sufficient reason to support Kerry.

Second-Term Blues

Despite no longer having to run for reelection, there was no indication in Bush's second term that he had changed his free-spending ways. Compared to Bill Clinton, Bush was a "big government liberal," conservative blogger Andrew Sullivan wrote in March 2005. A Cato Institute analysis in May again fingered unified Republican control of Congress and the White House as the key source of budgetary profligacy: "United government under Republicans has ratcheted up the budget for domestic programs considerably. Between fiscal years 2002 and 2005 Congress passed, and Bush signed into law, nondefense budgets that were a total of $91 billion more than the president proposed."[70]

Commenting on this study, Ryan Sager of the conservative *New York Post* said, "It's not always easy to see how radically Bush has transformed the GOP—from Reagan's admonition that 'government is the problem' to Dubya's own assertion that 'when somebody hurts, government has got to move.' But it's a real transformation—and an expensive one."[71]

Bush's abandonment of conservatism was evident as well to nonpartisan political analysts. *National Journal* columnist John Maggs searched and could find little evidence of conservatism in Bush's agenda:

Based on his actions, Bush has abandoned many traditional conservative causes. Instead of trying to rein in entitlements, he has created a costly new one; instead of trying to reduce the reach of the federal government in education, Bush has extended it; instead of trying to control discretionary spending, Bush has agreed to virtually every expansion that Congress has sought. Familiar targets of conservative budget cutters—farm subsidies, job training, import tariffs—have all gotten healthy increases under Bush.[72]

In July 2005, *Wall Street Journal* columnist George Melloan complained, "Mr. Bush has few peers among American presidents in his willingness to let Congress spend as freely as it always wants to do. And the Republican Congress has few peers in history in its willingness to take advantage of the president's generosity."[73] That same month, American Enterprise Institute economist Kevin Hassett pleaded, "Bring back the Clinton administration. Well, maybe not all of it, but at least its spending habits."[74]

Also in July, economists Veronique de Rugy and Kathryn Newmark of the American Enterprise Institute pointed out that despite a real increase in education spending of 82.5 percent through 2005, Bush was continuing to ask for still more. The only thing that it seems to have gotten for him, they argued, was ever more shrill demands from Democrats and the National Education Association that he spend more yet.[75] It only goes to prove the folly of trying to buy off your ideological enemies. It only emboldens them and increases their demands.

In August, conservatives were appalled when President Bush signed into law a heavily pork-laden highway bill costing $295 billion, despite his oft-stated insistence that any bill larger than $256 billion would meet his veto.[76] The National Taxpayers Union identified some 6,500 pork barrel projects costing more than $24 billion in the package. Just three years earlier, Bush's own budget had attacked such earmarks, saying, rightly, that they undercut the Transportation Department's ability to target projects with the most merit, diverted funds into those with low priority, and increased costs.[77]

Conservative columnist Jeff Jacoby noted that Ronald Reagan had vetoed a similar pork fest in 1987. Said Reagan on that occasion, "This bill is a textbook example of special interest, pork-barrel politics at work, and I have no choice but to veto it."[78] Jacoby wished that Bush's admiration of Reagan's foreign policy extended as well to his fiscal policy. [79]

The few fiscal conservatives left in Congress complained that Bush's commitment to sign the highway bill cut their legs out from under them. A veto might have been sustained if Democrats thought they could embarrass the White House by voting en bloc against the bill. In the end, only eight House members voted against it. Rep. Jeff Flake (R-AZ), one of the eight, lamented that Republicans "don't even pretend" to be fiscally conservative anymore.[80]

In truth, they do pretend, but only pretend. Because the highway bill was $8.5 billion larger than allowed by the congressional budget resolution, the legislation "rescinds" that $8.5 billion on the last day the legislation is in effect: September 30, 2009, the last day of the fiscal year.[81] In all my years in Washington, I don't think I have ever seen a more transparently phony budgetary gimmick. By this same method, Congress could technically balance the budget every year just by taking back an amount equal to the deficit on the last day of the fiscal year, which would have no effect because all the money was already spent. This is one reason why balanced budget requirements don't work.[82]

In September 2005, conservatives were again dismayed by Bush's open-checkbook response to Hurricane Katrina.[83] Within days he asked for and received from Congress virtually a blank check for $62.3 billion—equivalent to $62,300 for each of the 1 million people affected by the hurricane—with more to follow. Yet there was no request for offsets, as had been the case with relief for the Northridge earthquake in 1994, merely a promise to look for future savings.[84] When conservatives in Congress suggested budget savings, they were rebuffed.[85]

Of course, there is always the chance that President Bush and Republicans in Congress will get religion and give up their spending ways. But absent either a major economic or political reversal, that is extremely unlikely. As long as they think it is keeping them in office and there is no alternative on the Democratic side, we can expect inertia to operate.

By 2008, however, some Democrat may be smart enough to revive the gridlock argument, which by then could have more potency, especially if Hillary Clinton is the Democratic presidential nominee. She may not in her heart be any kind of conservative, but she can rightly point to a far more conservative fiscal performance on her husband's watch than that which followed. If gridlock was the reason, so be it. It's still a good reason for conservatives to vote for her, she may persuasively argue. Unless her Republican opponent has a long and consistent record of fighting to reduce government spending, that candidate is going to have a difficult time defending Bush's record and may find the Republican base as dispirited as it was in 1992, when another Democrat named Clinton was able to capitalize on it and gain the White House.

CHAPTER 8

Is Bush Another Nixon?

T HERE HAS BEEN AN INTERESTING TRANSFORMATION OF RICHARD Nixon over the last twenty years or so. Whereas once he was viewed as an archconservative, increasing numbers of historians now view him as basically a liberal, at least on domestic policy.[1] They have learned to look past Nixon's rhetoric and methods to the substance of his policies, and discovered that there is almost nothing conservative about them.

I believe that in time, George W. Bush may come to be viewed the same way. Although he infuriates liberals the same way Nixon did, he has also pursued what could be described as a Nixonian agenda using Nixon's methods. The danger, of course, is that Bush could end up having the same negative effects on himself and the economy as Nixon brought on.

BUSH AS NIXON

THE FIRST PERSON to draw a parallel between Bush and Nixon was someone who knew Nixon well: then–*New York Times* columnist

William Safire, who had been a speechwriter for Nixon. In a July 2003 column, Safire imagined a conversation with the late president, who spoke approvingly about Bush's strategy of moving left domestically while keeping the Republican base preoccupied with an external threat. Nixon had done this successfully with Vietnam and Bush was doing it with Iraq.[2]

In October, *Newsweek* columnist Robert Samuelson picked up on the theme. He saw Bush as following the same reelection strategy going into 2004 that Nixon had followed in 1972: boosting the economy any way he could regardless of the long-term consequences. Samuelson's biggest concern was the explosion of domestic spending, and he didn't even mention the Medicare drug bill.[3] The following month, Jacqueline Doherty of *Barron's* saw a dismal replay of the 1970s in the works:

A surge in government spending and persistently low interest rates have revived the U.S. economy. The stock market has rebounded after a nasty fall. The dollar is weakening, gold prices are rising, and the federal deficit has ballooned. Does this sound like the U.S under George W. Bush? In fact, we're describing the state of the Union, or at least its finances, under a previous White House tenant, Richard M. Nixon. But the eerie parallels point to similar policies, and suggest to some sage observers that the Bush administration's efforts to stimulate the economy will lead to similarly sorry ends.[4]

In November, conservative columnist Jim Pinkerton, who had been a special assistant to George H. W. Bush, noted that Karl Rove, George W. Bush's chief political adviser, had gotten his start in politics during Nixon's 1972 campaign. Pinkerton saw similarities between Nixon's Vietnamization policy and Bush's Iraqification strategy. Both presidents hoped they could turn over the fighting in a messy foreign war to indigenous troops and pull American soldiers out fairly quickly. Nixon's effort failed and Pinkerton thought that Bush's would fail as well.[5]

That same month, conservative radio talk show host Rush Limbaugh argued that Bush's Medicare drug bill and total abandonment of spending restraint reminded him of Nixon. "He's following Richard Nixon's footsteps on domestic policy," Limbaugh told his radio audience on November 25.[6]

Reporters were starting to notice similarities between Bush's and Nixon's styles as well. Dana Milbank of the *Washington Post* noted that they both structured their White Houses the same way—relying heavily on a small inner circle of trusted aides who wielded enormous power while mostly ignoring everyone else, including the cabinet. Milbank also saw strong similarities in the way the two presidents managed the news—avoiding press conferences, proactively attacking the media for liberal bias whenever it reported something unfavorable to them, and taking great pains to withhold information from the press.[7]

There was growing commentary on Internet blogs about the extent to which Bush and Nixon governed in analogous ways. One commentator was Prof. David Bernstein of the George Mason University Law School, who wrote:

"Compassionate conservatism" seems to have turned out to be a replay of the Nixon strategy of buying off every conceivable interest group that is capable of being bought off by a Republican administration, while using social issues and conservative rhetoric to appease the Republican masses. Nixon, at least, had the excuse of governing in an era when liberalism was at its apex, and with the constraints imposed by the other two branches of government, dominated by liberal Democrats. What is George Bush's excuse?[8]

By December, Bush-Nixon parallels were becoming commonplace. *Wall Street Journal* columnist Alan Murray saw the two presidents as bookends to a conservative era—Nixon marking the beginning and Bush the end.[9] Conservative columnist Christopher Caldwell also saw Karl Rove as the linkage between Bush's style and Nixon's. He described both as building their reelections around policies that helped them personally in the short run but harmed the Republican Party in the long run.[10] "In the history of presidential politics, only Richard Nixon rivals George W. Bush's level of cynicism about the economy," the *New Republic*'s Noam Scheiber added.[11]

Going into the election in 2004, Bush tried hard to portray himself as the heir to Ronald Reagan in order to secure the Republican Party's base. But close observers knew different. "In truth, Bush looks less like Ronald Reagan than like Richard Nixon, a conservative who was consistent not in his conservatism but in his determination to poach all the best political real estate, wherever it lay," wrote Jonathan Rauch in the *Atlantic Monthly*.[12]

It's ironic that most of the Nixon-Bush comparisons came from those on the right side of the political spectrum. I thought that Democrats would find this to be an effective line of attack in 2004.[13] For some reason they didn't use it. But recently, Sid Blumenthal, a Clinton White House political operative, called Bush's White House "the highest stage of Nixonism," and accused him of "building a leviathan beyond Nixon's imagining."[14] So perhaps they were just holding it in reserve.

The balance of this chapter will look in more detail at some of Nixon's policies, because I think there is a similarity between his and Bush's that could also have similar economic and political consequences.

THE INFLATION GENIE IS RELEASED

TO UNDERSTAND NIXON'S economic policy, one has to go back to 1960, when he ran against John F. Kennedy for the White House after having served eight years as Dwight Eisenhower's vice president. As the de facto incumbent, Nixon took the blame for everything bad that happened on Eisenhower's watch. Although today the 1950s are remembered as a somewhat idyllic era economically, in fact growth was slow and there were three serious recessions during Eisenhower's presidency:

the first from July 1953 to May 1954, and the second from August 1957 to April 1958.[15] The third began in April 1960, in the midst of Nixon's first presidential campaign. Nixon explains how he first came to realize that he would have to campaign in a recession:

> Early in March [1960], Dr. Arthur F. Burns, the former chairman of the President's Council of Economic Advisers and probably the nation's top authority on the economic cycle, called me in my office in the Capitol. In January, virtually all the economists in the country had been bullish about the prospects for the economy throughout 1960. But when Burns came to see me in March, he expressed great concern about the way the economy was then acting. . . . Burns' conclusion was that unless some decisive governmental action were taken, and taken soon, we were headed for another economic dip which would hit its low point in October, just before the elections.[16]

Nixon urged Eisenhower to take action. He pointed out that the two previous recessions on his watch had led to significant Republican losses in the 1954 and 1958 elections.[17] But he was overruled, in part because Eisenhower's other economic advisers did not share Burns' pessimistic forecast. Of course, Burns turned out to have been almost exactly correct—something Nixon never forgot.

Nixon appears to have cared little for economics and paid almost no attention to his appointments in that area after finally achieving the presidency in 1968. There was one exception, however, and that was the Federal Reserve Board, which was still chaired by William McChesney Martin. Martin had been chairman continuously since 1951 and Nixon blamed him more than anyone else for his defeat in 1960. He believed that ill-timed Fed tightening of monetary policy had brought on the recession that cost him the election. Consequently, Nixon was absolutely determined to get Martin out as soon as his term expired and replace him with someone who would guarantee an easy money policy going into the 1972 election. That man was Arthur Burns, who replaced Martin on January 31, 1970.

Nixon's determination to control the Federal Reserve was heightened by the onset of another recession in December 1969 that ran through November 1970. Nixon had made clear to Burns that the independence of the Fed and the goal of price stability were to take a back seat to political considerations. The "need for a Republican Congress," Nixon said, must be "superior" to the goal of fighting inflation, he told his staff in December 1969.[18]

The problem was that rising prices were already a problem when Burns took over the Fed. Inflation, which had been in the 1 percent to 2 percent range for many years, suddenly jumped to 3 percent to 4 percent between 1967 and 1968, and then jumped again to 6 percent in 1969 and 1970. This was especially worrisome to economists because recessions normally caused inflation to fall sharply. When that didn't happen during the 1969–70 recession, they realized that inflation was not a temporary problem, but something deeper.

The Federal Reserve should have tightened when Burns came in. His former student, economist Milton Friedman, strongly urged him to do so.[19] But under political pressure from Nixon, to whom he owed his appointment, Burns resisted it, thus allowing the situation to get out of control at a critical moment in time. By 1971, concerns about inflation were so great that Nixon imposed wage and price controls and eliminated the last vestiges of the gold standard in August of that year.[20] Although Burns must have known that this was a bad policy that would screw up the economy while doing nothing to stem underlying inflationary forces, he did nothing to talk Nixon out of it.[21]

Herb Stein, a member of the Council of Economic Advisers at the time, has made it clear that Nixon and the others, including himself, didn't really have a clue as to what they were doing. He calls the theory under which they were operating "flaky."[22] In 1980, I had the opportunity to ask former treasury secretary John Connally why he had supported price controls, after he had just given a speech explaining why they never work. His response, basically, was that there had been a unique set of circumstances in 1971 that had never existed before and would never exist again, in which controls could have worked.

Nixon's strategy was poor economics, but at least for a while was good politics. Measured inflation moderated and economic growth strengthened going into the election, helping give him a stunning victory in 1972. But the chickens soon came home to roost. As the price controls inevitably broke down, inflation spurted, finally forcing the Fed to tighten. The fall in the dollar also spurred oil-exporting countries to demand sharply higher prices for their oil.[23] Together, these factors brought on the deepest postwar recession in November 1973, which ran through March 1975. The weakness of the economy in 1974 made it untenable for Nixon to survive the unwinding Watergate scandal, which might have been possible if the economy had been strong.

The record shows that the declining economy was much more important to the fall in Nixon's poll ratings than Watergate.[24] Bill Clinton subsequently survived the Lewinsky scandal in large part because the economy was booming. As Nixon himself later put it, "It is very rare in history to see a political leader touched by scandal who is brought down during an expanding economy."[25]

The verdict of history is that Arthur Burns was a very poor Federal Reserve chairman, who unleashed inflationary forces that took a decade to tame.[26] The only real disagreement among economists is whether Burns fully understood the mistakes he was making, or was so wedded to incorrect Keynesian theories that he didn't realize what he was doing.[27] The only alternative is that he was under irresistible political pressure from Nixon and had no choice.[28] Neither explanation is very favorable to Burns.[29]

Economists now recognize the Nixon era as Exhibit A in how the adoption of bad economic policies in pursuit of short-term political gain eventually turns out to be bad politics as well.

TAXES AND SPENDING EXPLODE

WHEN INFLATION BEGAN to become a serious problem late in Lyndon Johnson's administration, economists misunderstood its cause. Because they were still largely operating under Keynesian economic theories, they thought that the federal budget deficit was the prime cause of inflation. In fact, the deficit had nothing to do with inflation; its root cause was an excessively easy monetary policy. Not realizing this, they pushed Johnson to raise taxes to reduce the deficit and, thereby, tame inflation.[30]

In 1967, Johnson asked Congress to enact a temporary surtax of 6 percent of each taxpayer's and corporation's regular liability. Congress did not act and so Johnson renewed his request in 1968, upping the surtax to 10 percent. Rising inflation spurred Congress to action and the surtax was enacted on June 28, 1968, retroactive to January 1 for corporations and April 1 for individuals. The surtax was scheduled to expire on June 30, 1969, the end of the fiscal year in those days. This was a significant tax increase, equaling about 1 percent of the gross domestic product.[31]

Nixon had campaigned on allowing the surtax to expire on schedule. But almost immediately after taking office, he switched gears, endorsing Johnson's request to extend the surtax in his last budget. Democrats in Congress played hardball, however, demanding repeal of the Investment Tax Credit as well, a measure first initiated by John F. Kennedy. But when Nixon acceded to this demand, Democrats raised the price, demanding action on fundamental tax reform as well.[32]

What had the Democrats so exercised was a Treasury Department study released just three days before Nixon took office showing that 155 tax returns in 1967 reported an income of at least $200,000 ($1.2 million in 2005 dollars), including 21 with an income of $1 million or more, and no income tax liability.[33] The scandal was that this had been done perfectly legally by taking advantage of legitimate tax deductions, exemptions, and exclusions.

Pressure had been building for some years to restrict "tax loopholes" that were allowing the rich to avoid paying their "fair share."[34] The Treasury study was the final impetus to action, aided by the creation of the first "tax expenditures" list, which Treasury had been working on for some years.[35] This led Nixon to propose the Tax Reform Act of 1969, based largely on ideas that had been developed during the Kennedy and Johnson administrations. As one observer put it, "Nixon was becoming the Republican Robin Hood."[36]

Nixon eventually got his precious surtax extension, but the price was extremely high. Not only did the Tax Reform Act of 1969 eliminate the ITC, it also raised the tax rate on long-term capital gains and imposed a minimum tax for the first time. The result was to sharply raise the cost of capital. Especially harmful was the increase for capital gains, on which the maximum long-term tax rate had been 25 percent since 1942. The Tax Reform Act of 1969 raised this to 35 percent. Interactions with the minimum tax and other tax provisions could raise it as high as 49.1 percent.[37] Economists later fingered this action as a key factor in the economic malaise of the 1970s, leading a Democratic Congress and a Democratic president to cut the maximum capital gains rate to 28 percent in 1978.[38]

The reason why Nixon was so keen on raising taxes—even soaking the rich—is that he wanted to greatly expand government spending to buy votes for reelection. In August 1969, Nixon proposed two expensive new programs: revenue sharing for the states and a guaranteed annual income for poor people. The following month he proposed a 10 percent across-the-board increase in Social Security benefits, plus automatic indexing of benefits to inflation thereafter. Congress bumped this to 15 percent and attached it to the Tax Reform Act of 1969, which Nixon signed into law in December.

Nixon was still adamant about indexing, which had not been enacted, and pressed ahead for it in 1970. Congress did not complete action on the legislation that year, but did find time to pass another Social Security benefit increase of 10 percent in early 1971, which

Nixon dutifully signed. Finally, in 1972, Congress approved the automatic indexing provision Nixon had strenuously sought, along with yet another across-the-board benefit increase of 20 percent, payable in October of that year, just before the election.[39]

One argument made for indexing was that increasing benefits automatically would preclude the ad hoc increases that Congress was enacting. It's worth remembering that between February 1970 and October 1972, Nixon and Congress raised everyone's Social Security benefits by 52 percent, compounded. But over this period, inflation went up only 11.3 percent. The inflation increase was 23.3 percent starting from the point at which Congress last raised Social Security benefits in March 1968. So benefits were raised far more than necessary just to compensate for inflation. Real benefits increased significantly at a time when most Americans were having difficulty making ends meet.

The argument that indexing would actually hold down future benefit increases would have been more persuasive if Congress hadn't screwed up the indexing formula, which inadvertently overindexed benefits to inflation.[40] In the absence of action, the average worker would see his benefits rise from 44 percent of his last year's wages in 1980 to 68 percent by 2050. A low-income worker would have seen his replacement rate rise from 56 percent to 106 percent. Even high-income workers would have seen an increase, with their replacement rate rising from 34 percent to 56 percent.[41]

In 1977, Congress changed the law to stabilize replacement rates at 55 percent for low-income workers, 43 percent for average workers, and 29 percent for high-income workers. In the process, it changed the way initial benefits are calculated so that they became indexed to wages rather than prices. Since real wages rise over time, the result was to program into Social Security an automatic increase in real benefits every year for new retirees. A panel of experts recommended price indexing back in 1976, but this advice was ignored.[42] We are still dealing with the consequences of that decision.[43]

If we look at the data today, there was not much of an increase in total federal spending on Nixon's watch—spending as a share of GDP was about the same in 1972 as it had been in 1969—although he did take all the money saved by winding down the Vietnam War and channeled it into domestic spending. Defense spending fell from 8.7 percent of GDP in 1969 to 6.7 percent in 1972 while domestic discretionary spending rose from 3.6 percent to 4.2 percent, Social Security went up from 2.8 percent to 3.3 percent, and other entitlements increased from 0.9 percent to 1.4 percent.

But Nixon's real legacy as a spender is that he put into place a huge permanent increase in Social Security spending that continues to raise spending even today.[44] And he did it all to buy a single election. Subsequently, most retirees came to believe that automatic annual increases in benefits had always been part of Social Security, and it became almost impossible even to slow the growth of benefits no matter how serious the nation's fiscal and economic problems.

Toward the end of his presidency, Nixon tried to put the spending genie back in the bottle by signing the Congressional Budget and Impoundment Control Act of 1974. It is not now remembered, but the impetus for this legislation was to take away budget impoundment authority, a kind of line-item veto that had been exercised by every president since George Washington, which Democrats hated.[45] Republicans added all of the budget process reforms as their price for support, in hopes that it would get spending under control. Those reforms turned out to do almost nothing to hold down spending, but every president since Nixon has lamented the loss of impoundment authority. Unfortunately, every effort since to give the president line-item veto power has failed.[46]

BIRTH OF THE REGULATORY STATE

PERHAPS THE BIGGEST impact of Nixon's economic policies was in the area of government regulation. He created the Environmental Protection Agency (July 1970), the Occupational Health and Safety Administration (December 1970), and the Consumer Product Safety Commission (October 1972). In addition, the energy price regulation established by the wage and price control program in 1971 remained in effect long after the rest of the controls expired, and were not ended until Ronald Reagan took office in 1981.[47] As Herb Stein has remarked, "Probably more new regulation was imposed on the economy during the Nixon administration than in any other presidency since the New Deal."[48]

Economists saw the impact of this new regulation in declining productivity almost immediately. Brookings Institution economist Edward Denison estimated that by 1975, output in the nonresidential business sector was 1.8 percent smaller than it would have been under the regulatory environment of 1967. He estimated that regulation was reducing the annual productivity growth rate by 0.5 percent per year, about one-fourth of the historical productivity growth rate.[49]

Looking back from today, it is even clearer that something profound happened in 1973 that dramatically reduced the growth of productivity. Labor productivity averaged 2.85 percent per year from 1959 to 1973. This fell to 1.49 percent per year from 1973 to 1995, when the advent of computers and information technology boosted productivity growth to 3 percent per year. About three-fifths of the decline was due to a reduction in technological advancement and the rest due to a decline in capital formation.[50]

Regulation contributed to this result in several ways, but mainly by diverting capital investment and research and development from areas dictated by markets to those demanded by government. For example, in 1972, the first year for which we have data, businesses were forced to spend $16.6 billion on pollution abatement and control. This represented 20 percent of all investment in business equipment that year. And this sort of thing went on year after year. In 1994, the last year for which there is data, outlays for pollution abatement and control came to $121.8 billion. Over that twenty-two-year period, businesses and governments spent at least $1.5 trillion to reduce pollution.[51]

Among studies documenting the negative effect of Nixon-era regulation on productivity and economic growth are these:

- A study of electric utilities found that restrictions on sulfur dioxide emissions over the 1973–79 period reduced productivity by 0.59 percentage points per year.[52]
- The diversion of research and development expenditures into pollution abatement in the 1970s reduced the effectiveness of overall R&D spending, thereby contributing significantly to the decline in productivity.[53]
- Environmental regulation had especially negative effects on the chemical, primary metals, and stone, clay, and glass industries, reducing both capital and labor productivity, accounting for almost all of the decline in productivity growth between the 1961–73 period and the 1973–80 period.[54]
- EPA and OSHA regulations reduced productivity growth by 0.44 percent per year for manufacturing industries, about 30 percent of the overall decline in productivity in the 1970s.[55]
- For every $1 invested in pollution abatement by oil refineries, productivity fell by $1.35. For paper mills the decline was $1.74, and for steel mills the decline was $3.28.[56]
- Environmental regulation imposes a cost on the private sector equivalent to about 10 percent of the total cost of government purchases of goods and services.[57]

Nixon's economic regulation was not limited to safety and the environment. He also promoted trade protection and was responsible for initiating affirmative action, which continues to bedevil race relations to this day.

Like the current president, Nixon was keen on buying the votes of South Carolina textile workers with trade protection. This led him to support the Multi-Fiber Agreement, which took effect January 1, 1974. It established rigid quotas on textile imports that lasted until the end of

2004. Nixon also initiated an embargo on soybean exports to Japan in order to hold down domestic food prices and imposed a 10 percent surtax on all imports at the same time he imposed price controls. In short, "He was quite prepared to sacrifice liberal trade principles whenever it suited his domestic political purposes."[58]

To buy the votes of blacks, Nixon came up with something called the "Philadelphia Plan," which established strict quotas for minorities on federal construction projects. Later, this was extended to all government contracts. Thus, it was Nixon who converted affirmative action from a benign program to make an extra effort to help minorities, as it had been during the Kennedy and Johnson administrations, into a de facto race quota system.[59]

MEN OF THE LEFT?

SPACE PROHIBITS LISTING every leftward policy of the Nixon Administration. One still worth mentioning, however, was his initiation of what today we call "industrial policy"—active government intervention in the economy on behalf of big businesses. These efforts included the bailout of the Penn Central Railroad in 1970, which eventually begat Amtrak, a money sieve to this day; a bailout of the Lockheed Corporation in 1971; and Nixon's efforts to subsidize development of a commercial supersonic jet aircraft, which Congress rejected and the Europeans went ahead with.[60] They lost their shirts on it, finally abandoning Concorde service in 2003.

At the time, leftists like economist John Kenneth Galbraith praised Nixon's actions in these areas as heralding the dawn of American socialism. He saw parallels to the Conservative Party's conversion to socialism in England in the 1950s. Galbraith noted that socialists in England had also started by nationalizing the railroad system.[61]

This did not go unnoticed on the right side of the political spectrum. Among the strongest Nixon-haters was the ultraconservative John

Birch Society, which routinely published attacks on Nixon's liberal policies.[62] Indeed, in 1972 a member of the society, Congressman John
Schmitz (R–CA), ran against Nixon for president and garnered more
than a million votes, including mine. Interestingly, Schmitz was actually
Nixon's own congressman by virtue of representing San Clemente,
where Nixon maintained his voting address.

All along, there have been some sophisticated liberals and conservatives who have viewed Nixon's domestic program as essentially liberal.
For example, just before the 1972 election, *New York Times* columnist
James Reston wrote, "It would probably be wrong to say that the reelection of President Nixon marked a swing to the right. In comparison with the policies he offered the American people four years ago, he
has been going to the left ever since."[63]

By 1992, it was becoming conventional wisdom that Nixon had
governed as a liberal. As conservative columnist George Will explained:

> Nixon's wage-and-price controls constituted the largest peacetime
> intrusion of government in the economy in American history, surpass-
> ing even the dreams of the New Dealers. Nixon, saying, "We are all
> Keynesians now," had an industrial policy (subsidizing the SST), and he
> got government into running a railroad (Amtrak). He initiated revenue
> sharing, which weakened spending restraints at the state and local lev-
> els. . . . The Environmental Protection Agency and the Occupational
> Safety and Health Administration were born under Nixon. The seeds
> of today's deficit explosion were sown in Nixon's competition . . . to
> see who could be most lavish with Social Security.[64]

Will misquotes Nixon's words about Keynes. What he actually said
was, "I am now a Keynesian in economics." Nixon made this statement
to broadcaster Howard K. Smith off-camera after a televised interview
on January 4, 1971. It was reported shortly thereafter.[65] It was economist
Milton Friedman who said, "We are all Keynesians now." This observation was made in an interview with *Time* magazine in 1965.[66] Still, it

is revealing that Nixon said what he said. At the time, people viewed it as the equivalent of the Pope saying he had converted to Islam.

It is too soon to say if history will put Nixon and Bush side by side, as two superficially conservative presidents who enacted liberal programs in order to buy votes for reelection. But the parallels are strong, as many observers have attested. Here is a summary of the case as I would make it:

- Nixon was obsessed with avenging his loss in 1960, which he blamed on the Federal Reserve for bringing on a recession. Bush was obsessed with avenging his father's loss in 1992, which resulted from a recession in 1990 and 1991 that was brought on by a tight Federal Reserve policy.
- Nixon initiated a massive, permanent increase in Social Security spending to buy the votes of the elderly in 1972. Bush initiated a massive, permanent increase in Medicare spending to buy the votes of the elderly in 2004.
- Nixon imposed massive new government regulation on the economy in the form of EPA, OSHA, and the CPSC. He also used protectionism to buy votes at every opportunity. Bush imposed massive new government regulation on the economy in the form of the Sarbanes-Oxley bill and also used protectionism to buy votes at every opportunity.
- Both engaged in controversial foreign wars and invoked "national security" at every opportunity to stifle criticism on the right.

The result of Nixon's policies was that the economy was severely weakened, making it harder for him to survive the Watergate scandal. He is now viewed as one of the worst presidents in American history.[67] Bush's legacy will depend on whether we survive the many financial and economic risks that abound and whether people in the future see him as responsible for the explosion of spending that is coming and the inevitable tax increase that I discuss in the next chapter.

CHAPTER 9

THE INEVITABLE
TAX INCREASE

G EORGE W. BUSH'S BEST-KNOWN DOMESTIC POLICY MAY BE HIS relentless effort to cut taxes. Yet ironically, he may ultimately be responsible for enactment of the largest tax increase in American history. It may not come on his watch, but it is inevitable and will be the direct result of Bush's policies.

BALANCED BUDGETS

AS NOTED EARLIER, there is really little economic rationale for the way Bush cut taxes. Unlike Ronald Reagan, he was not trying to implement supply-side economic policies that would increase work and investment incentives. The bulk of the Bush tax cuts were simple giveaways, little different, economically, from government spending.

But tax cuts are different politically. Increased spending ratchets up the size of government, eventually leading to tax increases. Tax cuts, on the other hand, can have the opposite effect: bringing down the size of government as lower revenues lead to spending cuts. This has become known as the starve-the-beast theory of taxation.

Throughout most of the postwar era, Republican fiscal policy was based on the idea of achieving a balanced federal budget. In practice, this mostly meant opposing tax cuts rather than trying to bring down spending. It was very hard to cut spending and much easier just to keep revenues on automatic pilot—putting off tax cuts until the budget was balanced.[1] Dwight Eisenhower clearly articulated this Republican philosophy at a February 17, 1953, press conference:

> Whether we are ready to face the job this minute or any other time, the fact is there must be balanced budgets before we are again on a safe and sound system in our economy. That means, to my mind, that we cannot afford to reduce taxes, reduce income, until we have in sight a program of expenditures that shows that the factors of income and of outgo will be balanced. Now that is just to my mind sheer necessity.[2]

Toward this end, Eisenhower firmly rejected all efforts to cut taxes on his watch—even by a Republican Congress in 1953. Despite suffering for it at the polls in 1954, when Republicans lost control, not to regain it again until 1994, the GOP embraced the Eisenhower philosophy. Most even went so far as to oppose the Kennedy tax cut on the grounds that it would increase the deficit.[3] In the House of Representatives, Republicans overwhelmingly voted against the tax cut by almost a three-to-one margin: 48 for and 126 against. Although a majority of Republican senators supported the tax cut, a third voted against it (21 for, 10 against).

The strange result was that by today's standards, Eisenhower was behaving like a Democrat while John F. Kennedy acted like a Republican.[4] This did not go unnoticed at the time. In a 1964 paper, UCLA economist Neil Jacoby, a member of Eisenhower's Council of Economic Advisers, pointed out how in practice Eisenhower was really quite liberal and Kennedy was really quite conservative:

> Federal performance under the Kennedy-Johnson Administration has been much different from the fiscal policy pronouncements of the

Democratic Party. Just as fiscal performance under the Eisenhower Administration was decidedly *less* conservative than Republican preachments, so has fiscal performance under the Kennedy Administration been *more* conservative than Democratic orthodoxy. In fact, this Administration's proposal of a massive reduction in Federal taxation, accompanied by an effort to hold the line on expenditures, is an essentially conservative adjustment to the working of a progressive Federal tax system in a growing economy. The orthodox Democratic adjustment would be a further expansion of federal expenditures![5]

Both Richard Nixon and Gerald Ford continued the balanced budget orthodoxy as Republican dogma. This led Nixon to renew the Vietnam War surtax in 1969 and to sign the Budget Act of 1974, even though it stripped the president of his power to impound funds. Because the Budget Act put in place procedures making it harder to cut taxes, Republicans thought the legislation would help bring about a balanced budget. Ford strenuously resisted congressional Republican efforts to cut tax rates, supporting only a temporary tax rebate in 1975 because it would not permanently impair the government's revenue-raising ability.

STARVE THE BEAST

AFTER FORD'S DEFEAT in 1976, Republicans in Congress were forced to rethink their doctrinaire opposition to tax cuts. They were down to just 143 seats in the House (out of 435) and 38 (of 100) in the Senate, and there was serious talk about the Republican Party literally ceasing to exist.

It was only because their backs were up against a wall that Republicans became at all receptive to the idea of tax cutting. Although many Republicans were uncomfortable with the idea of making the deficit worse at a time of high inflation, they were also convinced that the

American people were overtaxed and that they wanted a tax cut.[6] After the passage of Proposition 13 in California on June 6, 1978, most Republicans jumped aboard the tax-cut bandwagon being led by Congressman Jack Kemp, Republican of New York, Sen. Bill Roth, Republican of Delaware, and others. Their signature legislation would have cut statutory income tax rates by about 30 percent across the board.[7]

Kemp and Roth were not terribly worried about the deficit. They were more concerned with getting the economy moving again, and if a deficit happened to emerge, then so be it. A larger deficit wasn't the goal, as it had been with Kennedy, only a necessary consequence, an investment in the American economy that was expected to lose money for a while. And Kemp truly believed that the economy would expand enough to recoup the revenue loss from the tax cut, as predicted by the Laffer Curve.

But the vast majority of Republicans were less sure than Kemp was that revenues would really rise from a tax cut. They needed a more conventional rationale for supporting a politically popular tax cut in a way that was consistent with traditional Republican fiscal policy. From this was born the starve-the-beast theory of taxation.[8] Higher deficits from the tax cuts, it was said, would bring about political support for spending cuts.

The great economist Milton Friedman was undoubtedly the most outspoken advocate of this philosophy. In his view, the deficit was never very important, as it was to Keynesian economists. In the Friedman model, the money supply, which is controlled by the Federal Reserve, is far more important to business cycles, inflation, and interest rates. Keeping government as small as possible was also important, but as much for moral reasons as economic ones.

Hence, Friedman argued that shrinking the size of government, as measured by spending, was far more important than reducing the deficit. If tax cuts caused spending to be cut, then this was a good thing even if they raised the deficit. In a *Newsweek* column shortly after passage of Proposition 13, Friedman said, "I have concluded that the only effective way to restrain government spending is by limiting government's explicit tax revenue—just as a limited income is the only effective restraint on any individual's or family's spending."[9]

Other Republican intellectuals, like columnist George Will and economists Herb Stein and Alan Greenspan, quickly endorsed this view. Writing in the *Wall Street Journal* just after the Friedman column appeared, Irving Kristol said that Republicans had "learned the lesson on Proposition 13, which is that tax cuts are a prerequisite for cuts in government spending."[10]

Thus it was possible to support tax cuts without believing in the Laffer Curve or abandoning fiscal conservatism as long as one saw them as essentially forcing spending cuts down Congress's throat. Ronald Reagan skillfully played on this theme to gain support for his 1981 tax cut. Said Reagan in a nationally televised address early in his presidency, "There were always those who told us that taxes couldn't be cut until spending was reduced. Well, you know, we can lecture our children about extravagance until we run out of voice and breath. Or we can cure their extravagance by simply reducing their allowance."[11]

Although the deficit rose to 6 percent of the gross domestic product in 1983, its highest level since World War II, there was little evidence in Reagan's first term that this put much downward pressure on overall federal spending, which rose from 21.7 percent of GDP in 1980 to 23.5 percent in 1983. However, this was largely due to Reagan's increase in defense spending even as he tried to cut domestic spending, and because much spending, such as for Social Security and interest on the debt, cannot be controlled through the appropriations process.

By Reagan's second term, both deficits and spending were trending downward. In his last fiscal year, spending was down to 21.2 percent of GDP and the deficit was down to 2.8 percent. And during Reagan's presidency there was a significant decline in domestic discretionary spending, which fell from 5.2 percent of GDP in 1980 to 3.4 percent by 1989.

REAGAN'S TAX INCREASES

ONE REASON WHY there was such a small impact on spending from the 1981 tax cut is that Reagan subsequently endorsed a number of major tax increases that effectively took back about half of the tax cut.

The big Reagan tax cut, modeled on the Kemp-Roth tax bill, was signed into law in August 1981. But almost immediately, work began on a tax increase that would take back much of it.[12] A key reason was pressure from the Federal Reserve, which feared that rising deficits would be inflationary, forcing it to keep monetary policy tight and interest rates high.

As early as October 1981, work had started on what came to be known as the Tax Equity and Fiscal Responsibility Act of 1982. It focused mainly on business provisions of the 1981 tax cut that were widely viewed as excessive, particularly one known as "safe harbor leasing." In effect, it allowed companies to sell their tax losses to other companies. As a result, a number of very large, very profitable corporations like General Electric were able to reduce their corporate tax liability virtually to zero. Regardless of the economic merits of safe harbor leasing in principle, it became politically intolerable.

TEFRA, as it was called, was the largest peacetime tax increase in American history, according to a study by Treasury Department economist Jerry Tempalski.[13] He figures that it raised federal revenues by about 1 percent of GDP, equivalent to about $120 billion per year in today's economy. With the 1981 tax cut reducing revenues by an average of 2.9 percent of GDP, TEFRA alone took back one-third in the form of higher taxes.

Nineteen eighty-two also saw passage of the Highway Revenue Act, which raised the gasoline tax to pay for new highways. It raised taxes by about $3 billion per year.

In 1983, there was a Social Security crisis that led to appointment of a commission chaired by economist Alan Greenspan. The principal recommendation of this commission, which was enacted by Congress, was to raise the payroll tax rate and the wage base to which it applied. This raised revenues by about $9 billion per year.

The Deficit Reduction Act of 1984 was the second largest tax increase of the Reagan Administration, raising revenues by $18 billion per year. The Consolidated Omnibus Budget Reconciliation Act of 1985 increased revenues by another $2.4 billion per year.

The Tax Reform Act of 1986 was designed to be revenue-neutral, but in the short run it, too, was a revenue raiser, adding almost $20 billion to federal coffers in the first two years. The Superfund Amendments, also enacted that year, were another small, but explicit, tax increase.

There were two more tax increases in 1987, the Omnibus Budget Reconciliation Act of 1987 and the Continuing Resolution for 1987. And finally, the Reagan tax increases ended with another one in the Continuing Resolution for 1988.

Reagan's last budget, put forward in January 1989, contained a table that summarized the net effect of all the tax changes during his eight years in office. According to this table, reproduced in Appendix III, in 1988 federal revenues were lower by $275.3 billion as the result of legislation Reagan signed into law. But in that same year, revenues were higher by $132.7 billion as the result of explicit tax increases he also signed into law—about half of the tax cut. Thus there was a net tax cut of just $142.6 billion.

It's worth noting as well that federal revenues as a share of GDP rose significantly in Reagan's second term, from 17.4 percent in fiscal year 1984 to 18.4 percent in 1989. On average, federal revenues as a share of GDP were actually a little higher in the 1980s than they had been in the 1970s—18.3 percent versus 17.9 percent. The postwar average is 17.9 percent of GDP (1945–2004).

In a 1993 *Wall Street Journal* article, Reagan complained that he basically had been tricked into supporting many of these tax increases. They were part of budget deals with Democrats, who controlled the House of Representatives throughout his presidency, which included promises to cut appropriations. There was supposed to be $3 of spending cut for every $1 of tax increase in the 1982 legislation, he said, but "Congress never cut spending by even a penny."[14]

LESSONS LEARNED

BY THE END of the Reagan presidency, most Republicans had come to believe that not only did tax increases do nothing to reduce the deficit, they actually make it worse by encouraging more spending. In other words, despite all the evidence to the contrary, the starve-the-beast theory was still very much alive.

In a radio address on October 24, 1987, Reagan even put a precise figure on the taxes/spending effect: every $1 of tax increase since 1980 had been matched by $1.25 in increased spending, he said.[15] This suggests that spending in 1988 was $166 billion higher, about 3 percent of GDP, than it would have been if taxes had not been raised. But this is not really plausible, given the fact that federal outlays as a share of GDP were exactly the same in 1987 as they had been in 1980.

That same year, Republicans in Congress issued a study by economists Richard Vedder, Lowell Gallaway, and Christopher Frenze estimating that between 1947 and 1986 every $1 of new federal taxes or nontax revenue led to an increase in spending of $1.58. A second edition of this study in 1991 upped the number slightly to $1.59, a figure that is still widely cited on Capitol Hill.[16]

Some academic research finds that higher revenues do lead to higher spending. However, the bulk of the evidence for this proposition comes from the states, which operate under balanced budget requirements, or from years before the 1970s at the federal level, during which a de facto balanced budget rule largely prevailed.[17] Most research now supports the reverse idea, that excessive spending leads to higher taxes—sort of a "late charge" for profligacy, as one study put it.[18]

Nevertheless, the idea that holding down taxes will hold down spending is now deeply ingrained in the Republican psyche.[19] When running for the White House in 2000, George W. Bush publicly disagreed with Federal Reserve chairman Alan Greenspan that budget surpluses were a good thing for the economy. "Mr. Greenspan believes that money around Washington will be spent on a single item—debt reduction," Bush said. "I think it will be spent on greater government. He has got greater faith in the appropriators than I do."[20]

Conservative politicians and pundits continue to endorse the idea as well:

- George Will, syndicated columnist: "Even when tax cuts are not stimulative, they are justified as the most effective restraint on government spending."[21]
- Holman Jenkins, *Wall Street Journal* columnist: "What Republicans have understood . . . is that the only effective long-term form of fiscal discipline is tax cuts."[22]
- Sen. Rick Santorum, Republican of Pennsylvania: "I came to the House as a real deficit hawk, but I am no longer a deficit hawk. I'll tell you why—I had to spend the surpluses. Deficits make it easier to say no."[23]

Somewhat surprisingly, a number of reputable Republican economists also make the same argument:

- Robert Barro, Harvard University: "One attraction of tax cuts and deficits is that they starve the government of revenue and thereby promote spending restraint."[24]
- Gary S. Becker, Edward P. Lazear, and Kevin M. Murphy, all of Stanford's Hoover Institution: "Economic theory and empirical evidence suggest that spending often adjusts to available tax revenue rather than the other way around."[25]
- Milton Friedman, Hoover Institution: "How can we ever cut government down to size? I believe there is one and only one way: the

way parents control spendthrift children, cutting their allowance. For government, that means cutting taxes. Resulting deficits will be an effective—I would go so far as to say, the only effective—restraint on the spending propensities of the executive branch and the legislature. The public reaction will make that restraint effective."[26]

No Longer Effective

ONE THING THAT is clearly missing from these starve-the-beast advocates is any empirical evidence supporting their position. The fact is that if one has only recent data upon which to base one's analysis, it is all in exactly the opposite direction—tax cuts actually seem to cause spending increases. Between 2000 and 2005, there were five major tax cuts and federal revenues as a share of GDP fell from 20.9 percent to 16.8 percent. But over that same period, outlays rose from 18.4 percent of GDP to 20.3 percent. There may be particular reasons why this was the case—homeland security needs after 9/11, the recession, the war in Iraq—but the result, nevertheless, is totally contrary to the idea that tax cuts ratchet down spending.

One of the few conservative economists to actually look at the data is William Niskanen, a member of Reagan's Council of Economic Advisers and now chairman of the libertarian Cato Institute. In several recent papers he has concluded, flatly, that the starve-the-beast theory does not work. But continued belief in the idea that it does has unfortunately weakened what little support there was for spending cuts on the right side of the political spectrum.

Says Niskanen, "Acceptance of the 'starve the beast' position has led too many conservatives and libertarians to be casual about the sustained political discipline necessary to control federal spending directly and to succumb to the fantasy that tax cuts will solve this problem."[27]

In effect, the whole starve-the-beast theory has been turned on its head. Instead of bringing about spending cuts by deliberately raising the deficit, as the original theory supposed, tax cuts have become a substitute for spending cuts. Increasingly, members of Congress have come to believe that cutting taxes is all that is necessary to control the size of government.[28] Yet even the strongest advocate of the starve-the-beast theory, Milton Friedman, has always maintained that the burden of government is best measured by spending, not taxation.

Thus Republicans have raised spending for education, agriculture price supports, and Medicare along with innumerable pork barrel projects at the same time they were enacting more tax cuts than at any time in American history. Indeed, according to Tom Schatz of Citizens Against Government Waste, an independent watchdog group, pork barrel spending was worse in 2005 than at any time for which there are records. And Republicans like Sen. Ted Stevens, Republican of Alaska and chairman of the Senate Committee on Commerce, Science, and Transportation, rival the worst Democratic spenders in their pursuit of wasteful spending.

But the real nub of the problem is entitlement spending—programs that grow automatically and are not subject to annual appropriations. In the 1980s, when the baby boom generation was still relatively young and the baby bust generation born during the low-birth years of the Great Depression and World War II was moving into retirement, the entitlement problem was relatively benign compared to what is in store when the first member of the giant baby boom generation retires in 2008. When that happens, the floodgates will open and there will be an explosion of spending that has been long predicted by the U.S. Government Accountability Office (formerly the General Accounting Office), Congressional Budget Office, and independent analysts like financier Pete Peterson.[29]

Knowing that this flood of spending was on its way even with no change in law, Congress and the White House should have been enacting entitlement reform during the flush years of the late 1990s. But even though Bill Clinton committed himself to saving Social Security, he took no actions that would actually bring this about. He simply hoarded federal surpluses to protect them from Republican tax cutters, and this was deemed sufficient.

In retrospect, a unique political opportunity was tragically lost when Clinton became consumed by the Monica Lewinsky affair. As budget surpluses began to emerge in 1998, many in the Clinton Administration were talking about investing the Social Security trust fund in the stock market and creating new retirement savings accounts. Such ideas were not terribly far from the Republican position and there was definitely a deal to be made, in my opinion. But unfortunately, Clinton and congressional Republicans became hopelessly entangled in a bitter impeachment battle instead and a historic opportunity was lost.[30]

The loss ultimately hurt everyone. The American people lost a chance to get Social Security on a permanently sound financial footing with new opportunities to save for their retirement, which could easily have been financed at the time with budget surpluses. Republicans lost their best chance to reform Social Security, which really needs to be led by a Democrat for the same reason that only a Republican like Richard Nixon could go to China. Bill Clinton lost his chance at a legacy. And if the surplus had been committed to Social Security, Democrats could probably have been able to block Bush's tax cut in 2001.

Bush's Inevitable Tax Increase

UNTIL PASSAGE OF the Medicare drug bill in 2003, I thought there was still some hope that a budget crisis could be avoided. But passage of that legislation not only put spending on an unsustainable upward course, it also cost Bush any credibility he might have as a fiscal conservative, which doomed his effort to save Social Security in 2005.

To recap some numbers mentioned earlier, the long-term unfunded liability of just the drug benefit, excluding the rest of Medicare, is $18.2 trillion, according to the 2005 Medicare trustees report.[31] Adding up all of Medicare's unfunded costs yields a total as of 2005 of $68.1 trillion—six times Social Security's unfunded liability. The Social Security trustees put the long-term unfunded liability of that program at just $11.1 trillion. Thus Bush's own action in ramming the drug bill through Congress raised the national indebtedness by an amount two-thirds greater than Social Security's total unfunded liability.

To make these very large numbers somewhat more concrete, Social Security's unfunded liability comes to 1.2 percent of GDP in perpetuity (1.4 percent without the trust fund)—about what is raised by the corporate income tax. The comparable number for Medicare is 7.1 percent—about what is raised by the individual income tax. And remember that these figures are for the unfunded portion of these programs, so they are over and above payroll taxes.

The chilling conclusion, therefore, is that virtually 100 percent of all federal taxes, on a present value basis, do nothing but pay for Social Security and Medicare. Unless there are plans to abolish the rest of the federal government, large tax increases are inevitable.

Passage of the drug bill convinced me that there was no longer any hope that Republicans would even hold the line on spending, let alone cut it. Therefore, it was inevitable that the increased spending demands from retirement of the baby boomers would ultimately be addressed by tax increases. I first said so in a column on October 20, 2003.[32]

I was much criticized at the time by conservatives who felt that I had thrown in the towel on spending—in effect becoming a defender of the welfare state. But I felt that it was my party that had thrown in the towel when it created a vastly expensive, unfunded new entitlement program. I was just accepting the logical consequences.

I was not the only one to recognize that the political/fiscal situation had fundamentally changed. Columnist David Wessel made the point in the *Wall Street Journal*.[33] In a November 23, 2003, commentary, Heritage Foundation budget analyst Brian Riedl echoed my analysis. "Higher taxes are coming," he said, the result of a collapse of fiscal discipline by the Republican Party.[34]

Liberal economist Max Sawicky of the Economic Policy Institute wrote an op-ed article on December 17, 2003, in which he made this prediction: "You heard it here first: If George W. Bush wins a second term, he will sign a tax increase into law. If a Democrat wins, you can expect the same. The budget is too far out of whack for any other outcome."[35]

In January 2004, *Financial Times* columnist Amity Shlaes joined the chorus. "A tax increase is coming in America—and Republicans will be among those who preside over that increase," she said.[36]

In March, economist Dan Mitchell of the Heritage Foundation wrote a memo entitled "Medicare: A Ticking Time Bomb for Tax Increases."[37] Later in the year, Stuart Butler, also of Heritage, gave a briefing entitled "How Uncurbed Entitlements Will Force Large Tax Increases" and told the *New York Times* that the Medicare drug bill made tax increases inevitable.[38]

By September 2004, it was virtually conventional wisdom that the foreseeable debate in tax policy was likely to be more about how taxes would be increased than about how to cut them. As *Wall Street Journal* columnist Alan Murray put it:

> Not for decades will a Republican candidate be able to run on an agenda of broad-based tax cuts. In the short term, budget deficits make that position untenable. In the longer term, the retirement of the baby boomers will do the same.
>
> The fight for the next half century will be over how to prevent taxes and spending from being swollen to European dimensions by government-retirement programs. And politically, that puts conservatives back to where they were before quarterback Kemp abandoned the football field three decades ago—playing defense.[39]

WILL BUSH DO IT?

OF COURSE, ALL this speculation runs up against Bush's and the Republican Party's known antipathy for tax increases. But as NYU law professor Dan Shaviro notes, "The enactment of substantial future tax increases should not be discounted just because the current political environment is strongly anti-tax. Things may look very different once the payment of Social Security and Medicare benefits is at risk."[40]

And one cannot help but remember that Bush's father was forced to reverse his position on taxes when compelled by necessity. Similar circumstances have also forced many Republican governors—even those closely aligned with Bush—to raise taxes.[41] A particularly interesting example is that of Mitch Daniels, who served as director of the Office of Management and Budget for Bush before being elected governor of Indiana in 2004. Although Daniels was known for taking a hard line on federal spending while at OMB—Bush nicknamed him "The Blade"— he concluded that raising taxes in Indiana was the least bad way of dealing with the state's fiscal crisis.[42]

Others point out that even if Bush should change gears, there is no chance that a Republican Congress will ever accede to a tax increase. However, one would have said the same thing about Republicans in the Virginia legislature in 2003, where they controlled both houses. But when asked to raise taxes by Democratic governor Mark Warner in 2004, not only did the Republicans support it, they actually raised taxes more than he asked for. It appears that GOP legislators were more worried about losing their ability to spend than about conservative voter retaliation.[43]

In my opinion, the most likely scenario for Bush to reverse course on taxes would be some sort of financial crisis on the order of the stock market crashes of 1987 or 1989, both of which led to budget deals involving tax increases, dutifully signed into law by Republican presidents. When such events occur, it doesn't really matter what their cause is; political elites always respond by demanding that the budget deficit be reduced. It is the one thing within the government's control that might help and upon which a consensus can quickly be built.

Since the budget deficit is, in effect, negative saving, it bears much of the blame for inadequate domestic saving. Consequently, it would be quite reasonable to conclude that a reduction in the federal budget deficit would help redress the financial crisis when it occurs.[44]

When this day comes, it will be necessary to cut the budget deficit by a lot. I would estimate that a deficit reduction package on the order of 2 percent of GDP—about $250 billion per year—will be necessary to get the attention of markets and show political resolve.[45] That will be impossible to achieve just by cutting discretionary spending, especially when defense and homeland security are likely to be off limits. Nor is it realistic to think that entitlements can be cut enough to achieve the budget target. Even if it were politically possible to do so—which is highly doubtful—it is extraordinarily difficult to achieve large savings in these programs quickly without doing things like cutting Social Security benefits for current retirees, which is inconceivable.

Finally, it will be necessary for any large budget deal to be bipartisan if it is to be enacted rapidly. For these reasons it is an absolute certainty that probably half of any deficit reduction target will involve taking in higher revenues. This is typical of the budget deals of the 1980s and early 1990s and also standard in the foreign experience with fiscal adjustment, according to economists Alberto Alesina of Harvard and Roberto Perotti of Columbia University.[46]

THE ROAD AHEAD

IN 2005, THERE was evidence that a fiscal course reversal was starting to take shape. There was increasing resistance to further tax cuts in Congress, and a growing number of Washington insiders, including many conservatives, were starting to see the end of tax cuts and the inevitability of higher taxes.[47] Federal Reserve chairman Alan Greenspan opened the door in April 21 testimony.[48] And President Bush himself even suggested that raising the Social Security wage cap—which Newt Gingrich characterized as a major tax increase on the core Republican base—was a viable option to finance his Social Security reform plan.

"Nobody is talking publicly about tax hikes," Jeffrey Birnbaum reported in the *Washington Post* on March 21. "But tax experts are quietly preparing for all sorts of tax enhancements anyway. With a budget deficit that last year exceeded $400 billion, no other action makes sense."[49]

Even activist conservatives were becoming resigned to the inevitable. Writing in Pat Buchanan's right-wing *American Conservative* magazine on May 9, assistant editor Jim Antle laid out the predictable political dynamic. "When neither party wants to cut spending and only one is interested in holding the line on taxes," he wrote, "whenever the deficit has become a salient issue it has generally been the anti-tax forces who have lost."[50]

As American Enterprise Institute economist Kevin Hassett puts it, "It is undoubtedly true that in the end we shall have to pay for everything we spend. Ultimately, the budget will have to approximately balance. If we enter a trajectory with ever-increasing deficits, then some drastic policy action will necessarily ensue."[51]

Even if no financial crisis occurs, the trend toward an aging society and higher spending for Social Security and Medicare will put relentless pressure on Congress and the president to raise revenues down the road. It is simply impossible to run ever-larger deficits to cover about a 50 percent increase in spending as a share of GDP over the next generation, which is what is already baked into the cake, according to the CBO and GAO.

Many on the left believe that Bush's tax cuts are solely responsible for our fiscal dilemma, and they have even projected the cost of tax cuts seventy-five years into the future to prove it. But as history shows, tax cuts are much less permanent than tax increases—just look at all the tax increases signed into law by Ronald Reagan. Moreover, taxes rise automatically over time as inflation and real growth push taxpayers into higher brackets. But entitlements for the elderly live forever. And with the huge baby boom generation close to retirement, there is simply too much spending in the pipeline to avoid a large future tax increase even if the Bush tax cuts had never been enacted.

Bush may turn out to be extraordinarily lucky and avoid having to face the consequences of his own fiscal actions, especially the hugely ill-conceived Medicare drug bill, and the burden of enacting a major tax increase may fall on his successor. But it will be Bush's fault even if someone else ends up paying the political price.

CHAPTER 10

THE SHAPE OF
TAXES TO COME

As PREVIOUS CHAPTERS HAVE MADE CLEAR, I BELIEVE THAT THE United States is on an unsustainable fiscal course and that higher taxes are inevitable. The question thus becomes, how will taxes be raised? Many on the political left wish simply to repeal the Bush tax cuts. However, just as Republicans didn't undo all of Bill Clinton's 1993 tax increase as soon as they got the chance, I don't think Democrats would just repeal George W. Bush's tax cuts if they were suddenly given the power to do so. For one thing, a lot of Democrats voted for those tax cuts and continue to support specific elements of them, such as the child credit.

It is much more likely and far more desirable to use the necessity of raising taxes to substitute new revenue sources for the taxes that were previously cut. In particular, we need taxes that impose a lower economic burden on the economy than higher income tax rates, which almost all economists view as the most economically debilitating form of taxation.

If a "good" new tax substituted for an existing bad tax, the burden of taxation could conceivably fall even as taxes were rising. In other words, it is possible that the tax system could be improved enough such that the total economic burden of taxation would be less—even with a higher tax burden—than it is now. The current debate over tax reform may become the vehicle through which these goals are accomplished.

There are growing calls to fundamentally reform the U.S. tax system. It is conceivable that this debate could trigger adoption of new taxes, like a value-added tax, that could both finance reform and raise net revenue as well.

BASIC OPTIONS

GENERALLY SPEAKING, THERE are two basic approaches to fundamental tax reform that have long been debated among economists and tax theorists. The first is known as a comprehensive income tax. It is based on what is called the Haig-Simons definition of income, which is consumption plus the change in net worth between two points in time.[1]

Under such a tax system, there would be no special treatment for dividends, capital gains, or saving. All income would be taxed, but only once. There would be no place for any sort of special deductions, credits, 401(k) and Keogh accounts, or the corporate income tax, which constitutes a double tax on income generated in the corporate sector.

The idea is to have gross income and taxable income be as close to each other as possible. Under our current system, the two can diverge dramatically. This creates unfairness, because two taxpayers in similar circumstances can pay quite different tax rates. And it creates inefficiency, because investment and other economic activities are being dictated by the tax code instead of market forces.

The Brookings Institution has long been associated with this particular approach to tax reform. Dating back at least forty years, it has published innumerable books and conference proceedings with detailed analyses of ways in which the tax system diverges from a comprehensive income tax and ways in which it can be reformed along these lines.[2] In 1969 and 1976, Congress passed major tax reform legislation designed to bring the tax code more into line with a comprehensive tax base.

The other major approach to tax reform would be a pure consumption tax.[3] In 1976, the Treasury Department issued a report known as the Blueprints study that explained how a consumption tax could be implemented.[4] Previously, it had been assumed that a consumption-based tax system was theoretically desirable, but unworkable. As John Maynard Keynes once remarked, "An expenditure tax, though perhaps theoretically sound, is practically impossible."[5]

It is often wrongly thought that a consumption tax must necessarily take the form of a direct tax on consumption. In Europe, this is done via the value-added tax and in the states by a tax on retail sales.[6] The former is collected at each stage of production and distribution and embedded in prices that consumers pay. The latter is collected only on final sales.

However, economists know that a consumption-based tax system need not necessarily look like a VAT or a sales tax. It can appear very much like an income tax. All that is really necessary is that saving be entirely exempted from taxation. If that is the case, then all that is left is consumption. Hence, the burden of taxation will necessarily fall on consumption even though consumption is not taxed directly.[7]

In the early 1980s, the idea of taxing consumption by eliminating taxation of saving was married to the idea of getting rid of progressivity and instituting a flat rate or single-rate tax schedule. This resulted in the well-known Hall-Rabushka flat tax proposal. Named for Hoover Institution economists Robert Hall and Alvin Rabushka, it is in fact a pure consumption tax because there would be no taxation of saving or investment.[8] However, there is no reason why we could not have progressive rates on a consumption base.[9] Alternatively, we could have a flat rate on a comprehensive income tax base. In other words, the tax base and the rate structure are separate issues.

The principal virtue of a consumption-based tax system is that it is much less burdensome to the economy than an income tax raising the same revenue.[10] That is because saving, investment, and risk-taking are especially critical to growth. Even small burdens in these areas can be very detrimental to economic progress. Indeed, optimal tax theory says that there should be no taxes on capital at all. For this reason, it is probably safe to say that most economists these days favor a consumption-based tax system.[11]

As one can see, there are certain similarities between a comprehensive income tax and a consumption-based tax system. Both would support elimination of the corporate income tax and the elimination of tax subsidies and other special interest provisions in the tax code. As Henry Simons, an originator of the comprehensive income tax, once put it, "There should be no levies on business or concerns as such."[12] Supporters of each approach could travel down the road a long way together before reaching a fork.[13]

Tax Rates

THE RATE SCHEDULE is also an important factor in tax reform. Some recent studies have found that most of the benefits of tax reform come from flattening rates, irrespective of the tax base.[14] Other studies suggest that the economic cost of using progressive tax rates is very high.[15] Thus growth would be enhanced by reducing progressivity even if no changes are made to the tax base.

The Tax Reform Act of 1986, which was enacted with wide bipartisan support, was in essence a merger of the comprehensive income tax approach and the flat-rate idea. The former was embodied in the Bradley-Gephardt bill and the latter in the Kemp-Kasten bill. After a Treasury study reviewed all the options, the White House sent a proposal to Congress in 1985 that largely split the difference between the two.[16] Loopholes were closed and rates were cut in a revenue-neutral manner that was widely applauded across the political spectrum.

Unfortunately, under pressure to raise taxes for deficit reduction in 1990 and 1993, the deal that constituted the 1986 effort broke down.

Taxpayers had been promised lower tax rates in return for giving up loopholes. With the top rate reduced to just 28 percent by the legislation, it was a deal they were willing to make. But when rates were hiked in 1990 and 1993, raising the top rate to 39.6 percent, the loopholes were not restored. Many taxpayers felt that they had been double-crossed. Consequently, it will be harder to put together the same sort of coalition today.

Any new tax reform effort must also contend with the fact that the 1997, 2001, 2002, 2003, and 2004 tax bills radically changed the tax code. We now have a tax system that looks very different from the one we had in 1985. Rates are much lower, there are many new provisions like the child credit that didn't exist then, and the tax burden on capital is much lower—as is the overall burden of taxation—than it was in the mid-1980s.

It is important to understand that the tax code has in fact undergone major reforms over the last several years that have moved it considerably in the direction of a consumption base. Since 1997 the tax rates on capital gains and dividends have been sharply reduced, business depreciation allowances are much larger, and the estate tax has been abolished (at least temporarily in one year, 2010), among other things. Consequently, we are much closer to a consumption tax base than we were before 1997.

The main objection to a consumption-based tax system is distributional fairness. A direct consumption tax such as a VAT is assumed to take more out of the pockets of the poor than the rich in percentage terms, since the former consume a greater portion of their income.[17] A switch from an income tax to a consumption tax would also penalize the elderly, whose incomes were taxed during their working lives and would then find their consumption taxed when they drew down their savings during retirement. Many would view this as a kind of double tax.[18]

If a consumption-based tax system is achieved by eliminating taxes on saving and investment, most people would also view this as extremely unfair. Allowing investors to receive interest, dividends, capital gains, and rent tax-free while working people are fully taxed on their wages is not viable politically, regardless of the economic merits.

A pure income tax is equally unviable, however. If carried to its logical extreme, it would require people to be taxed on unrealized capital gains, the imputed rent homeowners receive for living in their own homes, and employee benefits such as health insurance as well as the abolition of Individual Retirement Accounts, Keogh plans, and 401(k) accounts. The annual tax expenditures list published by the Treasury Department essentially lists all of the deviations from a Haig-Simons tax base currently in the tax code.[19]

Thus the choice between an income tax and a consumption tax basically boils down to a choice between equity and efficiency.[20] An income tax is generally viewed as more fair, but diminishes economic growth below what a consumption tax of the same magnitude would achieve, owing to the income tax's harsh treatment of capital income. A consumption tax would raise growth by encouraging more saving, investment, and risk-taking, but at the cost of a tax system that would be viewed as grossly unfair to most people.

In practice, the U.S. tax system has never come close to either ideal. It is and always has been a hybrid system, with certain elements of an income tax and a consumption tax. It has swung back and forth from one ideal to the other depending on economic conditions and political circumstances. Republicans tend to favor consumption taxes, while Democrats generally support the income tax. In the 1960s and 1970s, Democrats made considerable progress in achieving their ideal. In recent years Republicans have been successful in moving the tax system toward theirs.

One way of compromising between the goals of equity and efficiency is through the rate schedule. Although the flat tax is primarily associated with those favoring a consumption tax, there is no reason why the two are necessarily linked together. Similarly, there is no necessary linkage between progressive rates and an income tax base. We could have a flat rate on an income tax base or progressive rates on a consumption base.[21]

Interestingly, a number of political liberals have suggested both approaches. As long ago as the 1950s, economist John Kenneth Galbraith suggested that it was socially desirable to tax sales more heavily in order to suppress conspicuous consumption, a view echoed more recently by economist Robert H. Frank.[22] Other liberals have supported a single tax rate on an income base. For example, in 1982, then-congressman Leon Panetta, Democrat of California, introduced such a bill.[23] The great liberal philosopher John Rawls thought a proportional expenditure tax was the fairest tax system.[24]

RETAIL SALES TAX VERSUS A VAT

UNFORTUNATELY, IN RECENT years the movement for consumption-based taxation has been hijacked by a group of extremists whose only real interest is abolishing the Internal Revenue Service. They believe that if virtually all federal taxes are eliminated and replaced with a retail sales tax like those in the states, then the states can simply collect the federal government's revenue for it, thereby allowing for abolition of the IRS.[25]

There are many reasons to oppose this particular tax system, but the most important is administrative. It simply will not work. It would require a minimum tax rate of 30 percent on all retail sales, with state and local sales tax on top.[26] But even this rate assumes far broader coverage than any existing sales tax and no evasion whatsoever. For example, new home sales, local government services (except education), all Internet sales, and medical care would be taxed. Using more realistic assumptions of what could be taxed, economists have estimated that a rate twice as high would be necessary.[27] A long list of economists and tax experts have testified that a rate much more than 10 percent is simply not feasible and would quickly break down.[28]

For this reason, every country that has seriously considered a national retail sales tax has concluded that a VAT makes more sense.[29] A key benefit of a VAT is that it is embodied in prices at each stage of production or distribution and thus is collected incrementally rather than being paid entirely on final sales. Thus, if a retailer fails to collect the tax, all that is lost is the tax increment that would apply to the final markup, whereas with retail sales tax 100 percent of the revenue would be lost.

To see how a classic VAT works in practice, a farmer produces wheat and sells it to the miller. He pays VAT on the sale and gives the miller an invoice showing that the tax was paid and included in the sale price. The miller makes flour and sells it to the baker. The miller multiplies the VAT rate times the sale to calculate his tax and then subtracts the tax he paid when he bought the wheat, as shown on the invoice from the farmer, sending the balance to the government. The miller sells the flour to the baker, including his tax on the invoice, and so on. Thus the VAT is largely self-enforcing because there is always an invoice trail and because businessmen need to pay the tax in order to claim credits for taxes that were embodied in the goods and services they purchased.

A key benefit of the VAT is that it is rebated at the border on exports. That is, the exporter is able to claim a refund from the government for all of the taxes embodied in the goods he sells abroad without having to collect the tax himself. (Conversely, a VAT will apply at the border on imports.) This is allowed under World Trade Organization rules, but only for direct consumption taxes. Indirect taxes, such as the corporate income tax, cannot be rebated.[30] Many American exporters view this asymmetrical tax regime as a hindrance to them and a benefit to nations with VATs.[31]

The benefits of a VAT on the trade balance tend to be overstated, however. Rather than subsidizing exports and penalizing imports, as it appears to do, rebating a VAT at the border on exports and applying it at the border on imports is necessary for tax neutrality and does not affect trade.[32] Indeed, that was the principal reason why the VAT was developed in the first place. And if it did create a trade advantage, exchange rates would adjust so as to eliminate it. In the end, the main impact of a VAT on trade is that the revenue could be used to reduce taxes on capital, which would make U.S. firms more productive and therefore more competitive.[33]

VAT OPTIONS

ANOTHER IDEA THAT has been put forward lately is to use a VAT to eliminate the Social Security payroll tax.[34] It is thought that the reduction in taxes on labor would expand employment. Research, however, indicates that the payroll tax is much less of a disincentive to employment than is commonly believed.[35] That is because workers view it as being more of a forced saving requirement, akin to putting money in a 401(k) plan, than a tax for which nothing specific in return is expected or received. Moreover, the benefit formula gives most workers more in future benefits than they pay in taxes, thus reinforcing work incentives.

Consequently, the impact on economic growth of replacing the payroll tax with a VAT would be minimal. Moreover, one really cannot fiddle with the payroll tax without simultaneously making major changes to the Social Security benefit structure. Therefore, changes in the payroll tax should be considered only in the context of overall Social Security reform rather than as part of tax reform.

What would make more sense is using a VAT to replace the corporate income tax. This is a proposal that has been made many times in the past.[36] What has made the issue more acute today is growing international investment, trade, and capital mobility that is making it harder and harder for all governments to tax corporate income. It is too easy for companies to shift their assets around to take advantage of tax regimes that give them the best deal. Thus, global tax competition is in the process of destroying the corporate income tax as a viable source of revenue.[37]

At the same time that the corporate income tax is being undermined largely by legal tax avoidance, the personal income tax is increasingly being eroded by tax evasion. The best data we have on this comes from comparing the Internal Revenue Service's measure of adjusted gross income taken directly from tax returns to the Commerce Department's measure of AGI compiled from data on wages, interest, and dividends paid by businesses. In 2002, the gap between these two figures reached $961 billion or 13.7 percent of the Commerce Department's estimate of AGI. This is the largest gap since figures began to be collected in 1959. It suggests that the federal government is losing at least $100 billion per year just due to the nonreporting of taxable income on personal tax returns.[38]

In March 2005, the IRS released new estimates of what it calls the "tax gap"—the differences between what taxpayers legally owe and what it is able to collect. The report put the tax gap for tax year 2001 at between $312 billion and $353 billion. The IRS eventually collected about $55 billion of the money owed, reducing the net tax gap to between $257 billion and $298 billion.[39]

Moving toward a VAT could solve both problems. Replacing the corporate income tax with a VAT would utilize corporations as tax collectors rather than as objects of taxation. Since the burden of the VAT is passed through to the final consumer, corporations really have no reason to evade it. And because the tax is collected incrementally at all stages of production and distribution, it is largely self-enforcing. It would even be possible to exempt most small retailers from collecting the tax without much revenue loss, since they would still pay the bulk of the tax when they purchased their inventory.

A VAT would also provide enough revenue both to fix glaring problems with the personal income tax, such as the rising burden of the Alternative Minimum Tax, and make a down payment on deficit reduction.[40] According to the International Monetary Fund, the average VAT in the advanced economies covers about 37 percent of GDP.[41] This means that a U.S. VAT would have raised about $46 billion for each percentage point in 2005. Thus a 10 percent VAT would raise about $460 billion per year. A 20 percent rate—the average rate in Europe—would raise close to $1 trillion. A narrower tax base covering 30 percent of GDP, which would allow things like food and medical care to be exempted, would raise $370 billion per year from a 10 percent rate and $740 billion from a 20 percent rate.

Even a 10 percent VAT on a narrow tax base could provide enough revenue to replace the corporate income tax, which will not raise more than 2 percent of GDP in revenue for the foreseeable future according to the Congressional Budget Office. There would be enough revenue to reform the AMT and still leave almost $100 billion per year left over for deficit reduction. A VAT could also finance significant tax simplification, relieving millions of taxpayers from having to file any tax returns at all.[42]

DEFICIT REDUCTION

ALTHOUGH THERE HAS not been much interest in tax increases or deficit reduction in recent years, this could change suddenly if interest rates were to spike or some other dramatic market event were to focus public attention once again on the deficit, as was the case in the 1980s and early 1990s. Moreover, even if one takes a benign view of the short-run deficit situation, the longer-term situation resulting from the aging of society will clearly require higher revenues at some point.

In conclusion, there is a pressing need for tax reform, but it will require a significant new revenue source to finance needed tax changes unless Congress is prepared to see a further reduction in federal revenues and a further rise in the deficit. This is unlikely. The deficit is already a serious problem and the impending retirement of the baby boom generation is going to put upward pressure on the federal budget for many years to come. It is completely unrealistic to think that tax increases can be avoided given this fact, not to mention the likelihood of higher defense spending for the foreseeable future to deal with the war on terror.

Therefore, it is my belief that a federal VAT is the best way to raise net new revenue to pay for tax reform and deficit reduction at the same time. This is an issue that has been debated on many occasions previously.[43] It has always failed because liberals view a VAT as regressive and conservatives fear that it would be a money machine that would finance the expansion of government. However, it is clear that the latter argument is no longer valid since the whole point of adopting a VAT today would be to raise federal revenue to reduce deficits and pay for the growth of entitlement programs, rather than as an element of tax reform, as was the case previously. It could also finance other tax or benefit changes that would minimize the impact on those with low incomes.

A Money Machine?

ECONOMIC THEORY TELLS us that the more efficient a tax system is, the more revenue it will raise, which could fuel demands for increased spending. As one study concluded, "A better tax system may lead to more wasteful spending."[44] This has led to the "money machine" fear.[45] The *Wall Street Journal* routinely rails against the VAT on these grounds.[46] As President Reagan put it in a February 21, 1985, press conference, "A value-added tax actually gives a government a chance to blindfold the people and grow in stature and size."[47]

While there is no question that most countries with VATs are high-tax countries, the fact is that almost all were high-tax countries before they adopted this tax. And while it is true that most countries have raised their VAT rates over time, it is important to distinguish among those countries. In general, those countries where the money machine argument is most valid are those that instituted a VAT before the great inflation of the 1970s, which disguised tax increases from public view. It was too easy for governments to raise VAT rates a percent at a time when inflation was raising all prices at double-digit rates.

By contrast, countries that have adopted VATs since inflation subsided have been much more restrained in raising their rates. And those that have adopted VATs during the era of relative price stability that we have enjoyed for the last twenty years show no money machine evidence at all. Indeed, some of them are even starting to cut their VAT rates. Slovakia and the Czech Republic have both recently cut their VATs from 23 percent to 19 percent.

Looking at the data, we see that the average increase in VAT rates for countries where the tax was established before 1974 is 7 percentage points and the median is 6.5 percent. For those where the VAT was established later, the average is just 1 percent and the median is zero.[48]

Furthermore, not all countries introducing VATs have seen their overall tax burden rise. Taxes as a share of GDP have fallen from 29.8 percent in Japan the year its VAT was introduced to a current level of 25.8 percent. In Canada the tax/GDP ratio fell from 36.4 percent to 33.9 percent. Other countries where the ratio has fallen since the VAT was introduced include Australia, the Czech Republic, Finland, Ireland, and Poland.

Serious academic studies have concluded that the VAT cannot be blamed for raising the overall burden of taxation, even in countries where it was a new tax and not a replacement for some existing tax. Writing in the prestigious *National Tax Journal,* economist J. A. Stockfisch found no support for the view that VATs raise either the tax level or government spending.[49]

A study for the American Petroleum Institute by Diana Furchtgott-Roth, formerly chief economist for the U.S. Department of Labor under George W. Bush, came to the same conclusion: "VAT rates and revenues have increased in OECD countries with VATs. However, these increases have been offset by a slower growth of other forms of taxes, leaving the aggregate growth rate of taxes the same."[50]

The VAT may or may not be a good idea for the U.S. But it should not be casually dismissed as a money machine without serious analysis of the trade-offs. It may turn out to be the least bad way of financing needed tax reforms and the massive growth of federal health care spending that neither the White House nor Congress shows any interest in restraining.

OTHER OPTIONS

OTHER REFORM OPTIONS are also possible. One would be, in effect, to replicate the 1986 tax reform effort—close loopholes and use the revenue to cut tax rates. Flattening the rate schedule will be beneficial for growth even if there is no movement toward a consumption tax base. The problem with this approach is that it requires a bipartisan consensus that no longer exists. Also, the fact that rates were raised so shortly after 1986 will undoubtedly make a similar deal much more difficult today.

Neither major party has had much to say about tax reform in recent years. Of course, in principle, everyone is for reform. But as soon as any specific reform is put on the table, those who would lose out are much more vocal in stating objections than those who would benefit are in voicing support.[51]

It is my belief that eventually financial markets will force some action on the deficit. And any significant deficit reduction will necessarily require higher revenues.[52] This may make options like a VAT politically viable. I think policymakers will inevitably be led toward adoption of this tax for the same reason that every other industrial country has done so—its proven ability to raise large revenues at a low economic cost.

The United States has been able to bear the cost of an inefficient tax system for a long time because we are a relatively low-tax country—according to the latest data, taxes as a share of GDP here are about 10 percentage points below the average for other industrialized countries.[53] By inefficient, I mean that we have provisions with a high deadweight cost—those that discourage a lot of economic activity for every dollar raised.[54] But as our tax/GDP ratio rises, such inefficiencies are a luxury that can no longer be afforded.

My conclusion that a VAT should be the foundation of a new tax reform effort is controversial. But given the twin problems of a large federal deficit and rising pressure for entitlement spending on the one hand, and the need to fix glaring problems in the tax code that will require further reductions in revenue on the other, I see no alternative except to add a significant new revenue source in order to deal with both simultaneously.[55]

VAT Time

THE IDEA OF a VAT for the United States has come up many times in the past. Richard Nixon commissioned a major study of the subject and various members of Congress have promoted it, most notably Congressman Al Ullman (D-OR) when he was chairman of the House Ways and Means Committee. His defeat in 1980, however, was widely blamed on his support for the VAT, which is always mentioned whenever the idea has come up again.

What might make circumstances in the future different? First would be a financial crisis. Another might be the need for a large new revenue source to pay for tax reform and Social Security reform.[56] In any event, the growing cost of Medicare is going to force Congress's hand someday. And historically, it has always found it easier to deal with entitlement problems by enacting higher taxes, as was the case with the Social Security fix of 1983.

It is also possible that liberals might one day relax their opposition to a VAT's regressivity if they fear that the alternative is cuts in programs for the poor to deal with a budget crisis. Alternatively, liberals might support a more regressive form of taxation in return for new benefits, as was the case in Europe, where socialists imposed VATs to create welfare states.[57]

In my view, the VAT lends itself to dealing with our long-term budget problem because it can be raised a little bit at a time without causing serious economic repercussions. If people knew that income tax rates would be higher in the future, they would engage in a lot of inefficient economic transactions designed solely to bring future income into the present. This happened in 1992, when many people saw Bill Clinton's tax increase coming and sped up bonuses and other payments that otherwise would have been paid in 1993.

But if people know that a sales tax rate will be 1 percent higher a couple of years from now, there is a severe limit to how much consumption they can move forward. Certainly there will be some of that, and when VATs are first imposed they can be disruptive as people buy as much as they can before the tax takes effect, leading to a collapse of consumption immediately afterward. But this is a onetime effect that can be anticipated and that leaves no permanent damage.

The start-up costs of a VAT are large. A new bureaucracy will be needed to collect it, a broad educational campaign will be necessary to inform consumers and businesspeople how it works, and a lot of new accounting will be required.[58] For these reasons, it probably wouldn't be worth the effort to impose a VAT at less than a 5 percent initial rate. But once in place, rates could be raised even tenths of a percentage point and produce large new revenues for the government.

While all taxes are burdensome and there is no such thing as a perfectly neutral tax, there are taxes that are burdensome and unneutral to greater and lesser degrees. Hence, the form in which taxes are paid can greatly affect their burden. Henry George expressed this point well in his great book *Progress and Poverty*, back in 1880:

> The mode of taxation is, in fact, quite as important as the amount. As a small burden badly placed may distress a horse that could carry with ease a much larger one properly adjusted, so a people may be impoverished and their power of producing wealth destroyed by taxation, which, if levied another way, could be borne with ease.[59]

No one likes paying taxes and no one likes admitting the need for higher taxes. But the reality is that spending cannot be cut enough to forestall this necessity at some point. Even if no new programs are enacted and discretionary programs are cut to the bone, entitlement programs will grow beyond the ability to fund them without higher revenues.

We can raise those revenues in a smart way or we can raise them in a stupid way. The smart way minimizes the economic burden of taxes so that they are as small as possible. Since the income tax is already stretched to the breaking point, an effort to raise significant new revenues from this source would be extremely debilitating to the economy, reducing growth far more than would be the case with an equivalent VAT.

So we are left with the unpleasant reality that a VAT is the least bad way of paying for the inevitable growth of government.

CHAPTER 11

THE POST-BUSH ERA: REPUBLICAN OR DEMOCRATIC?

M Y PRIMARY MOTIVATION IN WRITING THIS BOOK IS TO RESCUE the Republican Party from what I see as a coming political debacle resulting from George W. Bush's policies. His budgetary actions, especially strong-arming the Medicare drug benefit into law, are going to force a massive fiscal retrenchment starting very soon—the first baby boomer starts drawing Social Security benefits in 2008. I believe that the most likely scenario when the bills start coming due is a huge tax increase, probably involving establishment of a value-added tax. But whatever is done will certainly be unpopular and the Republican Party will, rightly, be blamed. President Bush didn't destroy the budget all by himself. He had a lot of help in Congress.

Well before the torrent of entitlement spending on retiring baby boomers begins, however, I expect to see some sort of market correction that will force Congress and the White House to adopt severe belt-tightening measures. I don't know when or how this event will be triggered. But there are so many ways and places it could occur that it will be a miracle if all of them can be avoided. Probably sooner rather than later, something is going to rivet everyone's attention on the budget deficit in a way that we haven't seen since the early 1990s. This will spell the final end of the era of tax cutting. Since tax cuts are the glue that holds the Republican coalition together, it is going to put great strain on that coalition, creating an opening that a smart Democrat can exploit.

NO SUCCESSOR

I ALSO BELIEVE that Bush has unnecessarily handicapped the Republican Party going into 2008 by failing to anoint a successor. It is extremely unlikely that Dick Cheney will seek the Republican presidential nomination, which will leave an enormous vacuum in the party.[1] Whoever ends up as the Republican nominee will certainly be in a much weaker position than a sitting vice president would have been.

It is not uncommon for presidents to change vice presidents—FDR had three different ones. As recently as 1976, Gerald Ford replaced Nelson Rockefeller with Bob Dole. So it would have been perfectly possible for Bush to have replaced Cheney in 2004 with someone better suited to run for president in 2008. This could easily have been done in a way that respected Cheney's contribution to his presidency. For example, Bush could have named him counselor and given him a West Wing office just as he had as vice president. Ultimately, one's influence with a president has little to do with one's formal title. If he wants you to have influence, then you have it, period.

However, the real value of naming his own successor this way is that Bush could have created an opportunity for someone new, someone who is not a governor or a senator, someone who has not necessarily spent their life working their way up through traditional electoral politics and therefore would never otherwise have a chance at the nomination—perhaps Colin Powell or Condoleezza Rice. Paving the way for the first black or the first female president (or both in the case of Rice) would have been a historic legacy that would have had the added benefit of giving the Republican Party a fighting chance at keeping the White House in 2008 against what will likely be a very strong Democratic challenger.

Although one can never underestimate the Democratic Party's ability to seize defeat from the jaws of victory, I think that by 2008 Democrats will have been out of office long enough that they will pull themselves together, nominate someone who can win, and not overburden him or her with too much ideological baggage, as was the case in 2000 and 2004. And even if Bush hadn't undermined the Republican Party, as I believe he has, voter fatigue would play in the Democrats' favor anyway.

I think 2008 will be a lot like 1968. The Republican nominee will, like Hubert Humphrey, be burdened by his predecessor. The Democrats will nominate someone they may not necessarily like very much, as Republicans did with Richard Nixon, but who is nevertheless in a position to unify the party by virtue of being almost everyone's second choice and who is also widely viewed as a winner. Whether 2012 resembles 1972, with the Democratic incumbent being reelected in a blowout, depends vitally on how Republicans interpret the experience of the Bush years and react to it.

I think they will eventually think of Bush the way earlier Republicans thought of Nixon—as someone who severely undermined the party and its principles just to get reelected. Not only did Nixon come close to exterminating the Republican Party with Watergate, he put in place policies that continue to burden the economy to this day—all to win one lousy election in 1972. I think Bush and his congressional enablers basically did the same thing in 2004. Bush's motives may have been higher than Nixon's—Bush believes he is fighting a holy war against terrorism, whereas Nixon was simply selfish—but the results may be the same.

CONSERVATIVE REVOLT

THE RUMBLINGS OF a conservative revolt are starting to be heard. A common cocktail party joke among conservatives is that the latest budgetary outrage in Congress never would have occurred if only the Republicans were in control. Some conservatives continue to blame

Bush's "compassionate conservatism" for getting Republicans on the wrong track. As *National Review*'s Jonah Goldberg explains:

> I have no problem with some of the specific policy proposals which have earned the [compassionate conservative] label. But as a school of thought and political action, I hate it more now than I did in 2000. It has become a rationale for patronage, for overspending and for the sort of rhetoric which romanticizes the State. Besides, political ideas are about moments. To the extent Compassionate Conservatism made sense in 2000, that was due to the fact that we had surpluses, we had peace and Republicans (though not necessarily conservatives) felt the need to out-Clinton Clinton on soccer mom politics. . . . But that was then, this is now. Government is way too bloated. There's a war on. And compassionate conservatism is now synonymous—in my mind—with the runaway spending and some of the worst lurches to the center of the Bush years.[2]

Writing in the tenth anniversary issue of the *Weekly Standard*, Andrew Ferguson lamented that conservatism itself had been corrupted by power. Although this was written in an evident state of crankiness, conservatives have long observed the tendency of right-wing politicians to declare Washington a cesspool and then go there and treat it like a hot tub. As Ferguson put it, "Conservative activists came to Washington to do good and stayed to do well."[3]

Unfortunately, there is really no one out there representing the "Republican wing" of the Republican Party, to paraphrase Howard Dean. But I believe it is only a matter of time before such a person emerges, around whom people like myself can rally, as conservatives unified behind Ronald Reagan in the wake of the Nixon debacle. I hope Republicans don't have to lose the White House in 2008 before a strong conservative leader emerges. On the other hand, it took Gerald Ford's defeat in 1976 before Reagan could emerge as leader of the Republican Party and not just its conservative wing.

In 1976, conservatives had no choice except to stand with Ford against Jimmy Carter because as bad as Ford was, Carter was worse. Most conservatives adopted this attitude in 2004 as well. They voted for Bush not so much because they supported his policies, but mainly because the alternative, John Kerry, was an order of magnitude worse. Kerry was a fool, in my opinion, for not throwing a bone to disaffected conservatives by attacking Bush for his utter abandonment of fiscal restraint. Although Kerry complained about the deficit, he never offered anything of substance that would correct the problem. More often than not, he attacked Bush for not spending enough.

The general political climate of 2004 also served to insulate Bush against conservative discontent. The shrillness and nastiness of liberal attacks on Bush kept conservatives from voicing concerns about his policies for fear of giving aid and comfort to the enemy. They kept their misgivings to themselves, held their noses, and pulled the lever for Bush.

But Bush is now past the election and in his final term. He cannot run for reelection and has no successor who will be forced to defend him in 2008. The Republican nominee will be someone with the freedom to chart a new course.

Bring Back Gridlock

ONE OF THE most powerful arguments that a Democratic presidential candidate will have in 2008 is the virtue of gridlock. Owing to gerrymandering and their edge in fund-raising, Republicans are likely to control Congress for the foreseeable future. Therefore, someone from the other party is needed in the White House to keep them in check, the Democrat can argue. Even many Republicans will find this argument compelling, given the extraordinarily poor fiscal record of unified Republican control of Congress and the White House since 2001.

It is counterintuitive to think that gridlock is desirable. It is regularly denounced by political scientists and party leaders who believe that it promotes stalemate and is a barrier to dealing with pressing national problems.[4] However, their idea of effectiveness—lots of legislation being passed—doesn't necessarily jibe with that of the general public, financial markets, or fiscal conservatives. For them, "effectiveness" often translates into unnecessary government meddling, declining stock and bond prices, and expanded government.

Polls have long shown that most Americans like the idea of divided government, which explains why we have had it throughout so much of the postwar era. Since 1986, the Hart-Teeter poll done for the *Wall Street Journal* has regularly asked voters if they prefer one party to control Congress and the White House or different parties. Those favoring different parties have always exceeded those favoring one-party control, usually by a large margin. In December 1999, 60 percent of people said they favored divided government versus only 33 percent favoring unified government.[5]

"Most voters don't trust either political party; they want the presidency in the hands of one while the other controls the Congress. The old principle of checks and balances has found new meaning in this deliberate partisan division of political power," says political consultant Dick Morris.[6]

I think he is right. The first thing every schoolchild learns about the U.S. government is that the Founding Fathers intentionally divided power among the legislative, executive, and judicial branches; separated the legislative power between the House and Senate; and created a federal system with strong state governments as a check on the national government.[7] They deliberately avoided creation of a parliamentary system such as they have in England, where party control of the legislative and executive branches is necessarily the same. The Founding Fathers wanted legislation to be slow and difficult to pass, not easy. This would weed out ill-advised measures that have momentary popularity and would ensure, for the most part, that those making their way into law had been thought through and had broad support.

Some analysts argue that rather than creating stalemate, gridlock actually contributes to effective legislating. Because each party has veto power over the other, one cannot run roughshod over the other and must therefore reach out to the other at an early stage of the legislative process and draw it in, thus creating stable compromises that can become good, lasting law. When one party is completely shut out, as Republicans were in 1993 and 1994 and Democrats are now, they have no reason to cooperate and a strong incentive to conduct a scorched-earth policy. This forces the governing party to pass legislation using only its own members, which often means compromising with the most extreme elements within the party, when better legislation would have resulted from forging a deal with the other party.[8]

As Jonathan Rauch of the Brookings Institution explains, "Unified control pushes policy to unsustainable extremes, poisons politics, and embitters politicians and voters. Divided control, in contrast, draws policy toward the center; and by giving both parties a stake in governing, it can lower the political temperature so that even daring changes (tax reform, welfare reform) *seem* moderate. In other words, divided control makes the country more governable."[9]

From the point of view of political conservatives, gridlock is clearly preferable to unified government. As noted in chapter 7, divided government from 1994 to 2000 is a key reason for the slow growth of spending and emergence of budget surpluses. According to economist Bill Niskanen of the Cato Institute, this is not an isolated example. The growth of federal spending is almost always slower during periods of divided government than unified government.[10] It is also worth noting that every entitlement program in American history was enacted by unified governments. Divided government, therefore, might have saved us from the monstrosity of the Medicare drug program.

For this reason, financial markets always cheer the prospect of gridlock. Every election cycle, one sees stories and commentaries in the financial press extolling its virtues. In 2000, *Time* magazine financial columnist Daniel Kadlec said gridlock "is the one candidate investors should vote for." Kenneth Fisher of *Forbes* magazine said the optimum outcome for markets was for Bush to win the White House and Democrat Dick Gephardt of Missouri to become speaker of the House. In 2004, *Wall Street Journal* columnist Holman Jenkins suggested that gridlock would have saved the business community from the awful effects of Sarbanes-Oxley, which Republicans rammed through in unseemly haste.[11]

As long as they were held in check by gridlock, with a Democrat in the White House, there was reason to believe that Republicans were sincere in their desire to control spending and reduce the size of government. Once released from gridlock by the election of a Republican president who refuses to veto any spending bill, no matter how pork-laden, the truth became clear—Republicans aren't opposed to spending, only spending money on things Democrats want to spend money on. But when the money is being spent on Republican pork or to buy reelection for Republicans, it is okay, so it seems.

HIGHWAY BILL WAKE-UP CALL

THE GROTESQUE HIGHWAY bill, enacted in August 2005, was a wake-up call to many conservatives in this regard. The American Enterprise Institute's Veronique de Rugy said that President Bush "gave up what was left of his credibility as a fiscal conservative" when he signed it.[12] Sen. John McCain (R-AZ) called the legislation "terrifying in its fiscal consequences."[13] Bush did himself no favors at the signing ceremony by saying that the main purpose of the bill was to increase demand and create jobs.[14] A more Democratic rationale for government spending is hard to imagine.

Some of the Republican Party's major donors started to revolt. The Club for Growth now complains bitterly about out-of-control Republican spending with the same venom it previously heaped on out-of-control Democratic spending.[15] "For fiscal conservatives, it's frustrating to watch," says Dave Keating, the Club's executive director.[16] Even though it is an explicitly Republican organization, I can see its members so sympathizing with the idea of gridlock that they wouldn't necessarily mind seeing a Democrat in the White House as long as Republicans keep Congress.

Throughout 2005, some conservatives overlooked Bush's utter lack of control over the budget because they strongly supported his plan to reform Social Security. But although he put an extraordinary amount of personal time into the effort, by midyear it was on life support, effectively dead but technically still breathing. As early as May, *Weekly Standard* editor Fred Barnes was saying that Bush needed an "exit strategy" on Social Security. By July, *New York Post* columnist John Podhoretz decreed that the reform effort was "a colossal political flop."[17]

The failure to gain traction on this issue owed much, I believe, to two factors discussed earlier: a deep weakness in the administration's policy development process and enactment of the Medicare drug bill.

Bush appointed a commission to study Social Security reform on May 2, 2001, early in his first term. It did its work quickly and issued a solid report on December 21, 2001. By all accounts, it was a credible effort that did a good job of laying out the options for fundamental reform, including the creation of private accounts, which would allow young workers to save for their own retirement.[18] But Bush did nothing with the report. Even after he started his big push for Social Security reform in 2005, little, if anything, was ever heard about the Social Security Commission. In the meantime, its report sat gathering the Internet equivalent of dust, with members of the Commission occasionally wondering what its purpose was if it never was going to be used.

Meanwhile, the vast resources of the Social Security Administration, Treasury Department, and other agencies were seldom utilized to flesh out the administration's plans and respond to valid criticisms. Instead, a couple of midlevel White House staffers did all the heavy lifting.[19] But lacking sufficient resources, the result was mostly vague speeches, sound bites, and talking points, with little meat for those who really wanted to understand what the president was trying to do. And because no formal proposal was ever put on the table, the gap couldn't be filled by think tanks or congressional committees. They had no details to analyze and could only make assumptions about what Bush would ultimately support, which necessarily left a lot of questions unanswered. The too-clever-by-half political people apparently thought they would have more room to maneuver if they weren't tied down to a specific plan. They leaked and then withdrew various options, which only added to confusion and a loss of momentum. The result was not to build support for Social Security reform, but rather to dissipate it as every group supporting reform devised its own plan.

"There is widespread belief in Republican ranks that Bush has made a mess of Social Security reform," Robert Novak wrote in June 2005. "Besides failing to come up with an administration plan, the president has blundered in his 'let a thousand flowers bloom' injunction on Republican members of Congress—urging them to come up with their own ideas."[20]

The early abandonment of the Social Security Commission report appears to have resulted from a high-level White House decision to concentrate on Medicare first. There was a clamor in Congress to do something to aid retirees in their purchases of prescription drugs. Advocates of true Medicare reform saw the drug benefit as a once-in-a-lifetime opportunity to buy support for fundamental restructuring of that program. In return for drug subsidies, seniors would be forced to accept Health Savings Accounts with which to pay for routine medical services covered by Medicare. Since they would be allowed to keep the money not spent, it would create a powerful incentive for those covered by the program to economize, which is the fairest and most effective way of controlling costs.

Unfortunately, Bush made little effort to push for HSAs, and their inclusion in the final bill was more token than real reform. Instead, he simply signed the drug bill after having repeatedly made clear his intention to sign *anything* sent to him by Congress, thereby giving up any negotiating power he might have had.

Why Social Security
Reform Died

By vastly increasing Medicare's liabilities, Bush lost the strongest argument he had for Social Security reform: the need to rein in out-of-control federal entitlement programs. Most analysts thought that Social Security would be easier to reform than Medicare. So the thinking was that if Social Security could be fixed successfully, then it might create some political capital that could be used to reform Medicare. But Bush got the cart in front of the horse by doing Medicare first. And then he screwed up the Medicare legislation by making it nothing but a vast new giveaway with little if anything in terms of real reform.

Consequently, Bush couldn't convincingly talk about reforming Social Security to reduce the cost of entitlements because he himself had just made the Medicare problem vastly worse by an amount far greater than could ever hope to be saved by reforming Social Security. Even if a perfect Social Security bill were enacted that completely eliminated its unfunded liability, the drug benefit would still have left the national indebtedness $7 trillion higher.

Moreover, Bush generally avoided talking about stabilizing Social Security's long-term finances, because that would have required him to discuss either tax increases or benefit cuts, neither of which was politically popular. Instead, he talked exclusively about private accounts, which, by themselves, would do nothing to improve Social Security's finances. They would help only if packaged with benefit cuts that would be compensated for by the return on the accounts. If done properly, workers would have as much retirement income, but have the added benefits of ownership and control of their Social Security wealth.

Early on, political consultant Dick Morris warned that Bush's strategy wasn't going to work. Said Morris, "Bush won't pull off Social Security reform if he bases his plan only on privatization and claims that simply letting individuals invest a portion of their tax payments will solve the system's problems. Americans won't buy it, and Bush will be accused of borrowing his way into disaster if he diverts Social Security revenues without any offset in cuts."[21]

Yet rather than talk about restoring Social Security's solvency—an issue with wide public support—Bush talked only about private accounts. In other words, it was all sugar and no medicine. This caused some prominent conservative economists, such as Robert Barro, to reject the Bush plan.[22]

The failure of Social Security reform created a lot of restlessness among conservatives and the Republican rank and file, especially since its demise almost exactly coincided with passage of the pork-laden highway bill and subsidy-loaded energy bill. Although the White House never officially announced the end of the Social Security campaign, it was widely perceived throughout Washington that President Bush was shifting gears during the congressional recess in August 2005. A meeting with his economic advisers signaled a shift in emphasis toward still more tax cuts. But even among hard-core tax cutters, there was a growing feeling that maybe Bush had gone back to that well once too often.

"It was bound to happen eventually," said Brendan Miniter of the *Wall Street Journal's* editorial board, "but Republicans may now be concluding that there is no longer any political benefit to pushing for deep tax cuts. . . . The reason is that the Laffer Curve applies to politics too. There's a point after which they won't win any more elections. . . . On both the national and state level, some Republicans are starting to bet that they know where the point of diminishing political returns is, and that for tax cuts, we've already reached it."[23]

Further reducing the demand for tax cuts was the increasingly difficult time the White House was having with the economy. It continually claimed that it was swimming along nicely, but average Americans nevertheless felt deep unease about their personal economic condition, as indicated by public opinion polls. If all the tax cuts already enacted hadn't been enough to sufficiently revive the economy and dispel doubts about the quality of the economic expansion, it was difficult to see how still more tax cuts were going to do so.

KATRINA

HURRICANE KATRINA WAS the final nail in the coffin. The relief effort and rebuilding of New Orleans clearly required considerable direct spending. Even the most dogmatic tax cutters had trouble figuring out a way of using the tragedy for their purpose. Most conceded that the pendulum was now moving in the opposite direction.

The ineptness of the federal government's response to Hurricane Katrina also brought to a head long-simmering conservative frustration with the Bush Administration. More and more conservatives began asking themselves what the point of unified Republican control of government was, particularly if there was no conservative agenda in place and Republicans were failing to competently manage even the basic functions of government.

Writing on *National Review* magazine's blog, Rod Dreher of the *Dallas Morning News* voiced what many conservatives were thinking. "This is a scandal, a real scandal," Dreher wrote. "How is it possible that four years after 9/11, the president treats a federal agency vital to homeland security as a patronage prize?"

Continuing, Dreher said, "The main reason I've been a Bush supporter all along is I trusted him (note past tense) on national security—which, in the age of mass terrorism, means homeland security too. Call me naïve, but it's a real blow to learn that political hacks have been running FEMA, of all the agencies of the federal government! What if al-Qaeda had blown the New Orleans levees? How much worse would the crony-led FEMA's response have been?"

Dreher concluded by asking, "Would conservatives stand for any of this for one second if a Democrat were president? If this is what Republican government means, God help the poor GOP congressman up for re-election in 2006."[24]

Writing on his blog, UCLA law professor Stephen Bainbridge echoed Dreher's comments. He pointed to news reports showing that the deployment of so many Louisiana and Mississippi National Guard troops to Iraq delayed the Guard's response to the hurricane, and statements by White House officials indicating that political considerations delayed the White House response.[25]

Bainbridge, a respected conservative commentator, wrote, "It's time for real conservatives and RINOs [Republicans in Name Only] to unite in holding this administration's feet to the fire. As I've said multiple times, Bush is pissing away the conservative moment with his incompetence and tone deafness."[26]

Conservatives were already angered by the vast, pork-laden highway bill, but it soon became clear that money allocated for flood control in New Orleans had routinely been siphoned off and wasted on local pork barrel projects.[27] Although they demanded that the highway bill be reopened to help pay for Katrina, congressional leaders were steadfast in their refusal to do so.

Bush supporters said that a crisis like Katrina demanded that we act first and worry about paying for it later. But *Wall Street Journal* editorial writer John Fund pointed out that previous presidents like Franklin D. Roosevelt and Harry Truman paid for World War II and the Korean War by slashing nondefense spending rather than increasing it, as Bush had done for the last five years.[28]

IMMIGRATION AND IRAQ
BACKLASH?

ADDING TO CONSERVATIVES' unease over Bush in 2005 was his renewed push for liberalized immigration rules. They worried about the cost in terms of welfare and other expenditures, and the impact on the culture as the Spanish-speaking population became so large that it no longer needed to assimilate to prosper within the U.S. Liberals were concerned as well about the pressure on jobs and wages, and both liberals and conservatives fretted about porous borders being a threat to national security.

Bush had planned to make immigration reform a key initiative in 2001.[29] It was part of a plan to increase his share of the Hispanic vote in 2004, but was put on hold by security concerns following 9/11.[30] However, by 2004, Bush was again promoting the idea of allowing America's 8 to 12 million illegal immigrants to have legal residency by applying for guest worker status. As in other cases, no formal proposal was ever prepared and Congress was left to figure out for itself what the White House actually wanted.[31]

There was an immediate outcry against the plan from conservatives.[32] Harvard economist George Borjas said it would encourage more illegal immigration and was "half-baked" because it was impractical to give green cards to every illegal immigrant already in the U.S. Even if the annual number of green cards granted were tripled from 150,000 to 450,000, he said, it would take thirty-two years to process all the existing illegals without any new ones arriving.[33] Although Bush stressed that his program was not an amnesty—illegals would have to earn permanent residency—it was nevertheless widely interpreted as an amnesty among illegal immigrants, leading to an increase in their numbers according to a government study.[34]

Congressional opposition kept the immigration plan on the back burner in 2004, but in 2005 Bush made another effort at passage. Conservative hostility, led by Republican Congressman Tom Tancredo of Colorado, was intense.[35] Democrats and independents also increasingly joined the opposition.[36] It was widely believed that the main factor pushing Bush to forge ahead was pressure from the business community, which needed illegal immigrants for labor and as a growing source of sales.[37] This further contributed to the view that Bush was more interested in corporate interests than the national interest.

I myself am conflicted on the immigration issue. The free market economist in me wants to believe that we should have free flows of labor as well as free flows of capital, goods, and services. And I do believe that, historically, immigrants have been an enormously positive addition to the United States, economically, culturally, and in many other ways as well. I believe that our willingness to accept the best and brightest of other nations has incalculably added to America's well-being in too many ways to even begin to catalog.

But at the same time, I am disturbed by the way some illegal immigrants have abused our hospitality and the way some politicians have exploited them. It is insane that some communities have forbidden local police from enforcing the federal immigration laws, even when they could be used legitimately to expel criminals from our midst.[38] I cannot comprehend why some states would allow illegal immigrants to attend state universities and pay in-state tuition, when the native-born from other states must pay more. I am concerned about the ease with which people can become citizens, simply by being born on our soil, when they have no meaningful connection to this country otherwise. And I am bothered by the ability of terrorists to exploit the holes in our immigration system.

If I as a libertarian have such concerns, it is unsurprising that run-of-the-mill conservatives tend to have even more unease. Yet George W. Bush has conspicuously failed to address the immigration problem except by proposing initiatives that would make it worse. At a minimum, it is an issue that requires vastly greater thought and analysis than we have seen thus far. If nothing else, Bush has created a huge opening for Democrats on the immigration issue that could easily be exploited by a smart Democratic candidate in 2008.

Adding to Bush's political woes in 2005 was growing frustration with the Iraq operation. More and more conservatives had deep misgivings about the whole thing, including the growing cost, total lack of planning for the postwar task of rebuilding the country, growing evidence that the White House knowingly fudged the evidence on weapons of mass destruction, and the contribution of the war to bigger government. Bainbridge spoke for many conservatives in an August 2005 posting:

> It's time for conservatives to face facts. . . . We control the White House, the Senate, the House of Representatives, and (more-or-less) the judiciary for one of the few times in my nearly five decades, but what have we really accomplished? Is government smaller? Have we hacked away at the nanny state? Are the unborn any more protected? Have we really set the stage for a durable conservative majority?

Answering his own questions, Bainbridge said, "The conservative agenda has advanced hardly at all since the Iraq War began. Worse yet, the growing unpopularity of the war threatens to undo all the electoral gains we conservatives have achieved this decade. . . . In sum, I am not a happy camper. I'm very afraid that 100 years from now historians will look back at [George W. Bush's] term and ask, 'What might have been?' "[39]

REPUBLICAN CRACK-UP

IF REPUBLICANS HAVE any hope of holding the White House in 2008, it is essential, in my mind, that they repudiate the big government policies of George W. Bush and stop aping the Democrats by throwing money away on wasteful subsidies, pork barrel projects, and tax giveaways. Voters don't automatically reward the party that spends the most to buy their votes. On the contrary, research shows that they are more likely to reward presidential candidates that demonstrate fiscal restraint.[40]

Republicans shouldn't assume that the Democrats have permanently become the "stupid party," as John Stuart Mill once called the British Conservative Party. They won a lot of elections for a long time by doing some things right and shouldn't be dismissed out of hand, as many

Republicans are wont to do these days. It is exactly that sort of attitude that so often leads to upsets, both in sports and in politics. Failure to take one's opponent seriously is a time-tested recipe for defeat.

I hope that a serious conservative challenger for the Republican nomination emerges soon. Conservative discontent with President Bush needs a leader to articulate its concerns, formulate a respectful criticism, and build a movement through which a traditional conservative message can be delivered.

That person should also be aware that the deepest discontent with Bush is among the conservative intelligentsia.[41] Such people tend to be dismissed by political-types as dreamers with no understanding of political realities or getting elected. Maybe so. But neither do intellectuals delude themselves that polls and focus groups are a substitute for thought, analysis, and a well-crafted vision of where the country ought to be going, as political hacks do. It is not hopelessly utopian to believe that we can do better, that the great thinkers of the past still have something to offer us today, or that people crave having their political passions stirred by someone with conviction, who really believes what he says and isn't just mouthing the words of some clever speechwriter.

Finally, I only hope that the Republican Party doesn't have to suffer a serious defeat of some sort before its current leadership is sufficiently discredited to allow new faces, voices, and ideas to emerge. Historically, both parties have found people to fill this role when their backs were against the wall. But, sadly, they sometimes had to have their backs against the wall first.

There is no doubt in my mind that the ideas about tax cutting and supply-side economics would have died in the crib without the political decimation of the Republican Party in 1974 and 1976. Nor could someone as conservative as Ronald Reagan have been a viable presidential candidate under less stressful economic and political circumstances than we had in the late 1970s.

Things are not quite as bad today, but neither are they so good that

Republicans can afford complacency. The Republican Party needs to start a dialogue that will get it back on track as the party of small government before it loses what is left of its principles, reputation, and heritage. If the American people conclude that it stands for nothing except payoffs for those on its team, it will have lost something precious that, like one's virtue or good name, is awfully hard to get back once lost.

PRESIDENTIAL VETOES

President	Years	Total Vetoes*
George Washington	1789–1797	2
John Adams	1797–1801	0
Thomas Jefferson	1801–1809	0
James Madison	1809–1817	7
James Monroe	1817–1825	1
John Quincy Adams	1825–1829	0
Andrew Jackson	1829–1837	12
Martin Van Buren	1837–1841	1
William Henry Harrison	1841	0
John Tyler	1841–1845	10
James K. Polk	1845–1849	3
Zachary Taylor	1849–1850	0
Millard Fillmore	1850–1853	0
Franklin Pierce	1853–1857	9
James Buchanan	1857–1861	7
Abraham Lincoln	1861–1865	7
Andrew Johnson	1865–1869	29
Ulysses S. Grant	1869–1877	93
Rutherford B. Hayes	1877–1881	13
James A. Garfield	1881	0
Chester A. Arthur	1881–1885	12
Grover Cleveland	1885–1889	414
Benjamin Harrison	1889–1893	44
Grover Cleveland	1893–1897	170
William McKinley	1897–1901	42

* Regular and pocket vetoes

President	Years	Total Vetoes
Theodore Roosevelt	1901–1909	82
William H. Taft	1909–1913	39
Woodrow Wilson	1913–1921	44
Warren G. Harding	1921–1923	6
Calvin Coolidge	1923–1929	50
Herbert Hoover	1929–1933	37
Franklin D. Roosevelt	1933–1945	635
Harry S. Truman	1945–1953	250
Dwight D. Eisenhower	1953–1961	181
John F. Kennedy	1961–1963	21
Lyndon B. Johnson	1963–1969	30
Richard M. Nixon	1969–1974	43
Gerald R. Ford	1974–1977	66
Jimmy Carter	1977–1981	31
Ronald Reagan	1981–1989	78
George H. W. Bush	1989–1993	44
Bill Clinton	1993–2001	38
George W. Bush	2001–	0

Source: Congressional Research Service, available at http://clerk.house.gov

PORK BARREL SPENDING

Year	Number of Projects	Billions of Dollars
1995	1,439	10.0
1996	958	12.5
1997	1,596	14.5
1998	2,100	13.2
1999	2,838	12.0
2000	4,326	17.7
2001	6,333	18.5
2002	8,341	20.1
2003	9,362	22.5
2004	10,656	22.9
2005	13,999	27.3

Source: Citizens Against Government Waste

LEGISLATED TAX CHANGES BY RONALD REAGAN AS OF 1988

Tax Cuts	Billions of Dollars
Economic Recovery Tax Act of 1981	−264.4
Interest and Dividends Tax Compliance Act of 1983	−1.8
Federal Employees' Retirement System Act of 1986	−0.2
Tax Reform Act of 1986	−8.9
Total legislated tax cuts	−275.3

Tax Increases	Billions of Dollars
Tax Equity and Fiscal Responsibility Act of 1982	+57.3
Highway Revenue Act of 1982	+4.9
Social Security Amendments of 1983	+24.6
Railroad Retirement Revenue Act of 1983	+1.2
Deficit Reduction Act of 1984	+25.4
Consolidated Omnibus Budget Reconciliation Act of 1985	+2.9
Omnibus Budget Reconciliation Act of 1985	+2.4
Superfund Amendments and Reauthorization Act of 1986	+0.6
Continuing Resolution for 1987	+2.8
Omnibus Budget Reconciliation Act of 1987	+8.6
Continuing Resolution for 1988	+2.0
Total legislated tax increases	+132.7

Source: Budget of the United States Government for Fiscal Year 1990

VAT Rates in OECD Countries Establishing VATs Before 1975

(Ranked by Year of Inception)

	Country	Initial Rate	Year	2005 Rate	% Increase
1	Denmark	10	1967	25	150
2	France	16.66	1968	19.6	17.6
3	Germany	10	1968	16	60
4	Netherlands	12	1969	19	58.3
5	Sweden	11.11	1969	25	125
6	Luxembourg	8	1970	15	87.5
7	Norway	20	1970	24	20
8	Belgium	18	1971	21	16.7
9	Ireland	16.37	1972	21	28.3
10	Austria	16	1973	20	25
11	Italy	12	1973	20	66.7
12	U.K.	10	1973	17.5	75
	Average	13.3		20.25	52.2

Sources: EU, IMF, PricewaterhouseCoopers, and national sources

VAT Rates in OECD Countries Establishing VATs After 1975

(Ranked by Year of Inception)

	Country	Initial Rate	Year	2005 Rate	% Increase
13	Korea	10	1977	10	0
14	Mexico	10	1980	16.2	62
15	Turkey	10	1985	15.4	54
16	New Zealand	10	1986	12.5	25
17	Portugal	16	1986	19	18.7
18	Spain	12	1986	16	33.3
19	Greece	18	1987	18	0
20	Hungary	25	1988	25	0
21	Iceland	24	1989	24.5	2.1
22	Japan	3	1989	5	66.7
23	Canada	7	1991	7	0
24	Czech Rep.	23	1993	19	(17.4)
25	Poland	22	1993	22	0
26	Slovakia	23	1993	19	(17.4)
27	Finland	22	1994	22	0
28	Switzerland	6.5	1995	7.6	16.9
29	Australia	10	2000	10	0
	Average	14.8		15.8	6.7

Sources: EU, IMF, PricewaterhouseCoopers, and national sources

NOTES

1. On the liberal origins of big government conservatism, see Schlesinger (1983).

2. I am reminded of an incident of this. Early in the George H. W. Bush administration, the Commerce Department was very keen on the idea of subsidizing HDTV (high-definition television), because it thought it was essential to maintain the international competitiveness of the American electronics industry. I was at the Treasury Department and we were very skeptical of the Commerce plans, which eventually were dropped. Some years later, I ran into one of the Commerce people who had been pushing the subsidies for HDTV. He said that we turned out to be right—the technology that Commerce wanted to subsidize was already obsolete. If the subsidies had gone through, the newer, more promising technology might not have been developed, he said. On the political fight over HDTV subsidies, see Davis (1990) and Hart (1994).

3. For a powerful statement of this philosophy, see Hayek (1945).

4. Of course, conservatives still distrust pure democracy because they think people are too easily swayed by appeals to their emotions. But the U.S. has never been anything close to a pure democracy, but instead is a democratic republic, with theoretically severe limits to the legislature's power. Nevertheless, in today's America, those on the right are more likely to trust the will of the people than those on the left, and thus are more likely to be "small d" democrats. This is partially explained by public opinion polls that have long shown that many more

Americans describe themselves as "conservative" than "liberal." And over time, the conservative margin has tended to grow and the liberal percentage has tended to fall.

5. Some liberals have started to question the efficacy of achieving their policy goals by fiat through court decisions rather than doing the work necessary to build genuine popular support for them. See Starr (2005).

6. "President's Remarks on Labor Day," www.whitehouse.gov (September 1, 2003).

7. Let's not forget that as recently as 1961, a Republican president, Dwight Eisenhower, left office warning about the "military-industrial complex." See Taft (1951) for a statement of the traditional Republican view of a limited American foreign policy, in contrast to the expansiveness of Wilsonianism. See also Berger (1967, 1971, 1975), Paterson (1976), and Radosh (1975: 119–95). On Wilson's warmongering, see Bourne (1964), Karp (1979), and Powell (2005).

8. Posted on *National Review*'s blog, "The Corner" (September 11, 2005).

9. Grunwald (2002) and Rosenbaum (2002a). On Bush's disdain for federalism, see Yoo (2005).

10. Lichtblau (2005). The accuracy of the data, relating to racial profiling, was not in dispute.

11. Novak (2004e).

12. Quoted in Bumiller (2004).

13. Skinner, Anderson & Anderson (2001, 2003, 2004) leave no doubt that Ronald Reagan was exceptionally well read and informed.

14. In an interview with Brit Hume of Fox News that aired on September 22, 2003, Bush said he glanced at the headlines but rarely read the stories, preferring instead to be briefed by his staff on the news of the day.

15. For example, when I worked in the White House there were people who would not go home until they knew that President Reagan had retired from the Oval Office for the night, lest he need them for some purpose. It didn't matter that he had never once summoned them or that the White House operators could easily find them at home if he did. It was just vanity that kept them in the office. And of course, all their underlings were expected to stay around as well. This shows the way in which every little thing the president does is studied and responded to, even at the lowest levels of the White House bureaucracy.

16. In his memoir, Darman talks often about how he tried to restrain Reagan's conservative views and push him toward the political center. See Darman (1996).

17. For the curious, see Bartlett (1984a). Incidentally, I know that President Reagan saw it, because a staffer from the Council of Economic Advisers called me to confirm some of the statistics. He said Reagan had referred to the article in a cabinet meeting. On Reagan's affection for *Human Events,* see Hunt (1980).

18. His father had the same attitude, perhaps as a consequence of having served as director of Central Intelligence. See Dowd (1990). Richard Nixon's White House counsel, John Dean, has called George W. Bush's White House "the most secretive ever to run the United States." Quoted in Coman (2004). See also Dean (2004), McQuillan (2002), and Shane (2005).

19. Will (1992b).

20. On conservative enmity toward Bush in 1992, see Bartley (1992), Novak (1992), and Wessel & McQueen (1992).

21. Oreskes (1990).

22. As real incomes rise, people get pushed up into higher tax brackets, thus raising the tax burden without any legislated increase in taxes.

23. I sometimes suspected that I was kept around just so the Bush people could find out what conservatives were thinking since they didn't know any other conservatives personally.

24. Miniter (1999).

25. Posted on *National Review*'s blog, "The Corner" (June 29, 2005).

26. Speech before the Front Porch Alliance (July 22, 1999).

27. Crane (1999).

28. http://www.manhattan-institute.org/html/bush_speech.htm.

29. Writing in the liberal *New Republic* magazine just before the election, editor Andrew Sullivan said Gore was going to lose because he was too liberal for the country. "What voters have heard from Gore since August has been one leftist theme after another," he said, and it wasn't going to work. It didn't. See Sullivan (2000).

30. York (2001).

31. Gigot (2001b).

32. Of course, there were always those on the right-wing kook fringe who hated Bush since day one and for whom 9/11 was simply an excuse to hate him more, even implying that he had something to do with it. See, for example, the postings at www.lewrockwell.com. On June 9, 2005, this site published a column by Morgan Reynolds arguing that U.S. government demolition experts actually blew up the World Trade Center, not Muslim terrorists. The insanity of this argument is truly breathtaking. Amazingly, Reynolds had served as chief economist for the Department of Labor during Bush's first term, a political appointment.

33. See Will (2002a, 2002c). It is worth noting that academic research is highly skeptical of the premise behind campaign finance reform, finding little evidence that contributions significantly influence politicians' votes or election outcomes. See Bronars & Lott (1997) and Levitt (1994).

34. Milbank (2002).

35. Lambro (2002).

36. Allen (2002), Novak (2002a).

37. Broder (2002). See Rauch (2003) for an elaboration of this argument.

38. On the origins of neoconservatism, see Kristol (1995) and Steinfels (1979). As Kristol's book makes clear, neoconservatism has always been almost entirely about domestic policy and was originated principally by social scientists. A neoconservative foreign policy is a very recent development that really has nothing to do with historical neoconservatism, except that Kristol's son Bill, editor of the *Weekly Standard,* was one of the leading proponents of the war. Nevertheless, those who were supportive of the war with Iraq were popularly tagged as neoconservatives. See Kosterlitz (2003). This brought forth attacks from some on the traditional right, such as Pat Buchanan, who became an outspoken critic of the war. See Hitchens (2004), Kirkpatrick (2004d), and Omestad (2004). Neoconservatives have long been controversial among traditional conservatives, with some viewing them as ersatz conservatives. See, for example, Buchanan (2004: 37–59) and Gottfried (1993: 78–96). Unfortunately, some of these so-called paleoconservatives come dangerously close to anti-Semitism. (Many neoconservatives are Jewish.) Bill Buckley fired one, writer Joseph Sobran, as an editor of *National Review* for being excessively critical of Israel on too many occasions, giving the appearance of anti-Semitism even if he may not technically have been an anti-Semite. See Trueheart (1991).

39. Tanenhaus (2003). Nock is a pretty obscure character even among well-read conservatives these days and it's doubtful that he ever really thought of himself as a conservative, but rather as an individualist who today would be called a libertarian. See Nock (1935) for the book Tanenhaus refers to. On Nock's life, see Nock (1943), Powell (2000: 212–19), and Wreszin (1971).

40. Will (2003b).

41. Novak (2003b).

42. *National Review* (2003). See also Ponnuru (2003).

43. Podhoretz (2003a).

44. Barnes (2003a).

45. Dinan (2003).

46. Calmes (2004a), Novak (2004a), Rutenberg (2004), Andrew Sullivan (2004), Washington (2004).

47. Quoted in Dinan (2004).

48. Casse (2004).

49. Nofziger (2004a).

50. http://acuf.org/issues/issue10.asp

51. Balz & Morin (2004).

52. Novak (2004c).

53. Kirkpatrick (2004b). See also Wighton & Harding (2004).

54. Kirkpatrick (2004a).

55. Quoted in Kirkpatrick (2004c). My own view is the same. In 2005, one of the leading war "hawks," Eliot Cohen, a professor of strategy at Johns Hopkins University, said that he had also become ambivalent about the war because he never imagined beforehand that the Bush Administration would be so incompetent at handling its postwar role in Iraq. Much of this failure obviously stemmed from inadequate prewar planning. See Cohen (2005).

56. Academic research supports the idea that divided government helps keep spending under control. See Alesina & Rosenthal (1995).

57. Bandow (2004), Doherty (2004), George (2004), *Tampa Tribune* (2004). See also Micklethwait & Wooldridge (2004).

58. http://fairmodel.econ.yale.edu/vote2004/index2.htm

59. *Los Angeles Times* (November 4, 2004).

60. Nofziger (2004b).

61. On the drug bill, see Gleckman (2004), Novak (2004b, 2004d), and Meyerson (2004). On the education bill, see Harwood (2005d) and Kronholz (2004). On immigration, see Calmes (2004c).

62. Will (2004).

63. Fund (2005a). See also Lambro (2005).

64. Novak (2005a).

65. VandeHei (2005a).

66. Kirkpatrick (2005).

67. See Derbyshire (2005), Harwood (2005a), Nagourney (2005), Sager (2005a), and Sullivan (2005b).

68. Noonan (2005).

69. Ferguson (2005b).

70. Novak (2005f).

71. On the success of conservatives in exploiting new media, see Hewitt (2005).

72. Chait (2005).

73. Grimaldi (2005).

74. Weisberg (2005).

75. Lichtman (2004).

CHAPTER 2: THE END OF SERIOUS POLICY ANALYSIS

1. See Light (1991), Kingdon (2003), and Porter (1983).

2. I recall one incident late in the George H. W. Bush administration when I participated in a working group led by then–Transportation Secretary Andrew Card, who went on to be White House chief of staff in the George W. Bush administration, on how to aid the domestic shipbuilding industry. As the repre-

sentative from the Treasury Department, my orders were to oppose any new tax subsidies for shipbuilding or expansions of existing ones. In the course of doing research on this issue, I discovered a Treasury memo from the Truman Administration that exactly reflected Treasury's current view on this issue and whose analysis could have been reused without alteration. It just proves that in Washington some things never change.

3. On George H. W. Bush's lack of interest in domestic policy, see Harwood & Wessel (1991), Kolb (1993), McQueen & Harwood (1991), Pinkerton (1992), Podhoretz (1993), Walsh (1991), and Wildavsky (1991).

4. At one point during the campaign, President Bush visited a local supermarket and appeared to be unfamiliar with its computerized checkout scanner. The truth was that this was a new model and he knew perfectly well about scanners. Nevertheless, the incident became an unshakable metaphor for his disconnection from the economic problems of average Americans.

5. On the operation of economic policy during the Clinton Administration, see Orszag, Orszag & Tyson (2002), Rubin & Weisberg (2003), and Woodward (1994).

6. Wessel (1992).

7. Borrus & McNamee (1996) and Destler (1996).

8. Suskind (2003).

9. Unfortunately, the memo can no longer be found on the *Esquire* Web site. However, it does appear to be available on numerous other Web sites that can be located with a simple Internet search.

10. DiIulio (2002).

11. Novak (2002b).

12. Frum (2003: 20).

13. Kosterlitz (2001).

14. Schlesinger (1959: 243)

15. Blum (1967: 343–59).

16. Suskind (2004a: 165–66).

17. *Washington Post* (2004a).

18. Rich Karlgaard, publisher of *Forbes* magazine, had called for O'Neill to be fired in its July 23 issue on the grounds that he suffered from terminal foot-in-mouth disease.

19. Suskind (2004a: 268).

20. The online magazine *Slate* had a regular feature called "The O'Neill Death Watch" that cataloged all the rumors.

21. Cheney later described O'Neill as "a round peg in a square hole." See Keen (2004).

22. In August 2005, it was said that the White House was seriously consider-

ing Lindsey to become Federal Reserve chairman after the retirement of Alan Greenspan. See Ip (2005b). If this was true, then it makes Lindsey's earlier dismissal all the more bizarre.

23. Davis (2002).

24. Simendinger (2003).

25. Novak (2004f).

26. Friedman had also been head of Goldman Sachs, as was Rubin.

27. Ip (2005a) and Stevenson (2005).

28. Andrews (2005b), Shah & Jackson (2005), and Vieth (2005).

29. Scheiber (2003a).

30. Allen (2004c).

31. Allen (2004b).

32. Allen & Weisman (2004b).

33. Those on the career staff were frustrated as well, with many deciding to take early retirement rather than waste their time. See Weisman (2002).

34. Throughout 2005, most of Treasury's top vacancies were unfilled due to a "hold" by Sen. Max Baucus (D-MT), ranking Democrat on the Senate Finance Committee, on all Treasury nominees over an obscure trade regulation. Although this hold could have been broken fairly easily, there was no pressure to do so because everyone knew that Treasury wasn't really doing anything anyway. See Weisman (2005c).

35. Suskind (2004c).

36. Federal departments are ranked in the order they were established. The Department of State came first and Treasury second.

37. Internal Revenue Service (2005).

38. *Financial Times* (2005).

39. By custom, the World Bank president is always named by the United States, although it is an independent international institution technically affiliated with the United Nations. Similarly, the Europeans always name the managing director of the IMF.

40. On the role and history of the CEA, see Feldstein (1997), Flash (1965), Norton (1991), Porter (1997), and Weidenbaum (1986).

41. Hahn & Wallsten (2003), Milbank (2003a), and Murray (2003a).

42. U.S. Treasury Department (1992).

43. Weisman (2005a).

44. Murray (2004b). See also Reed (2004).

45. Taylor (2004: 99).

46. Hale (2003).

47. Weisman (2003c). Bodman went on to become secretary of energy in Bush's second term.

48. Boot (2004a).

49. Michael Brown, head of FEMA when Katrina hit, had been commissioner of judges for the International Arabian Horse Association before joining FEMA. Apparently, his only qualification for the FEMA job was that he was an old friend of Joseph Allbaugh, Bush's first appointment to head the agency, who made his pal general counsel of FEMA after he was fired from the horse group. See Arends (2005). Apparently, Brown was not the exception, with many of the agency's experienced disaster relief officials having been replaced by political hacks during the Bush Administration. See Hsu (2005).

50. Glanz (2004), Mooney (2005), Revkin (2004), and Smith (2005).

51. Easterbrook (2004b), *Economist* (2004).

52. Satel (2004).

53. Birnbaum (2002). See also Barro (2002), Bumiller (2002), Hoagland (2002), and Rosenbaum (2002b).

54. *Wall Street Journal* (2005a).

55. Balls (2005), Davis (2004b), Scheiber (2002, 2004), and Surowiecki (2004).

56. Miller, McNamee & Walczak (2004).

57. Allen & Weisman (2004a).

58. Andrews (2005a), Andrews & Becker (2005), and Blustein & Weisman (2005).

59. Fletcher (2005). See also James Barnes (2005).

60. Novak (2005c).

61. Tumulty, Thompson & Allen (2005).

62. *New York Times* (2005).

63. Quoted in Revkin (2004).

64. Suskind (2004b: 51). Ellipses in original.

65. Quoted in Lemann (2004: 158). See also Allen (2005).

66. Lemann (2004: 158).

67. Lemann (2004: 159). I can confirm that the "murder board" is indeed a Washington institution. For example, when I was at the Treasury Department, we would put the secretary through one of these before every congressional hearing at which he was testifying. It wasn't pleasant, either for him or the staff, but everyone understood that it was better for him to make a mistake or betray ignorance behind closed doors than in public. It might also be the only opportunity the staff had to brief the secretary on issues he might otherwise have preferred to avoid or put off.

68. Posted on *National Review*'s blog, "The Corner" (July 8, 2004). Brookhiser's comment is a play on Barry Goldwater's 1964 campaign slogan: "In your heart, you know he's right."

CHAPTER 3: WHY THE BUSH TAX CUTS
DIDN'T DELIVER

1. Keynes (1973: 129).

2. See Bartlett (1993b).

3. Joint Committee on Taxation (2005: 41). The reason is that the negative tax liability of those receiving the Earned Income Tax Credit offsets all of the taxes paid by everyone else with an income below $40,000. The EITC is refundable for those with no tax liability, thus creating negative tax rates where people receive rebates from the government even though they have no income tax liability.

4. Kennedy (1963: 869).

5. House Committee on the Budget and Joint Economic Committee (1978).

6. Congressional Budget Office (1978: 25).

7. Canto, Joines & Webb (1983) come closest to proving that the Kennedy tax cut paid for itself by including higher revenues that accrued to state and local governments with those obtained by the federal government.

8. Fortunately, Galbraith had been exiled to India, where he was the U.S. ambassador, making it hard for him to influence Kennedy's decision. In any case, his fears about the Republicans were unfounded. They mostly opposed the tax cut. See Galbraith (1969: 381).

9. Interestingly, the tax expenditures concept has only applied to provisions that reduce the tax burden. Those that would cause taxes to be higher than under an ideal tax system were ignored. In recent years, the chapter of the president's budget dealing with tax expenditures has been critical of this double standard.

10. For a comprehensive discussion of the tax expenditure concept, see Bartlett (2001b).

11. In an interview with Barbara Walters on ABC in 1992, Bush said that breaking the pledge was the biggest mistake of his presidency. However, in an interview with Carl Leubsdorf of the *Dallas Morning News,* Bush said that making the pledge in the first place was his real mistake. See Leubsdorf (2002) and Rosenthal (1992).

12. Bartley (1999).

13. Lindsey had been a special assistant to his father, who appointed him to be a governor of the Federal Reserve Board. In 1999, Lindsey was a senior fellow at the American Enterprise Institute in Washington, a well-known Republican think tank. Among the other economists involved in the tax effort were Michael Boskin, John Cogan, and John Taylor, all of Stanford's Hoover Institution, and Harvard's Martin Feldstein.

14. Gigot (2000).

15. Forbes campaign press release (December 1, 1999).

16. *Manchester Union Leader* (1999).

17. Novak (1999).

18. Real GDP rose by 7.3 percent in the fourth quarter of 1999, one of the highest rates ever recorded. The unemployment rate was just 4.1 percent in December, and the Dow Jones Industrial Average was well over 11,000.

19. Despite the good economic data, Lindsey was very bearish on the economy. See Schlesinger (1999).

20. Woodward (1994) explains the change in Clinton's thinking.

21. Suskind (2004a: 42).

22. Mallaby (2001).

23. Dionne (2001).

24. Reinhardt (2001).

25. For example, Broder (2001a, 2001b), Domenici (2001), Freeman & Appelbaum (2001), and Raspberry (2001).

26. Kiefer (1992).

27. Blinder (1981), Modigliani & Steindel (1977), and Steindel (2001).

28. Bartley (2001).

29. Forbes (2001).

30. Speech to the National Association of Business Economists (March 27, 2001).

31. U.S. General Accounting Office (2001).

32. Reddy (2001).

33. Moore (2001).

34. Bloomberg News (2001) and University of Michigan (2001).

35. See Johnson, Parker & Souleles (2004), and Shapiro & Slemrod (2003a, 2003b).

36. Feldstein (2001).

37. House & Shapiro (2004).

38. Donlan (2001).

39. Reynolds (2001).

40. Archer (2001).

41. On problems with the corporate AMT, which operates quite differently than the individual AMT, see Chorvat & Knoll (2003) and Lyon (1997).

42. Bartlett (2001c).

43. Barro (2001).

44. Bartlett (2001a).

45. Bartlett (1998).

46. In 2001, total welfare spending (federal and state) was $24.5 billion. The total cost of the EITC was $33.4 billion, of which $29 billion was the refunded portion. House Committee on Ways and Means (2004: 7–59, 13–14).

47. For example, Cherry & Sawicky (2000).

48. Macomber (2005).

49. *Wall Street Journal* (1978a).

50. *Wall Street Journal* (2001).

51. Ferguson (2005a).

52. Ture (1974).

53. Smith (1963).

54. Moore (2002).

55. The best case for the idea that a cut in dividend taxes would boost the stock market and hence economic growth can be found in Harris, Hubbard & Kemsley (2001). Although passage of the dividend tax cut did increase dividend payouts, there is little evidence that there was much of an impact on stock prices. One reason may be that the dividend tax cut was not enacted permanently and is due to expire in 2008. See Browning (2005), Chetty & Saez (2004), and Michel & Rector (2004).

56. See McLure (1979) for a thorough discussion.

57. Vickrey (1993).

58. Despite his strong disagreement with President Bush on almost all aspects of tax policy, Sen. John Kerry of Massachusetts, the Democratic Party's presidential candidate in 2004, agreed that the double taxation of dividends should be abolished. See his speech to the City Club of Cleveland (December 3, 2002).

59. See Carter's interview with *Fortune* magazine in May 1976, and his interview with *BusinessWeek* (May 3, 1976).

60. *New York Times* (1977).

61. Reagan (1984: 120) and *Wall Street Journal* (1985).

62. U.S. Treasury Department (1992).

63. Shlaes (2001).

64. Hubbard (1993).

65. Hassett (2003b). See also Gleckman (2003a).

66. Reynolds (2003).

67. See Bartlett (2004a).

CHAPTER 4: THE WORST LEGISLATION IN HISTORY?

1. Republican Study Committee (2003).

2. *Congressional Record* (November 21, 2003): H12295–H12296.

3. Common Cause (2004).

4. Pear & Toner (2003). Rep. Trent Franks (R-AZ) made this same argument. See Pear & Andrews (2004).

5. House Committee on Standards of Official Conduct (2004).

6. Novak (2003a).

7. Antos & Gokhale (2003). This is a "present value" calculation, meaning

that it is adjusted for the time value of money. In other words, it compensates for the fact that a dollar in the future is not worth as much as a dollar today even in the absence of inflation.

8. Connolly & Allen (2005), Pear (2005).

9. Holtz-Eakin (2005).

10. *Wall Street Journal* (2004b).

11. Goldstein (2004a).

12. Holtz-Eakin (2005).

13. For evidence that the White House and Republican congressional leaders knew about Foster's estimate well before the final vote on the legislation, see Goldstein (2004a, 2004b, 2004c), Pear (2004c), Rogers (2004), and Stolberg & Pear (2004).

14. U.S. Department of Health & Human Services (2004). A Congressional Research Service report concluded that laws probably were broken. See Maskell (2004). In any event, no one was ever prosecuted.

15. *Los Angeles Times* (2004).

16. Quoted in Pear (2004a).

17. www.cms.hhs.gov/publications/trusteesreport

18. www.ssa.gov/OACT/TR/index.html

19. McClellan (2001) reviews the history of Medicare financing and the fact that it has regularly exceeded estimates of its cost since the day it was established. Interestingly, the author, who is a medical doctor and holds a Ph.D. in economics, was appointed head of the agency that oversees Medicare in 2004. He is also the brother of Scott McClellan, who is the White House press secretary in President Bush's second term.

20. See Super (2004).

21. Lichtenberg (2002–2003, 2003a, 2003b). See also Hensley (2003).

22. According to the Census Bureau, in November 2004, 70.8 percent of those aged 65 to 74 reported voting, compared with 66.6 percent for those aged 45 to 64, 52.2 percent for those aged 25 to 44, and a mere 41.9 percent of those aged 18 to 24. Little wonder that the elderly are so easily able to get benefits for themselves paid for by the young.

23. Altman (2003).

24. Gingrich (2003). Oddly, Gingrich had previously warned against passage of the drug bill on the grounds that it would be a budget-buster, would be deemed inadequate by elderly voters, and would depress the Republican Party's base. See Harwood (2003). The rationale for this 180-degree reversal of position is unknown.

25. Cook (2003).

26. Gleckman (2003b), Harris (2003).

27. Hulse (2003).

28. Martinez (2004).

29. AARP (2004).

30. Kaufman & Brubaker (2004).

31. Goldstein & Dewar (2004).

32. Lowry (2004).

33. Novak (2004b).

34. Gleckman (2004).

35. Novak (2004d).

36. Meyerson (2004).

37. Freudenheim (2003).

38. Francis (2004).

39. Pear (2004d).

40. Gleckman & Welch (2005).

41. Schultz & Francis (2004).

42. Berenson (2005).

43. Jacobzone (2000).

44. U.S. General Accounting Office (1992).

45. Salins & Mildner (1992).

46. Morton (2001), Vernon (2002–2003, 2004).

47. Baker & Allen (2005).

48. CBS News, *The Early Show* (September 20, 2005).

49. Oberlander & Jaffe (2003).

50. Armey (2005: 12).

51. Kuttner (2003).

CHAPTER 5: THE WORST RECORD ON TRADE SINCE HOOVER?

1. For recent research on the damaging effects of Smoot-Hawley, see Archibald & Feldman (1998), Crucini & Kahn (1996), and Irwin (1998).

2. *Congressional Record* (May 6, 1913): 1247.

3. The following review draws heavily on Destler (2005), which cannot be recommended too highly.

4. See Dam (1970) and Gardner (1969).

5. Brusse (1997), DeLong & Eichengreen (1993).

6. Although protectionists often cite Hamilton in defense of their policies, he was far less of a protectionist than they imagine. He didn't so much want to restrict trade as tax it for the revenue. This meant keeping tariffs at a moderate level so as not to discourage imports too much, lest it lead to lower tariff revenue.

See Irwin (2004). For protectionist praise of Hamilton, see Buchanan (1998: 131–33) and Eckes (1995: 15–16).

7. Mill (1909: 922). Bastable (1900: 139–40) likened infant industry protection to patent or copyright protection. However, Kemp (1960) points out that Mill's and Bastable's assumptions are actually quite restrictive. For criticism of infant industry protection on both theoretical and empirical grounds, see Baldwin (1969), Haberler (1936: 278–85), and Krueger & Tuncer (1982).

8. Barringer & Pierce (2000). It doesn't matter whether the goods were made with domestic steel or imported steel because tariffs cause domestically produced steel to rise in price by the same amount.

9. Congressional Budget Office (1986), Lenway, Morck & Yeung (1996).

10. U.S. Department of Commerce (2001).

11. Francois & Baughman (2001), U.S. International Trade Commission (2001).

12. Will (2002b). While in the House of Representatives, William McKinley had been the leading proponent of trade protection and was the principal author of the Tariff Act of 1890, popularly known as the McKinley Tariff. Will's reference to Bush's political advisers is primarily to Karl Rove, who often compared George W. Bush to William McKinley in terms of making the Republican Party politically dominant.

13. Rich (2002).

14. Wonacott (2002).

15. *Wall Street Journal* (2002).

16. The House Committee on Small Business held two hearings on the damaging impact of the steel tariffs on small steel users, on July 23, 2002, and September 25, 2002.

17. Francois & Baughman (2003).

18. Drucker (2005).

19. U.S. International Trade Commission (2003).

20. Hufbauer & Goodrich (2003).

21. *Wall Street Journal* (2003b).

22. Alden (2003).

23. Barnes (2002b).

24. Despite NAFTA, the United States has been limiting Canadian lumber imports for years, with significant effects on the cost of housing construction in the United States. See Lindsey, Groombridge & Loungani (2000).

25. Peterson (1979), Touré & Compaoré (2003).

26. Andrews (2003).

27. Lardy (2003).

28. International Monetary Fund (2003).

29. For reports of China's planned buying mission, see Goodman (2003), Hutzler (2003a), and Shirouzu (2003). On cancellation of the buying mission, see Hutzler (2003b) and Hutzler & Buckman (2003).

30. For sober analyses of outsourcing, see Amiti & Wei (2005), Bhagwati, Panagariya & Srinivasan (2004), Drezner (2004), and Schultze (2004).

31. Council of Economic Advisers (2004: 229).

32. Weisman (2004).

33. *Washington Post* (2004b).

34. Davis (2004a).

35. *New York Times* (2004b).

36. Bhagwati & Panagariya (2003).

37. See Congressional Budget Office (2003a), Krueger (1999), and Levy (1997). The classic analysis can be found in Viner (1950), in which he differentiated between trade agreements that expand trade and those that merely divert it.

38. U.S. General Accounting Office (2000).

39. Alden (2004).

40. *New York Times* (2004a).

41. Andrews (2005c), Blustein (2005).

42. Quoted in Hitt (2005b).

43. On use of the antidumping laws as backdoor protectionism, see Blonigen & Prusa (2001), Hindley & Messerlin (1996), Kelly & Morkre (2002), McGee (1993), and U.S. International Trade Commission (1995).

44. On the theory and history of dumping, see Viner (1923).

45. Mankiw & Swagel (2005) emphasize this point.

46. Ikenson (2004). The European Union used a similar system and it was ruled illegal by the WTO. The EU alleged that the U.S. is behaving unlawfully for the same reasons and the WTO agreed. The Bush Administration immediately appealed the ruling.

47. Ikenson (2005).

48. According to the WTO, seventy-four antidumping actions were taken against U.S. companies between 1995 and mid-2004. Only China, Korea, Taiwan, and Japan had more.

49. U.S. Government Accountability Office (2005c).

50. For an economic analysis of the Byrd Amendment, see Congressional Budget Office (2004b). For a litany of Bush's protectionist actions, see European Union (2004).

51. Carnahan (2003).

52. Langenfeld & Nieberding (2005) estimate that open trade added $2,500 to the median family income in 2002.

CHAPTER 6: IS ENRON A METAPHOR FOR
BUSH'S ECONOMIC POLICY?

1. McLean & Elkind (2003: 240), Simpson (2002). Krugman even wrote a puff piece about Enron in *Fortune* magazine. See Krugman (1999). He later became a harsh critic of the company.

2. Quoted in Suskind (2004a: 291).

3. Smith (1937: 250).

4. Smith (1937: 128).

5. Smith (1937: 250).

6. On historical business support for regulation, see Kolko (1963, 1965), Nordhauser (1973), Shaffer (1997), and Wood (1985).

7. *Economist* (1994), Hong & Peterson (1992).

8. Brophy (1981).

9. McCoy (1984).

10. Brooks (2001).

11. Andrews (1994).

12. See Riekhof & Sykuta (2004).

13. Council of Economic Advisers (1988: 199–229), Vietor (1990).

14. Stigler (1975: 114).

15. Simon (1978). For a powerful recent statement of the dangers of crony capitalism, see Rajan & Zingales (2003).

16. Murray (2004c).

17. Harwood & Chen (2001).

18. Becker (2001), Power & Schlesinger (2002).

19. Melloan (2001).

20. On Clinton's midnight regulations, see Dreazen (2000), Morgan (2000), and Skrzycki (2000).

21. Dudley (2004–2005: 4).

22. Morin (2002).

23. Ip (2002).

24. Revkin (2002).

25. *Federal Register* (March 28, 2002): 15014, 15038.

26. Dudley & Warren (2005).

27. *Federal Register* (February 3, 2003): 5494.

28. Crain & Hopkins (2001).

29. Crain (2005).

30. http://www.whitehouse.gov/omb/circulars/a004/a-4.pdf

31. Dudley (2004-2005: 7).

32. Sanger (2003).

33. Smith (1937: 700).

34. Berle & Means (1932).

35. On ways that government and politics came to shape today's corporation, see Roe (1994).

36. See Yago (1991).

37. Harvard Business School economist Michael Jensen was a strong proponent of this view. See Jensen (1984, 1986, 1988, 1989) and Jensen & Ruback (1983).

38. See Fischel (1995). By the same token, I've never figured out what Martha Stewart did wrong, either. Although people assume she was guilty of insider trading, she was not even indicted for this. Rather, she was convicted of lying to prosecutors and obstructing justice by proclaiming her innocence of insider trading.

39. A number of analysts suggested that the cure for the Enron problem was to bring back the hostile takeover. See Jenkins (2003a) and Manne (2002).

40. On accounting conventions that allowed Enron and Arthur Andersen to get away with what they were doing, see Mulford & Comiskey (2002). On the failures of financial analysts, see Cole (2001) and Gasparino (2005).

41. Brown & Opdyke (2001).

42. Ribstein (2002).

43. Bagehot (1999: 158).

44. Ribstein (2003: 78).

45. Bainbridge (2004).

46. It is named for Sen. Paul Sarbanes, Maryland Democrat, and Congressman Michael Oxley, Ohio Republican, who at the time chaired the respective committees with jurisdiction over securities laws.

47. Quoted in Drinkard (2002).

48. Quoted in Tucker & Parker (2005).

49. Romano (2005: 1523, 1526).

50. Strine (2005).

51. Kimmel & Vazquez (2003).

52. Quoted in Jones (2003).

53. Donaldson (2005), Solomon (2005).

54. Hartman (2004).

55. Financial Executives International (2004).

56. Politi, Michaels & Wighton (2004).

57. Michaels (2004).

58. Deutsch (2005), Engel, Hayes & Wang (2004), Ligos (2004), Thornton (2004).

59. Ascarelli (2004), Epstein (2005), Landler (2004), Pozen (2004).

60. Bellman (2005).

61. Bainbridge (2005), Cohen, Dey & Lys (2005), Hill (2002).

62. Ignatius (2004a).

63. Solomon & Peecher (2004).

64. Downloaded at www.number-10.gov.uk.

65. Hartman (2005).

66. Financial Executives International (2005).

67. Morgan (2005).

68. Zhang (2005).

69. Novak (2005d).

70. Tucker & Parker (2005).

71. Kuttner (2002), Public Citizen (2001).

72. McLean & Elkind (2003: 87-88).

73. Grimaldi (2002), Stevenson (2002), Sustainable Energy & Economy Network (2002).

74. Taylor (2002).

75. Reich (2001).

76. Stevenson (2001).

77. Power & Carey (2002).

78. Maynard (2004).

79. Congressional Budget Office (2002), Cummins & Lewis (2003), Gron & Sykes (2002–2003).

80. Brown, Cummins, Lewis & Wei (2004).

81. U.S. General Accounting Office (2004).

82. Meese & Gattuso (2004).

83. Crews (2005).

84. Singer (2005).

85. McKinnon (2005b), VandeHei (2005c).

86. Murray (2005).

87. McKinnon (2005c). In 2005, the National Conference of State Legislatures launched a "Preemption Monitor" to catalog the growing federal intrusions into state affairs.

88. "States Get Stuck with $29 Billion Bill," *NCSL News* (March 10, 2004). See also Congressional Budget Office (2005a).

89. Calvin Coolidge, "The Press under a Free Government" (January 17, 1925).

90. His father was the same way. See Saddler (1991).

91. Quoted in Edsall (2004).

CHAPTER 7: ON THE BUDGET, CLINTON WAS BETTER

1. It was called *Agenda for American Renewal*. I'm not sure when it came out because there is no date on it. But my memory is that it wasn't until well after Labor Day—too late to have done any good even if it had been brilliant and well distributed, which it wasn't.

2. Quoted in Woodward (1994: 35).

3. Clinton & Gore (1992: 27).

4. Clinton staffers knew that some of the revenue numbers were basically lies. See Woodward (1994: 46).

5. Samuelson (1992).

6. Thomas (1992).

7. Quoted in Byron (1992).

8. Vogel (1992).

9. Fuerbringer (1992).

10. Schmalz (1992).

11. Bush's comment was made on ABC's *Good Morning America* on October 6, 1992.

12. Wessel & Seib (1992).

13. Senate Committee on Governmental Affairs (1989: 29-30).

14. Woodward (1992a, 1992b, 1992c, 1992d).

15. The stimulus package was mostly a grab bag of pork barrel projects favored by congressional Democrats. See Harwood & Rogers (1993) and Wessel (1993).

16. Quoted in Woodward (1994: 84).

17. The Congressional Budget Office scored the premiums that would be paid for the health insurance as federal revenues that would have amounted to a $513 billion de facto tax increase by fiscal year 2004, making it the largest peacetime tax increase in American history. See Congressional Budget Office (1994: 38).

18. For a list of Clinton's vetoes, see Senate Library (2001: 15–24).

19. *Congressional Record* (October 10, 2000): H9576.

20. See, for example, Blinder & Yellen (2001). Both served on Clinton's Council of Economic Advisers and he appointed both to the Federal Reserve Board.

21. Meeropol (1998: 242–64), Pollin (2003: 21–47).

22. Stiglitz (2003: 49–55).

23. Reich (1999, 2000).

24. For a classic conservative critique of the welfare system, see Murray (1984).

25. For a history of the welfare reform effort, see DeParle (2004).

26. For some positive assessments of welfare reform, see Harden (2001), Moffitt (2002), O'Neill (2001), and Pear (2004b).

27. Congressional Budget Office (2001: 16–17).

28. Dawson & Seater (2005).

29. Stiglitz (2003: 19).

30. Boot (2004b).

31. Posted at www.marginalrevolution.com (June 16, 2004).

32. McTague (2004).

33. Bartlett (2004b).

34. See Appendix I.

35. See Ballou & Podgursky (1997), Dearden, Ferri & Meghir (2002), Hanushek (1986, 1998), Hanushek, Kain & Rivkin (1999), Hoxby (2000), and Lazear (1999).

36. Quoted in Gigot (2001a).

37. Kessler (2002), Riedl (2002), Rogers (2001, 2002).

38. Quoted in Cummings (2002).

39. See Appendix II.

40. Barnes (2002a).

41. Remarks at the Inter-American Development Bank (March 14, 2002).

42. Radelet (2003), New York Times (2002), Washington Post (2002).

43. Harris & Wright (2004).

44. New York Times (2004c).

45. Schneider (2005).

46. U.S. Treasury Department (1982).

47. Reagan (1982: 1052–55).

48. See Boone (1996), Burnside & Dollar (2000), and Easterly (2001, 2003).

49. Hitt (2005a).

50. Quoted in Rauch (2003).

51. De Rugy & DeHaven (2003).

52. Light (2003). See also Hamburger (2003) and Light (1999).

53. Rosenbaum (2003b), Weisman (2003a, 2003b).

54. Hook (2003).

55. Wall Street Journal (2003a).

56. Barnes (2003b).

57. Podhoretz (2003b).

58. Hallow (2004), Samuel (2004), Stevenson (2004).

59. Wall Street Journal (2004a).

60. Melloan (2004).

61. McKinnon (2004).

62. See Schmitt & Pear (2004).

63. Collender (2005). The Congressional Budget Office, which normally projects larger deficits than the administration, projected a fiscal year 2004 deficit $43 billion lower than the Bush Administration at the time the budget was released—a sure sign that the deficit was being highballed. See Congressional Budget Office (2004a).

64. Hitt (2004).

65. Allen (2004a), Hook & Vieth (2004).

66. Easterbrook (2004a).

67. Schultze (2005).

68. Ferguson (2004).

69. Scarborough (2004).

70. Slivinski (2005: 14). See De Rugy (2005a) for a similar analysis.

71. Sager (2005b).

72. Maggs (2005).

73. Melloan (2005).

74. Hassett (2005).

75. De Rugy and Newmark (2005).

76. See, for example, Statement of Administration Policy on S. 1072 (February 11, 2004).

77. Office of Management and Budget (2002: 263).

78. Reagan (1989: 297).

79. Jacoby (2005).

80. Quoted in Weisman (2005d). See also Novak (2005g).

81. Hulse (2005), Meckler (2005).

82. Even supporters of a constitutional balanced budget or spending limitation amendment admit that there is almost no limit to Congress's ability to get around it. See Wildavsky (1980: 84–105).

83. Calmes (2005).

84. Wessel (2005).

85. Murray & VandeHei (2005), Republican Study Committee (2005).

CHAPTER 8: Is Bush Another Nixon?

1. See Barone (1990: 487–89), Greenberg (2003: 304–37), Hoff (1994), Parmet (1990: 530–31), Small (1999: 213–14), Unger (1996: 300–47).

2. Safire (2003). One is reminded of Shakespeare's advice in *Henry IV,* part 2, to "busy giddy minds with foreign quarrels."

3. Samuelson (2003).

4. Doherty (2003).

5. Pinkerton (2003).

6. Transcript downloaded at www.rushlimbaugh.com.

7. Milbank (2003b).

8. Posted at www.volokh.com on November 24, 2003.

9. Murray (2003b).

10. Caldwell (2003).

11. Scheiber (2003b).

12. Rauch (2004b).

13. Bartlett (2003b).

14. Blumenthal (2005).

15. Real gross domestic product grew at only a 2.6 percent compounded growth rate between the fourth quarter of 1952 and the fourth quarter of 1960, a decent but hardly praiseworthy growth rate. On economic conditions in the 1950s generally, see Vatter (1963). On the 1953–54 recession, see Holmans (1958). On the 1957–58 recession, see Holmans (1961: 273–95).

16. Nixon (1962: 309–10). He was right about Burns' expertise on business cycles. He had been president of the National Bureau of Economic Research, which was established to study business cycles and is the organization that officially dates them. Nixon had an office in the Capitol because, as vice president, he was also president of the Senate.

17. Republicans lost 18 seats in the House and one in the Senate in 1954, which was enough for them to lose control in both bodies. The defeat in 1958 was much more severe, with a Republican loss of 48 seats in the House and 13 in the Senate. It was more than twenty years before the party really recovered from that debacle. See Ornstein, Mann & Malbin (2002: 66).

18. Matusow (1998: 7–33), Safire (1975: 491–95).

19. Burns had taught Friedman economics when he was an undergraduate at Rutgers. Burns was responsible for making him an economist and was the most important influence on his professional life for decades thereafter.

20. On the operation and failure of price controls, see Blinder & Newton (1981), Grayson (1974), Kosters (1975), Rockoff (1984: 200–33), and Stein (1991). On closing the gold window, see Gowa (1983).

21. Indeed, Burns may unintentionally have encouraged the price controls with his talk about the need for an "incomes policy," which he thought was necessary to curb "cost-push" inflation. See Friedman & Friedman (1998: 385) and Kettl (1986: 122–23).

22. Stein (1996).

23. Although conventional wisdom blames OPEC for causing the inflation of the 1970s, in fact it was reacting to the inflation, which was eroding the purchasing power of its oil revenues. See Bartley (1986, 1990, 1991) for details, quoting OPEC documents. As German chancellor Helmut Schmidt observed in 1978, "It is a fact that the worldwide inflation was one of the main causes of the explosion in oil prices and the world recession." Quoted in the *Wall Street Journal* (1978b). The latest research confirms that rising oil prices did not cause the stagflation of the 1970s, but rather easy money did. See Barsky & Kilian (2002).

24. Ladd (1998).

25. He told this to the late Jude Wanniski in a private meeting some years after leaving the White House. Wanniski told it to me in private correspondence in 1998.

26. See Gordon (1980), Hetzel (1998), Newton (1983), Pierce (1979), Poole (1979), and Rose (1974).

27. Reynolds (2004), Wells (1994).

28. Woolley (1984: 168–80).

29. His only real defender is his son. See Burns (2004).

30. The easy money policy really began in 1966, when Johnson threatened not to reappoint Martin as Fed chairman if he raised interest rates. Although Martin did raise rates a bit, he quickly cut them the following year after the modest rate rise brought on a credit crunch resulting more from Regulation Q, which limited the interest rates that banks could pay, than from the tightening itself. See Burger (1969), Greider (1987: 331), and Kettl (1986: 104–109). In Martin's defense, he may have thought Johnson's promise to raise taxes would obviate the need for a tighter monetary policy. He was wrong. See Bremner (2004: 209–51).

31. See Tempalski (2003).

32. Matusow (1998: 39–42).

33. See the testimony of Treasury Secretary Joseph W. Barr in Joint Economic Committee (1969: 46). It's worth noting that Barr had become secretary only on December 21, 1968. Since he left office on Inauguration Day 1969, his total service as Treasury secretary was just one month.

34. See, for example, Stern (1964).

35. It appears in Joint Economic Committee (1969: 11–31). On development of the tax expenditures budget, see Surrey (1973).

36. Matusow (1998: 43).

37. Burman (1999: 26).

38. See Bartlett (1982: 150–58).

39. See Ball (1973).

40. Kaplan (1977).

41. Snee & Ross (1978: 13).

42. Consultant Panel on Social Security (1976).

43. According to the Congressional Budget Office, adoption of price indexing—which means that future retirees will receive the same real benefits as those today, but not more—would be enough to keep Social Security solvent forever, with no need for benefit cuts or tax increases beyond those already in law. See Congressional Budget Office (2005b).

44. See Miller (1997), Ponnuru (1999), and Rauch (1994, 2004a).

45. On the history of impoundment authority, see Fisher (1975: 147–201) and McDonald (1988). Some scholars have argued that the Budget Act's restriction of impoundment is unconstitutional. See Glazier (1988).

46. Surprisingly, I've never heard any line-item veto supporter suggest simply

repealing the Budget Act of 1974 as an unambiguously constitutional means of giving the president this power by reinstating impoundment authority.

47. This was the primary reason for the energy crisis of the late 1970s. If prices had simply been allowed to adjust freely, there would have been no gas lines in 1979. See Chapman (1980).

48. Stein (1984: 190).

49. Denison (1978).

50. Jorgenson, Ho & Stiroh (2004).

51. Vogan (1996). The Commerce Department has discontinued collecting this data.

52. Gollop & Roberts (1983).

53. Link (1982).

54. Barbera & McConnell (1986).

55. Gray (1987).

56. Gray & Shadbegian (1995).

57. Jorgenson & Wilcoxen (1990).

58. Matusow (1998: 119).

59. Thernstrom & Thernstrom (1997: 428).

60. Lockheed got a loan guarantee of $250 million from the federal government after its effort to diversify out of military aircraft into the civilian market, by building the L-1011 passenger plane, failed. On Congress's rejection of Nixon's efforts to build the SST, see Joint Economic Committee (1973).

61. Galbraith (1970).

62. For example, see Allen (1971).

63. Reston (1972).

64. Will (1992a).

65. *New York Times* (1971).

66. *Time* (1965: 65). In a letter to the editor in the February 4, 1966, issue of *Time*, Friedman said his quote was taken out of context. What he actually said was, "In one sense, we are all Keynesians now; in another, nobody is any longer a Keynesian."

67. See Schlesinger (1997).

CHAPTER 9: THE INEVITABLE TAX INCREASE

1. It should be remembered that even without a legislated tax increase, the federal tax burden will rise over time as real growth pushes people up into higher tax brackets.

2. Eisenhower (1960: 48).

3. The Republican members of the House Ways and Means Committee said

the tax cut "is morally and fiscally wrong, and will do irreparable damage to the Republic." House Committee on Ways and Means (1963: c28).

4. On Eisenhower's resistance to tax-cutting, see Linder (1996).

5. Jacoby (1964: 368–69).

6. It's worth remembering that most economists thought that deficits were inflationary at this time. Today they recognize that inflation is almost entirely caused by the Federal Reserve's monetary policy.

7. Kemp and Roth explicitly modeled their legislation on the Kennedy tax cut.

8. Interestingly, John Kenneth Galbraith may have originated the starve-the-beast theory when he argued against the Kennedy tax cut on the grounds that "lower tax revenues will become a ceiling on spending." Galbraith (1969: 381).

9. Friedman (1978b). See also Friedman (1978a).

10. Kristol (1978).

11. Reagan (1982: 81).

12. In some ways, increased taxes were always implicit in the Reagan tax cut—and not because of the Laffer Curve. Inflation, which was very high when he took office, automatically raises taxes by pushing people into higher tax brackets. Although Reagan supported "indexing" to prevent this from happening, he did not want it to take effect until 1984. In essence, he wanted a few years of bracket creep to raise federal revenues even as he was cutting them. The problem was that inflation came down more quickly than anyone thought possible in 1981, thus depriving the government of revenue it had anticipated, which is a key reason why deficits were larger than expected. See Roberts (1987a, 2000).

13. Tempalski (2003).

14. Reagan (1993).

15. Reagan (1989: 1231).

16. Vedder, Gallaway & Frenze (1991).

17. Baack & Ray (1985), Blackley (1986), Holtz-Eakin, Newey & Rosen (1989), Hoover & Sheffrin (1992), Hoover & Siegler (2000), Joulfaian & Mookerjee (1990), Manage & Marlow (1986).

18. Anderson, Wallace & Warner (1986), Congressional Budget Office (1987), von Furstenberg (1991), von Furstenberg, Green & Jeong (1985, 1986).

19. Firestone (2003), Rosenbaum (2003a), Suskind (2004a: 300).

20. Wolffe (2000).

21. Will (2003a).

22. Jenkins (2003b).

23. Nichols (2003).

24. Barro (2003).

25. Becker, Lazear & Murphy (2003).

26. Friedman (2003).

27. Niskanen (2004). See also Niskanen (2002, 2005).

28. Again, liberal economist John Kenneth Galbraith was prescient. In congressional testimony in 1965 he warned against tax cuts because conservatives "would like it too much." He went on to say, "Tax reduction would then become a substitute for increased outlays on urgent social needs. We would have a new and reactionary form of Keynesianism with which to contend." Joint Economic Committee (1965: 13).

29. Bipartisan Commission on Entitlement and Tax Reform (1995), Congressional Budget Office (2003b), Fallows (1982), Kotlikoff & Burns (2004), Peterson (1999, 2004), U.S. Government Accountability Office (2005a).

30. Sam Beard says that a deal was in the making and that he met with Clinton about it. See Beard (2005). Others concur. See Elmendorf, Liebman & Wilcox (2002), and Hassett & MacGuineas (2005).

31. This is a present value calculation, which means that there would need to be $18.2 trillion invested in productive assets right now, earning a return, to pay the unfunded promises that have been made to current and future retirees.

32. Bartlett (2003a).

33. Wessel (2003).

34. Riedl (2003).

35. Sawicky (2003). I politely informed Max, with whom I went to college at Rutgers, that he was not the first to make this prediction. He agreed that I was first.

36. Shlaes (2004a).

37. Mitchell (2004).

38. Andrews (2004).

39. Murray (2004a). Before being elected to Congress, Kemp played professional football, principally for the Buffalo Bills of the old American Football League.

40. Shaviro (2004a).

41. Calmes (2004b), Miller (2004), Reid (2005), Yardley (2005).

42. Novak (2005b).

43. Dao (2004), Becker (2004), Shear & Jenkins (2004). In the 2005 primaries, all but one of the Republicans who had supported the tax increase were victorious, despite a strenuous effort by antitax forces to unseat them.

44. Cecchetti (2004).

45. Bartlett (2004c).

46. Alesina & Perotti (1995).

47. McKinnon (2005a), Stolberg & Kirkpatrick (2005), and VandeHei (2005b).

48. Henderson (2005).

49. Birnbaum (2005).

50. Antle (2005).

51. Hassett (2003a).

CHAPTER 10: THE SHAPE OF TAXES TO COME

1. The classic statements of a comprehensive income tax base can be found in Haig (1959) and Simons (1938). See Goode (1977) and Thuronyi (1990).

2. A good example is Break & Pechman (1975).

3. Classic statements of the case for a consumption-based tax system can be found in Fisher & Fisher (1942) and Kaldor (1955).

4. It also contained a proposal for a comprehensive income tax as well. See Bradford (1984) and U.S. Treasury Department (1977). Andrews (1974) was also influential.

5. Keynes (1981: 295).

6. The states and the federal government also have a few specific excise taxes on things like alcohol, tobacco, and gasoline.

7. See Bartlett (1997b) and Council of Economic Advisers (2003: 175–211).

8. Hall & Rabushka (1995). This plan was first put forward in 1981.

9. Advocates of this approach include Bank (2003), Graetz (1979), McCaffery (2002, 2005), and Shaviro (2004b). This idea is not new and was first advocated almost one hundred years ago. See Beale (1911).

10. For a recent estimate of the growth effects of switching to a consumption-based tax system, see Altig, Auerbach, Kotlikoff, Smetters & Walliser (2001).

11. Pechman (1990: 1). A growing body of research says that the optimal tax on capital is zero. See Atkeson, Chari & Kehoe (1999) and Chamley (1986).

12. Simons (1950: 20). Fullerton, King, Shoven & Whalley (1981) show large economic benefits to abolition of the corporate tax.

13. Slemrod (1997) provides a roadmap.

14. Cassou & Lansing (2004) and Castaneda, Diaz-Gimenez & Rull (1998).

15. Auerbach, Kotlikoff & Skinner (1983), Caucutt, Imrohoroglu & Kumar (2000), Gruber & Saez (2002), and Li & Sarte (2001).

16. U.S. Treasury Department (1984) and White House (1985).

17. Actually, the regressivity of consumption taxes is overstated. Because lifetime consumption is proportional to income, a consumption tax would also tend to be proportional. See Fullerton & Rogers (1993) and Sabelhaus (1993). Gramlich, Kasten & Sammartino (1989) conclude that imposition of a VAT would not alter the distribution of income.

18. Heller (2005). The author is a former member of the Federal Reserve Board. It should be remembered, however, that the burden of a VAT is imposed by raising the prices of goods. Since Social Security benefits are indexed to inflation, retirees would largely be compensated through higher Social Security benefits.

19. Bartlett (2001b).

20. A recent study suggests that there is less of a trade-off than might appear. Bankman & Weisbach (2005) argue that a consumption tax can be at least as redistributive as an income tax while being significantly more efficient.

21. Fullerton, Shoven & Whalley (1983) shows strong growth effects from switching to a consumption tax base even with progressive rates.

22. Applebome (1999), Frank (1999: 211–26), and Galbraith (1958: 315–21).

23. Panetta (1982). See also Cockburn & Pollin (1992) and Hitchens (1994).

24. Rawls (1999: 246). See also Sugin (2004).

25. Starobin (1995). It's worth remembering that the United States had a system similar to this during the Articles of Confederation. It broke down, leading to a constitutional convention, because the states didn't like paying taxes to the federal government any more than individuals do. See Ferguson (1961).

26. Supporters of the sales tax claim that their rate is only 23 percent. But this is calculated as if the tax were part of the sale price, which they call the tax-inclusive rate. Calculating the rate conventionally, as with state sales taxes, yields a tax-exclusive rate of 30 percent.

27. Bartlett (1995), Gale (1999, 2004, 2005), Gale, Koenig, Rogers & Sabelhaus (1998), Joint Committee on Taxation (2000), and Koenig (1999).

28. Hall (2004), OECD (1993: 78), Slemrod (1996: 370), Tait (1988: 18–19), and Tanzi (1995: 50–51).

29. Cnossen (2002: 242), McLure (1987: 107), Messere, Kam & Heady (2003: 152), OECD (1988: 103), Shoup (1973: 226), U.S. Treasury Department (1984: 1: 34), and Zodrow (1999).

30. Hufbauer & Gabyzon (1996: 21–26).

31. See Deal (1995).

32. Feldstein & Krugman (1990).

33. Joint Committee on Taxation (1991) and U.S. International Trade Commission (1998).

34. Halstead & MacGuineas (2004). Former house speaker Newt Gingrich first made this suggestion back in 1986.

35. Blinder, Gordon & Wise (1980), Burkhauser & Turner (1985), and Disney (2004).

36. Dresch, Lin & Stout (1977), Smith (1965), and U.S. General Accounting Office (1993a).

37. See Haufler (2001), Merrill (2004), Plender (2004), Razin & Sadka (2004), Martin Sullivan (2004), and Tanzi (2000).

38. Ledbetter (2004). Recent estimates of the underground economy range between 8.2 and 13.9 percent of GDP. See Schneider & Enste (2002).

39. Internal Revenue Service (2005).

40. There is a vast literature on problems with the AMT. For a good review see Burman, Gale & Rohaly (2003).

41. Ebrill, Keen, Bodin & Summers (2001: 41).

42. Committee for Economic Development (2005) and Graetz (2002).

43. It's worth remembering that George W. Bush proposed a VAT for Texas when he was governor. See Sullivan (1999).

44. Fischer & Summers (1989: 387). See also Becker & Mulligan (2003) and Holcombe & Mills (1994).

45. I have written a number of articles saying so myself. See Bartlett (1984b, 1985, 1993a). I still agree with all the substantive criticisms I made of the VAT in these articles. But fundamentally, my concern was always mainly that the VAT would be a money machine.

46. For example, *Wall Street Journal* (2005b).

47. Reagan (1988: 204).

48. The data can be found in Appendixes IV and V.

49. Stockfisch (1985).

50. Furchtgott-Roth (1990).

51. Tax preferences are capitalized into the value of existing assets, potentially leading to large losses in wealth if they are repealed. See Goetz (1978).

52. Every major budget deal of the last twenty-five years has had a significant revenue component. See Koitz & Harlan (1994) and Merski (1991).

53. In 2002, the total tax burden in the U.S. was 26.4 percent of GDP versus an OECD average of 36.3 percent. See OECD (2004: 68).

54. Jorgenson & Yun (1991) estimate that the U.S. tax system discourages 18 cents of production for each additional $1 raised. That is, the private sector loses $1.18 for every dollar of tax. See also Ballard, Shoven & Whalley (1985a, 1985b), Stuart (1984), and U.S. Government Accountability Office (2005b).

55. I first suggested the need for a VAT in a *Los Angeles Times* article in August 2004. I followed up with articles in *Fortune* and the *New York Times*. See Bartlett (2004c, 2004d, 2005b). I was heavily criticized by conservatives for this suggestion. However, subsequently, others have echoed my argument. See Allen (2004), Hufbauer & Grieco (2005), Ignatius (2004b), and Shlaes (2004b).

56. House Ways and Means Committee Chairman Bill Thomas (R-CA) has suggested this idea. See Bartlett (2005a).

57. Conley (2004).

58. The IRS has already studied these issues. See Internal Revenue Service (1993). See also U.S. General Accounting Office (1993b).

59. George (1975: 409).

CHAPTER 11: THE POST-BUSH ERA: REPUBLICAN OR DEMOCRATIC?

1. Although he will be only sixty-seven on Election Day 2008, Cheney will be an "old" sixty-seven given his heart problems, long years of government service, and position as a lightning rod for many of the Bush Administration's most controversial actions. I am also certain that he has heard enough about Halliburton and its alleged sins to last a lifetime, which he would certainly hear ad infinitum should he run. Although Cheney will be pushed to run in 2008 by some elements of the party, I simply don't believe that he will put himself through that and will instead retire and write his memoirs.

2. Posted on *National Review*'s blog, "The Corner" (June 29, 2005).

3. *Weekly Standard* (September 19, 2005): 45.

4. Binder (2003), Coleman (1999).

5. Crowley (1999).

6. Morris (2001).

7. It is now forgotten how important state governments were to the Founding Fathers, since they have now largely been reduced to administrative districts for federal programs. The main way that the states exercised restraint on the federal government was through the Senate, members of which were originally elected by state legislatures, which meant that they represented the states as states. Unfortunately, the Seventeenth Amendment to the Constitution abolished this system, making senators into little more than supercongressmen. For this reason, growing numbers of constitutional scholars lament this fundamental, but seldom appreciated, change in our system of government. See Amar (1996), Bybee (1997), Hoebeke (1995), Rossum (2001), and Zywicki (1997).

8. Political scientist David Mayhew of Yale finds that divided government is no barrier to enacting important legislation. See Mayhew (2005).

9. Rauch (2004b).

10. Niskanen (2003).

11. Fisher (2000), Jenkins (2004), Kadlec (2000).

12. De Rugy (2005b).

13. *Congressional Record* (July 29, 2005): S9398.

14. "President Signs Transportation Act," www.whitehouse.gov (August 10, 2005).

15. Lizza (2005: 39).

16. Quoted in Burek (2005).

17. Fred Barnes (2005), Podhoretz (2005).

18. The report can be found at http://www.csss.gov/reports.

19. Charles Blahous and Keith Hennessey, both with the National Economic Council.

20. Novak (2005e).

21. Morris (2005).

22. Barro (2005), Roberts (2005), Weisman (2005b).

23. Miniter (2005).

24. Posted on *National Review* magazine's blog, "The Corner" (September 9, 2005).

25. He cited an Associated Press report on September 9, 2005, quoting Lt. General Steven Blum as saying that a day or so of response time was lost because of so many Mississippi and Louisiana National Guard troops being in Iraq, and a *New York Times* report quoting an unnamed White House official as saying that it would have looked bad for Bush to preempt the authority of a female Democratic governor. See Lipton, Schmitt & Shanker (2005).

26. Posted at www.professorbainbridge.com (September 10, 2005).

27. Grunwald (2005).

28. Fund (2005c).

29. Schmitt (2001).

30. Frum (2003: 84).

31. Hitt & Millman (2004).

32. Richardson (2004), Swarns (2004).

33. Borjas (2004).

34. Branigin (2005).

35. Harwood (2005b).

36. Fund (2005b), Magnusson & Elgin (2005).

37. Grow (2005), McKinnon (2005d).

38. See MacDonald (2004, 2005).

39. Posted at www.professorbainbridge.com (August 20, 2005).

40. Cuzán, Heggen & Bundrick (2003). Bovitz (2002) finds that opposing pork barrel spending can improve the electoral prospects for members of Congress as well. Republican consultant Scott Reed noted that Republican members of Congress got "no bounce" from their passage of the energy and highway bills in 2005. See Harwood (2005c).

41. Balz & Harris (2004).

REFERENCES

AARP. 2004. *Trends in Manufacturer Prices of Brand Name Prescription Drugs Used by Older Americans, 2000 through 2003* (May).

Alden, Edward. 2003. "Tariff Defense That Bought Time for Industry Turnaround." *Financial Times* (December 5).

Alden, Edward. 2004. "Bush Acted to Protect Powerful Sugar Industry." *Financial Times* (February 11).

Alesina, Alberto, and Robert Perotti. 1995. "Fiscal Expansions and Adjustments in OECD Countries." *Economic Policy* (October): 207–48.

Alesina, Alberto, and Howard Rosenthal. 1995. *Partisan Politics, Divided Government, and the Economy.* New York: Cambridge University Press.

Allen, Gary. 1971. "Richard Nixon: Professor Galbraith Calls Him a Socialist." *American Opinion* (January): 1–22.

Allen, Jodie. 2004. "Tax Reform Tossup." *U.S. News & World Report* (November 29): 37.

Allen, Mike. 2002. "Bush Faces Sustained Dissention on the Right." *Washington Post* (April 22).

Allen, Mike. 2004a. "$3 Trillion Price Tag Left Out as Bush Details His Agenda." *Washington Post* (September 14).

Allen, Mike. 2004b. "Bush to Change Economic Team." *Washington Post* (November 29).

Allen, Mike. 2004c. "Snow's Status Remains Uncertain." *Washington Post* (December 7).

Allen, Mike. 2005. "Living Too Much in the Bubble?" *Time* (September 19): 42–45.

Allen, Mike, and Jonathan Weisman. 2004a. "Gutierrez Is Pick for Commerce Secretary." *Washington Post* (November 30).

Allen, Mike, and Jonathan Weisman. 2004b. "Treasury Secretary Is Asked to Stay: Bush Considered Others Before Extending Offer." *Washington Post* (December 9).

Altig, David, Alan Auerbach, Laurence Kotlikoff, Kent Smetters, and Jan Walliser. 2001. "Simulating Fundamental Tax Reform in the United States." *American Economic Review* (June): 574–95.

Altman, Daniel. 2003. "Some Doubts about Logic of Senate Plan for Drug Aid." *New York Times* (June 14).

Amar, Vikram David. 1996. "Indirect Effects of Direct Election: A Structural Examination of the Seventeenth Amendment." *Vanderbilt Law Review* (November): 1347–1405.

Amiti, Mary, and Shang-Jin Wei. 2005. "Fear of Service Outsourcing: Is It Justified?" *Economic Policy* (April): 309–47.

Anderson, William, Myles S. Wallace, and John T. Warner. 1986. "Government Spending and Taxation: What Causes What?" *Southern Economic Journal* (January): 630–39.

Andrews, Edmund. 1994. "Bell Companies Use Regulation to Stop Rivals." *New York Times* (July 26).

Andrews, Edmund. 2003. "U.S. Moves to Limit Textile Imports from China." *New York Times* (November 19).

Andrews, Edmund. 2004. "Whoever Wins, More Taxes May Be the Only Way Out." *New York Times* (September 26).

Andrews, Edmund. 2005a. "One Treasury Post Filled, But Others Remain Open." *New York Times* (March 24).

Andrews, Edmund. 2005b. "Treasury Takes Social Security to Airwaves." *New York Times* (April 7).

Andrews, Edmund. 2005c. "Bush Administration Will Ask China to Agree to Broad Limits on Clothing Exports." *New York Times* (August 2).

Andrews, Edmund, and Elizabeth Becker. 2005. "Economic Posts Unfilled Despite Big Pushes Ahead." *New York Times* (February 25).

Andrews, William D. 1974. "A Consumption-Type or Cash Flow Personal Income Tax." *Harvard Law Review* (April): 1113–88.

Antle, W. James. 2005. "The Taxman Cometh." *American Conservative* (May 9): 24–26.

Antos, Joseph, and Jagadeesh Gokhale. 2003. "A Benefit That Is Bad for America's Health." *Financial Times* (June 20).

Applebome, Peter. 1999. "Resisting a Society's Rage to Spend." *New York Times* (August 14).

Archer, Bill. 2001. "Cutting Taxes Will Be Harder the Next Time." *Wall Street Journal* (May 29).

Archibald, Robert B., and David H. Feldman. 1998. "Investment During the Great Depression: Uncertainty and the Role of the Smoot-Hawley Tariff." *Southern Economic Journal* (April): 857–79.

Armey, Richard. 2005. "Reflections on the Republican Revolution." In *The Republican Revolution 10 Years Later*, ed. Chris Edwards and John Samples, pp. 5–16. Washington: Cato Institute.

Arends, Brett. 2005. "Brown Pushed from Last Job: Horse Group: FEMA Chief Had to Be 'Asked to Resign.'" *Boston Herald* (September 3).

Ascarelli, Silvia. 2004. "Citing Sarbanes, Foreign Companies Flee U.S. Exchanges." *Wall Street Journal* (September 20).

Atkeson, Andrew, V. V. Chari, and Patrick J. Kehoe. 1999. "Taxing Capital Income: A Bad Idea." *Quarterly Review*, Federal Reserve Bank of Minneapolis (summer): 3–17.

Auerbach, Alan, Laurence Kotlikoff, and Jonathan Skinner. 1983. "The Efficiency Gains from Dynamic Tax Reform." *International Economic Review* (February): 81–100.

Baack, Ben, and Edward John Ray. 1985. "The Political Economy of the Origin and Development of the Federal Income Tax." In *The Emergence of the Modern Political Economy*, ed. Robert Higgs, pp. 121–38. London: JAI Press.

Bagehot, Walter. 1999 (1873). *Lombard Street: A Description of the Money Market.* New York: John Wiley.

Bainbridge, Stephen. 2004. "Does the SEC Know When Enough Is Enough?" www.techcentralstation.com (January 8).

Bainbridge, Stephen. 2005. "SOXing It to Small Businesses." www.techcentralstation.com (April 12).

Baker, Peter, and Mike Allen. 2005. "President Vows to Veto Any Changes to Medicare." *Washington Post* (February 12).

Baldwin, Robert E. 1969. "The Case Against Infant-Industry Tariff Protection." *Journal of Political Economy* (May–June): 295–305.

Ball, Robert M. 1973. "Social Security Amendments of 1972: Summary and Legislative History." *Social Security Bulletin* (March): 3–25.

Ballard, Charles, John Shoven, and John Whalley. 1985a. "General Equilibrium Computations of the Marginal Welfare Costs of Taxes in the United States." *American Economic Review* (March): 128–38.

Ballard, Charles, John Shoven, and John Whalley. 1985b. "The Total Welfare Cost of the United States Tax System: A General Equilibrium Approach." *National Tax Journal* (June): 125–40.

Ballou, Dale, and Michael Podgursky. 1997. *Teacher Pay and Teacher Quality.* Kalamazoo: W. E. Upjohn Institute for Employment Research.

Balls, Andrew. 2005. "Treasury Feels White House Heat on Policy." *Financial Times* (April 22).

Balz, Dan. 2005. "Clinton Angers Left with Call for Unity." *Washington Post* (July 27).

Balz, Dan, and John F. Harris. 2004. "Some Republicans Predict Upheaval within the Party." *Washington Post* (September 4).

Balz, Dan, and Richard Morin. 2004. "Bush Poll Numbers on Iraq at New Lows." *Washington Post* (May 25).

Bandow, Doug. 2004. "Why Conservatives Must Not Vote for Bush." www.salon.com (September 10).

Bank, Steven. 2003. "The Progressive Consumption Tax Revisited." *Michigan Law Review* (May): 2238–60.

Bankman, Joseph, and David A. Weisbach. 2005. "The Superiority of an Ideal Consumption Tax Over an Ideal Income Tax." John M. Olin Law & Economics Working Paper No. 251, University of Chicago Law School (July).

Barbera, Anthony J., and Virginia D. McConnell. 1986. "Effects of Pollution Control on Industry Productivity: A Factor Demand Approach." *Journal of Industrial Economics* (December): 161–72.

Barnes, Fred. 2002a. "Bush's Big Budget Conservatism." *Weekly Standard* (January 21): 13–14.

Barnes, Fred. 2002b. "The Pigs Return to the Trough." *Weekly Standard* (May 27): 12, 14.

Barnes, Fred. 2003a. " 'Big Government Conservatism': George Bush Style." *Wall Street Journal* (August 15).

Barnes, Fred. 2003b. "Hey, Big Spenders!" *Weekly Standard* (December 8): 9–10.

Barnes, Fred. 2005. "A Social Security Quagmire?" *Weekly Standard* (May 2): 13.

Barnes, James A. 2005. "Team Bush." *National Journal* (June 18): 1818–23.

Barone, Michael. 1990. *Our Country: The Shaping of America from Roosevelt to Reagan.* New York: Free Press.

Barringer, William H., and Kenneth J. Pierce. 2000. *Paying the Price for Big Steel.* Washington: American Institute for International Steel.

Barro, Robert J. 2001. "Why the War Against Terror Will Boost the Economy." *BusinessWeek* (November 5): 30.

Barro, Robert J. 2002. "Bush's Economics Team Is Broken, and It's Time to Fix It." *BusinessWeek* (August 26): 26.

Barro, Robert J. 2003. "There's a Lot to Like about Bush's Tax Plan." *BusinessWeek* (February 24): 28.

Barro, Robert J. 2005. "Why Private Accounts Are Bad Public Policy." *Business-Week* (April 4): 26.

Barsky, Robert B., and Lutz Kilian. 2002. "Do We Really Know that Oil Caused the Great Stagflation? A Monetary Alternative." In *NBER Macroeconomics Annual, 2001*, ed. Ben Bernanke and Kenneth Rogoff, pp. 137–83. Cambridge: MIT Press.

Bartlett, Bruce. 1982. *Reaganomics: Supply-Side Economics in Action*, 2nd ed. New York: Morrow/Quill.

Bartlett, Bruce. 1984a. "Do U.S. Deficits Cause High Interest Rates?" *Human Events* (February 18).

Bartlett, Bruce. 1984b. "Revenue-Raising Redux: It's VAT Time Again." *Wall Street Journal* (August 2).

Bartlett, Bruce. 1985. "The Case Against a Value-Added Tax." Heritage Foundation Backgrounder No. 468 (November 5).

Bartlett, Bruce. 1993a. "Not VAT Again!" *Wall Street Journal* (April 16).

Bartlett, Bruce. 1993b. "How Not to Stimulate the Economy." *Public Interest* (summer): 99–109.

Bartlett, Bruce. 1995. "Replacing Federal Taxes with a Sales Tax." *Tax Notes* (August 21): 997–1003.

Bartlett, Bruce. 1997b. "Tax Spending, Not Saving." *New York Times* (July 6).

Bartlett, Bruce. 1998. "Tax Aspects of the 1997 Budget Deal." *National Tax Journal* (March): 127–41.

Bartlett, Bruce. 2001a. "Recent Proposals Relating to Family Taxation." *Tax Notes* (April 2): 153–57.

Bartlett, Bruce. 2001b. "The End of Tax Expenditures as We Know Them?" *Tax Notes* (July 16): 413–22.

Bartlett, Bruce. 2001c. "Tax Rebates Won't Stimulate the Economy." *Wall Street Journal* (November 1).

Bartlett, Bruce. 2003a. "Deficit Pressure Points." *Washington Times* (October 20).

Bartlett, Bruce. 2003b. "Power of Perception." *Washington Times* (December 10).

Bartlett, Bruce. 2004a. "Explaining the Bush Tax Cuts." *Commentary* (June): 23–27.

Bartlett, Bruce. 2004b. "Those Were the Days." *New York Times* (July 1).

Bartlett, Bruce. 2004c. "A New Money Machine for the U.S." *Los Angeles Times* (August 29).

Bartlett, Bruce. 2004d. "Tax Advice for Mr. Bush: Consider the VAT." *Fortune* (December 13): 77.

Bartlett, Bruce. 2005a. "Want Reform? Talk to Bill." *Fortune* (February 21): 54.

Bartlett, Bruce. 2005b. "Feed the Beast." *New York Times* (April 6).

Bartley, Robert L. 1986. "The Monetary Source of Oil Boom and Bust." *Wall Street Journal* (December 29).

Bartley, Robert L. 1990. "The Great International Growth Slowdown." *Wall Street Journal* (July 10).

Bartley, Robert L. 1991. "Nixon's Worst Weekend." *Wall Street Journal* (August 15).

Bartley, Robert L. 1992. "Bush Comeback: Get Economics Back from Detour." *Wall Street Journal* (July 22).

Bartley, Robert L. 1999. "Checking in with the Frontrunner." *Wall Street Journal* (December 1).

Bartley, Robert L. 2001. "Rebates: A Séance with Keynes." *Wall Street Journal* (June 4).

Bastable, C. F. 1900. *The Theory of International Trade*, 3rd ed. London: Macmillan.

Beale, Truxton. 1911. "The Measure of Income for Taxation." *Journal of Political Economy* (October): 655–75.

Beard, Sam. 2005. "The Two Parties Must Put Aside Partisanship and Work for Solutions." *Newark Star-Ledger* (March 4).

Becker, Gary S. 2001. "The Best Thing Bush Is Doing for Business." *Business-Week* (July 9): 24.

Becker, Gary S., and Casey B. Mulligan. 2003. "Deadweight Costs and the Size of Government." *Journal of Law and Economics* (October): 293–340.

Becker, Gary S., Edward P. Lazear, and Kevin M. Murphy. 2003. "The Double Benefit of Tax Cuts." *Wall Street Journal* (October 7).

Becker, Jo. 2004. "Senate Tax Rise Is Too Steep, Warner Says." *Washington Post* (March 6).

Bellman, Eric. 2005. "One More Cost of Sarbanes-Oxley: Outsourcing to India." *Wall Street Journal* (July 14).

Berenson, Alex. 2005. "Cancer Drugs Offer Hope, But at a Huge Expense." *New York Times* (July 12).

Berger, Henry W. 1967. "A Conservative Critique of Containment: Senator Taft and the Early Cold War Program." In *Containment and Revolution*, ed. David Horowitz, pp. 125–39. Boston: Beacon Press.

Berger, Henry W. 1971. "Senator Taft Dissents from Military Escalation." In *Cold War Critics*, ed. Thomas G. Paterson, pp. 167–204. Chicago: Quadrangle.

Berger, Henry W. 1975. "Bipartisanship, Senator Taft, and the Truman Administration." *Political Science Quarterly* (summer): 221–37.

Berle, Adolf A., and Gardiner Means. 1932. *The Modern Corporation and Private Property*. New York: Macmillan.

Bhagwati, Jagdish, and Arvind Panagariya. 2003. "Bilateral Trade Treaties Are a Sham." *Financial Times* (July 14).

Bhagwati, Jagdish, Arvind Panagariya, and T. N. Srinivasan. 2004. "The Muddles over Outsourcing." *Journal of Economic Perspectives* (fall): 93–114.

Binder, Sarah A. 2003. *Stalemate: Causes and Consequences of Legislative Gridlock.* Washington: Brookings Institution.

Bipartisan Commission on Entitlement and Tax Reform. 1995. *Final Report to the President.* Washington: U.S. Government Printing Office.

Birnbaum, Jeffrey. 2002. "The Gang That Couldn't Shoot Straight: If Our President's National Security Team Is So Good, Why Is His Economic Team So Bad?" *Fortune* (September 2): 121.

Birnbaum, Jeffrey. 2005. "When Higher Taxes Loom, Lobbyists Realize Profit Potential." *Washington Post* (March 21).

Blackley, Paul R. 1986. "Causality between Revenues and Expenditures and the Size of the Federal Budget." *Public Finance Quarterly* (April): 139–56.

Blinder, Alan. 1981. "Temporary Income Taxes and Consumer Spending." *Journal of Political Economy* (February): 26–53.

Blinder, Alan, and William Newton. 1981. "The 1971–1974 Controls Program and the Price Level." *Journal of Monetary Economics* (July): 1–23.

Blinder, Alan, and Janet Yellen. 2001. *The Fabulous Decade: Macroeconomic Lessons from the 1990s.* New York: Century Foundation.

Blinder, Alan, Roger Gordon, and Donald Wise. 1980. "Reconsidering the Work Disincentive Effects of Social Security." *National Tax Journal* (December): 431–42.

Blonigen, Bruce A., and Thomas J. Prusa. 2001. "Antidumping." National Bureau of Economic Research Working Paper No. 8398 (July).

Bloomberg News. 2001. Bloomberg News Poll (September 25).

Blum, John Morton. 1967. *From the Morgenthau Diaries: Years of War, 1941–1945.* Boston: Houghton Mifflin.

Blumenthal, Sidney. 2005. "Nixon's Empire Strikes Back." *Guardian* (June 9).

Blustein, Paul. 2005. "Both Parties Propose to Punish China Trade." *Washington Post* (July 15).

Blustein, Paul, and Jonathan Weisman. 2005. "Treasury Struggles to Keep Influence: Role in Administration Diminished under Bush." *Washington Post* (January 15).

Boone, Peter. 1996. "Politics and the Effectiveness of Foreign Aid." *European Economic Review* (February): 289–329.

Boot, Max. 2004a. "Bush's Team Needs a Coach." *Los Angeles Times* (June 17).

Boot, Max. 2004b. "A Clever Fellow, to Be Sure, but Clueless about Character." *Los Angeles Times* (June 24).

Borjas, George J. 2004. "Making It Worse." *National Review* (February 9): 24–26.

Borrus, Amy, and Mike McNamee. 1996. "Bad Counsel at the Economic Council?" *BusinessWeek* (February 26): 34.

Bourne, Randolph S. 1964. *War and the Intellectuals: Collected Essays, 1915–1919.* New York: Harper Torchbooks.

Bovitz, Gregory L. 2002. "Electoral Consequences of Porkbusting in the U.S. House of Representatives." *Political Science Quarterly* (fall): 455–77.

Bradford, David F. 1984. *Blueprints for Basic Tax Reform,* 2nd ed. Arlington, VA: Tax Analysts.

Branigin, William. 2005. "Bush Proposal Prompted Surge in Illegal Immigrants." *Washington Post* (June 28).

Break, George F., and Joseph A. Pechman. 1975. *Federal Tax Reform: The Impossible Dream?* Washington: Brookings Institution.

Bremner, Robert P. 2004. *Chairman of the Fed: William McChesney Martin Jr. and the Creation of the American Financial System.* New Haven: Yale University Press.

Broder, David. 2001a. "Why Not a Tax Rebate?" *Washington Post* (January 31).

Broder, David. 2001b. "Saying Yes To a Quick Tax Rebate." *Washington Post* (April 1).

Broder, David. 2002. "Radical Conservatism." *Washington Post* (September 25).

Bronars, Stephen G., and John R. Lott, Jr. 1997. "Do Campaign Donations Alter How a Politician Votes? Or, Do Donors Support Candidates Who Value the Same Things That They Do?" *Journal of Law and Economics* (October): 317–50.

Brooks, Rick. 2001. "FedEx, UPS Join Forces to Stave Off Foreign Push into U.S. Market." *Wall Street Journal* (February 1).

Brophy, Beth. 1981. "Everybody Out of the Pool." *Forbes* (August 17).

Brown, Jeffrey R., J. David Cummins, Christopher M. Lewis, and Ran Wei. 2004. "An Empirical Analysis of the Economic Impact of Federal Terrorism Reinsurance." *Journal of Monetary Economics* (July): 861–98.

Brown, Ken, and Jeff D. Opdyke. 2001. "Analysts Were Once the Rock Stars of the Street, but Tunes Changed." *Wall Street Journal* (November 16).

Browning, E. S. 2005. "Dividend Stocks Haven't Caught Investors' Fancy." *Wall Street Journal* (January 31).

Brownstein, Ronald. 2005. "Clinton's New Job: Defining the Center." *Los Angeles Times* (July 26).

Brusse, Wendy Asbeek. 1997. "Liberalizing Intra-European Trade." In *Explorations in OEEC History,* ed. Richard T. Griffiths, pp. 123–37. Paris: Organisation for Economic Co-operation and Development.

Buchanan, Patrick J. 1998. *The Great Betrayal.* Boston: Little, Brown.

Buchanan, Patrick J. 2004. *Where the Right Went Wrong.* New York: St. Martin's Press.

Bumiller, Elisabeth. 2002. "A Role Unfilled: Authoritative Voice on the Economy Still Lacking in Bush Administration." *New York Times* (August 12).

Bumiller, Elisabeth. 2004. "Talk of Bubble Leads to Battle over Bulge." *New York Times* (October 18).

Burden, Barry C. 2002. "United States Senators as Presidential Candidates." *Political Science Quarterly* (spring): 81–102.

Burek, Josh. 2005. "Bush Makes History—A Five-Year Streak Without Saying 'No.'" *Christian Science Monitor* (August 16).

Burger, Albert E. 1969. "A Historical Analysis of the Credit Crunch of 1966." *Federal Reserve Bank of St. Louis Review* (September): 13–30.

Burkhauser, Richard, and John Turner. 1985. "Is the Social Security Payroll Tax a Tax?" *Public Finance Quarterly* (July): 253–67.

Burman, Leonard. 1999. *The Labyrinth of Capital Gains Tax Policy.* Washington: Brookings Institution.

Burman, Leonard, William G. Gale, and Jeffrey Rohaly. 2003. "The Expanding Reach of the Individual Alternative Minimum Tax." *Journal of Economic Perspectives* (spring): 173–86.

Burns, Joseph M. 2004. "Monetary Policy Wasn't Manipulated for Nixon." Letter to the Editor. *Wall Street Journal* (April 26).

Burnside, Craig, and David Dollar. 2000. "Aid, Policies, and Growth." *American Economic Review* (September): 847–68.

Bybee, Jay S. 1997. "Ulysses at the Mast: Democracy, Federalism, and the Sirens' Song of the Seventeenth Amendment." *Northwestern University Law Review* (winter): 500–72.

Byron, Christopher. 1992. "Depending on the Kindness of Strangers." *New York* (November 16): 30–31.

Caldwell, Christopher. 2003. "A President on the Path of Least Resistance." *Financial Times* (December 20).

Calmes, Jackie. 2004a. "Bush Finds Party Faithful in an Ugly Mood." *Wall Street Journal* (February 9).

Calmes, Jackie. 2004b. "Taxes Divide National, State Republicans." *Wall Street Journal* (February 20).

Calmes, Jackie. 2004c. "Bush's Gambit for Hispanic Vote Fizzles." *Wall Street Journal* (March 10).

Calmes, Jackie. 2005. "Conservatives Balk as Spending Soars in Katrina's Wake." *Wall Street Journal* (September 16).

Cannon, Carl. 2005. "Why Not Hillary?" *Washington Monthly* (July–August): 26–31.

Canto, Victor A., Douglas H. Joines, and Robert I. Webb. 1983. "The Revenue Effects of the Kennedy Tax Cuts." In *Foundations of Supply-Side Economics,* ed. Victor A. Canto, Douglas H. Joines, and Arthur B. Laffer, pp. 72–103. New York: Academic Press.

Carnahan, Ira. 2003. "Quota Factory: The International Trade Commission

Protects American Shores from the Ravages of Cheap Coat Hangers." *Forbes* (April 14): 110.

Casse, Daniel. 2004. "Is Bush a Conservative?" *Commentary* (February): 19–26.

Cassou, Stephen, and Kevin Lansing. 2004. "Growth Effects of Shifting from a Graduated-Rate Tax System to a Flat Tax." *Economic Inquiry* (April): 194–213.

Castaneda, Ana, Javier Diaz-Gimenez, and Jose-Victor Rull. 1998. "Earnings and Wealth Inequality and Income Taxation: Quantifying the Trade-offs of Switching to a Proportional Income Tax in the U.S." Federal Reserve Bank of Cleveland Working Paper No. 9814 (September).

Caucutt, Elizabeth, Selahattin Imrohoroglu, and Krishna Kumar. 2000. "Does the Progressivity of Taxes Matter for Economic Growth?" Federal Reserve Bank of Minneapolis Discussion Paper No. 138 (December).

Cecchetti, Stephen. 2004. "Say It Softly: The Solution Is a Tax Increase." *Financial Times* (November 23).

Chait, Jonathan. 2005. "Wages of Sin: Patronage, Bush-Style." *New Republic* (May 16): 21–28.

Chamley, Christophe. 1986. "Optimal Taxation of Capital Income in General Equilibrium with Infinite Lives." *Econometrica* (May): 607–22.

Chapman, Stephen. 1980. "The Gas Lines of '79." *Public Interest* (summer): 40–49.

Cherry, Robert, and Max Sawicky. 2000. "Giving Credit Where Credit Is Due: A 'Universal Unified Child Credit' that Expands the EITC and Cuts Taxes for Working Families." Economic Policy Institute Briefing Paper (April).

Chetty, Raj, and Emmanuel Saez. 2004. "Do Dividend Payments Respond to Taxes? Preliminary Evidence from the 2003 Dividend Tax Cut." National Bureau of Economic Research Working Paper No. 10572 (June).

Chorvat, Terrence R., and Michael S. Knoll. 2003. "The Case for Repealing the Corporate Alternative Minimum Tax." *SMU Law Review* (winter): 305–32.

Clinton, Bill, and Al Gore. 1992. *Putting People First*. New York: Times Books.

Cnossen, Sijbren. 2002. "Evaluating the National Retail Sales Tax from a VAT Perspective." In *United States Tax Reform in the Twenty-first Century*, ed. George Zodrow and Peter Miezkowski, pp. 215–44. New York: Cambridge University Press.

Cockburn, Alexander, and Robert Pollin. 1992. "Why the Left Should Support the Flat Tax." *Wall Street Journal* (April 2).

Cohen, Daniel A., Aiyesha Dey, and Thomas Z. Lys. 2005. "The Sarbanes-Oxley Act of 2002: Implications for Compensation Structure and Risk-Taking." Working Paper, Kellogg School of Management, Northwestern University (July 8).

Cohen, Eliot. 2005. "A Hawk Questions Himself as His Son Goes To War." *Washington Post* (July 10).

Cole, Benjamin M. 2001. *The Pied Pipers of Wall Street*. Princeton, NJ: Bloomberg Press.

Coleman, John J. 1999. "Unified Government, Divided Government, and Party Responsiveness." *American Political Science Review* (December): 821–35.

Collender, Stan. 2005. "Do Bad Estimates Make Good Politics?" www.nationaljournal.com (July 26).

Coman, Julian. 2004. "Bush's Administration Is Worse Than Nixon's, Says Watergate Aide." *London Daily Telegraph* (April 5).

Committee for Economic Development. 2005. *A New Tax Framework: A Blueprint for Averting a Fiscal Crisis* (September).

Common Cause. 2004. *Democracy on Drugs: The Medicare/Prescription Drug Bill: A Study in How Government Shouldn't Work* (May 18).

Congressional Budget Office. 1978. *Understanding Fiscal Policy* (April).

Congressional Budget Office. 1986. *Has Trade Protection Revitalized Domestic Industries?* (November).

Congressional Budget Office. 1987. *The Relationship between Federal Taxes and Spending: An Examination of Recent Research* (July).

Congressional Budget Office. 1994. *An Analysis of the Administration's Health Proposal* (February).

Congressional Budget Office. 1995. *Federal Financial Support of Business* (July).

Congressional Budget Office. 2001. *Changes in Federal Civilian Employment: An Update* (May).

Congressional Budget Office. 2002. *Federal Reinsurance for Disasters* (September).

Congressional Budget Office. 2003a. *The Pros and Cons of Pursuing Free-Trade Agreements* (July).

Congressional Budget Office. 2003b. *The Long-Term Budget Outlook* (December).

Congressional Budget Office. 2004a. *An Analysis of the President's Budgetary Proposals for Fiscal Year 2005* (March).

Congressional Budget Office. 2004b. *Economic Analysis of the Continued Dumping and Subsidy Offset Act of 2000* (March 2).

Congressional Budget Office. 2005a. *A Review of CBO's Activities in 2004 Under the Unfunded Mandates Reform Act* (March).

Congressional Budget Office. 2005b. *Projected Effects of Various Provisions on Social Security's Financial and Distributional Outcomes* (May 25).

Conley, Dalton. 2004. "Turning the Tax Tables to Help the Poor." *New York Times* (November 15).

Connolly, Ceci, and Mike Allen. 2005. "Medicare Drug Benefit May Cost $1.2 Trillion." *Washington Post* (February 9).

Consultant Panel on Social Security. 1976. *Report to the Congressional Research Service.* Prepared for the Committee on Finance of the United States Senate and the Committee on Ways and Means of the U.S. House of Representatives. Joint Committee Print, 94th Congress, 2nd session. Washington: U.S. Government Printing Office.

Cook, Charlie. 2003. "Off to the Races." www.nationaljournal.com (July 1).

Council of Economic Advisers. 1988. *Economic Report of the President, 1988.* Washington: U.S. Government Printing Office.

Council of Economic Advisers. 2003. *Economic Report of the President, 2003.* Washington: U.S. Government Printing Office.

Council of Economic Advisers. 2004. *Economic Report of the President, 2004.* Washington: U.S. Government Printing Office.

Crain, W. Mark. 2005. *The Impact of Regulatory Costs on Small Firms.* Washington: Office of Advocacy, Small Business Administration.

Crain, W. Mark, and Thomas D. Hopkins. 2001. *The Impact of Regulatory Costs on Small Firms.* Washington: Office of Advocacy, Small Business Administration.

Crane, Edward H. 1999. "The Clintonesque George Bush." *New York Times* (August 4).

Crews, Clyde Wayne. 2005. *Ten Thousand Commandments.* Washington: Competitive Enterprise Institute.

Crowley, Elizabeth. 1999. "Checks and Balances: Public Likes Executive-Legislative Control Split." *Wall Street Journal* (December 16).

Crucini, Mario J., and James Kahn. 1996. "Tariffs and Aggregate Economic Activity: Lessons from the Great Depression." *Journal of Monetary Economics* (December): 427–67.

Cummings, Jeanne. 2002. "Bush Keeps Veto Pen Pocketed." *Wall Street Journal* (June 11).

Cummins, J. David, and Christopher M. Lewis. 2003. "Catastrophic Events, Parameter Uncertainty and the Breakdown of Implicit Long-Term Contracting: The Case of Terrorism Insurance." *Journal of Risk and Uncertainty* (March): 153–78.

Curl, Joseph. 2005. "Hillary in the Middle on Value Issues." *Washington Times* (January 26).

Cuzán, Alfred G., Richard J. Heggen, and Charles M. Bundrick. 2003. *Voters and Presidents.* Philadelphia: Xlibris.

Dam, Kenneth W. 1970. *The GATT.* Chicago: University of Chicago Press.

Dao, James. 2004. "Virginia Political Shocker: Republicans for High Taxes." *New York Times* (March 28).

Darman, Richard. 1996. *Who's in Control?* New York: Simon & Schuster.

Davis, Bob. 1990. "High-Definition TV, Once a Capital Idea, Wanes in Washington." *Wall Street Journal* (June 6).

Davis, Bob. 2002. "Bush Economic Aide Says Cost of Iraq War May Top $100 Billion." *Wall Street Journal* (September 16).

Davis, Bob. 2004a. "Some Democratic Economists Echo Mankiw on Outsourcing." *Wall Street Journal* (February 12).

Davis, Bob. 2004b. "GOP Use of Treasury to Analyze Kerry Tax Plan Raises Questions." *Wall Street Journal* (March 31).

Dawson, John W., and John J. Seater. 2005. "Regulation and the Macroeconomy." Unpublished paper (February).

Deal, Christopher. 1995. "The GATT and VAT: Whether VAT Exporters Enjoy a Tax Advantage under the GATT." *Loyola of Los Angeles International and Comparative Law Journal* (April): 649–70.

Dean, John W. 2004. *Worse Than Watergate.* Boston: Little, Brown.

Dearden, Lorraine, Javier Ferri, and Costas Meghir. 2002. "The Effect of School Quality on Educational Attainment and Wages." *Review of Economics and Statistics* (February): 1–20.

DeLong, J. Bradford, and Barry Eichengreen. 1993. "The Marshall Plan: History's Most Successful Structural Adjustment Program." In *Postwar Economic Reconstruction and Lessons for the East Today,* ed. Rudiger Dornbusch, Wilhelm Nölling, and Richard Layard, pp. 189–230. Cambridge: MIT Press.

Denison, Edward F. 1978. "Effects of Selected Changes in the Institutional and Human Environment upon Output Per Unit of Input." *Survey of Current Business* (January): 21–44.

DeParle, Jason. 2004. *American Dream.* New York: Viking.

Derbyshire, John. 2005. "Twilight of Conservatism." www.nationalreview.com (May 10).

De Rugy, Veronique. 2005a. "So Many Missed Opportunities." www.techcentralstation.com (June 22).

De Rugy, Veronique. 2005b. "No Pork Left Behind." www.techcentralstation.com (August 18).

De Rugy, Veronique, and Tad DeHaven. 2003. "On Spending, Bush Is No Reagan." Cato Institute Tax and Budget Bulletin No. 16 (August).

De Rugy, Veronique, and Kathryn Newmark. 2005. "The Sinkhole Grows." www.techcentralstation.com (July 25).

Destler, I. M. 1996. *The National Economic Council: A Work in Progress.* Washington: Institute for International Economics.

Destler, I. M. 2005. *American Trade Politics*, 4th ed. Washington: Institute for International Economics.

Deutsch, Claudia H. 2005. "The High Price of Staying Public." *New York Times* (January 23).

DiIulio, John. 2002. Memorandum to Ron Suskind. www.esquire.com (October 24).

Dinan, Stephen. 2003. "Rumbling on the Hard-Line Right." *Washington Times* (December 30).

Dinan, Stephen. 2004. "Bush Policy Principles Easily Bent." *Washington Times* (January 12).

Dionne, E. J. 2001. "Bush: Fuzzy . . ." *Washington Post* (March 1).

Disney, Richard. 2004. "Are Contributions to Public Pension Programs a Tax on Employment?" *Economic Policy* (July): 267–311.

Doherty, Brian. 2004. "A Case for Kerry." *Orange County Register* (July 25).

Doherty, Jacqueline. 2003. "That '70s Show." *Barron's* (November 17).

Domenici, Pete. 2001. "Let's Cut Taxes Now." *USA Today* (March 28).

Donaldson, William H. 2005. " 'We've Been Listening.' " *Wall Street Journal* (March 29).

Donlan, Thomas G. 2001. "Witch's Brew." *Barron's* (April 16): 42.

Dowd, Maureen. 1990. "The Patrician's Way: Bush's Passion for Secrecy Runs Afoul of Public's Passion for Open Debate." *New York Times* (October 10).

Dreazen, Yochi J. 2000. "Ergonomic Rules Are the First in a Wave of Late Regulations." *Wall Street Journal* (November 14).

Dresch, Stephen, An-loh Lin, and David Stout. 1977. *Substituting a Value-Added Tax for the Corporate Income Tax*. Cambridge: Ballinger.

Drezner, Daniel W. 2004. "The Outsourcing Bogeyman." *Foreign Affairs* (May–June): 22–34.

Drinkard, Jim. 2002. "Scandal Publicity Drives Accounting Bill Forward." *USA Today* (July 25).

Drucker, Peter. 2005. "Trading Places." *National Interest* (spring): 101–107.

Dudley, Susan. 2004–2005. "The Bush Administration Regulatory Record." *Regulation* (winter): 4–9.

Dudley, Susan, and Melinda Warren. 2005. *Upward Trend in Regulation Continues: An Analysis of the U.S. Budget for Fiscal Years 2005 and 2006*. Arlington, VA: Mercatus Center, George Mason University.

Easterbrook, Gregg. 2004a. "Why We Shouldn't Go to Mars." *Time* (January 26): 51.

Easterbrook, Gregg. 2004b. "Politics and Science Do Mix." *Los Angeles Times* (April 6).

Easterly, William. 2001. *The Elusive Quest for Growth*. Cambridge: MIT Press.

Easterly, William. 2003. "Can Foreign Aid Buy Growth?" *Journal of Economic Perspectives* (summer): 23–48.

Ebrill, Liam, Michael Keen, Jean-Paul Bodin, and Victoria Summers. 2001. *The Modern VAT.* Washington: International Monetary Fund.

Eckes, Alfred E. 1995. *Opening America's Market: U.S. Foreign Trade Policy Since 1776.* Chapel Hill: University of North Carolina Press.

Economist, The. 1994. "Regulate Us, Please" (January 8): 69.

Economist, The. 2004. "Cheating Nature? Science and the Bush Administration" (April 10): 66–67.

Edsall, Thomas B. 2004. "In Bush's Policies, Business Wins." *Washington Post* (February 8).

Edwards, Chris. 2005. "Where's the Opposition?" *Washington Times* (August 22).

Eisenhower, Dwight. 1960. *Public Papers of the Presidents of the United States: Dwight D. Eisenhower, 1953.* Washington: U.S. Government Printing Office.

Elmendorf, Douglas W., Jeffrey B. Liebman, and David W. Wilcox. 2002. "Fiscal Policy and Social Security During the 1990s." In *American Economic Policy in the 1990s*, ed. Jeffrey A. Frankel and Peter R. Orszag, pp. 61–119. Cambridge: MIT Press.

Engel, Ellen, Rachel M. Hayes, and Xue Wang. 2004. "The Sarbanes-Oxley Act and Firms' Going-Private Decisions." Working Paper, Graduate School of Business, University of Chicago (October 29).

Epstein, Daniel. 2005. "Goodbye, Farewell, Auf Wiedersehen, Adieu . . ." *Wall Street Journal* (February 9).

European Union. 2004. *Report on United States Barriers to Trade and Investment* (December).

Fallows, James. 1982. "Entitlements." *Atlantic Monthly* (November): 51–59.

Feldstein, Martin. 1997. "The Council of Economic Advisers: From Stabilization to Resource Allocation." *American Economic Review* (May): 99–102.

Feldstein, Martin. 2001. "The 28% Solution." *Wall Street Journal* (February 16).

Feldstein, Martin, and Paul Krugman. 1990. "International Trade Effects of Value-Added Taxation." In *Taxation in the Global Economy*, ed. Assaf Razin and Joel Slemrod, pp. 263–78. Chicago: University of Chicago Press.

Ferguson, Andrew. 2004. "Has George W. Bush Killed Off Conservatism?" www.bloomberg.com (September 14).

Ferguson, Andrew. 2005a. "What a Tangled Web We Weave . . ." *Weekly Standard* (January 17): 10–12.

Ferguson, Andrew. 2005b. "Operation Overreach." *Weekly Standard* (May 16): 12–14.

Ferguson, E. James. 1961. *The Power of the Purse.* Chapel Hill: University of North Carolina Press.

Financial Executives International. 2004. "Sarbanes-Oxley Cost Estimates Soar 62% Since January '04." Press release (August 11).

Financial Executives International. 2005. "Sarbanes-Oxley Compliance Costs Exceed Estimates." Press release (March 21).

Financial Times. 2005. "Blair Kept Quiet over Wolfowitz World Bank Role." (March 26).

Firestone, David. 2003. "Conservatives Now See Deficits as a Tool to Fight Spending." *New York Times* (February 11).

Fischel, Daniel. 1995. *The Conspiracy to Destroy Michael Milken and His Financial Revolution.* New York: HarperBusiness.

Fischer, Stanley, and Lawrence H. Summers. 1989. "Should Governments Learn to Live with Inflation?" *American Economic Review* (May): 382–87.

Fisher, Irving. 1926. "A Statistical Relation between Unemployment and Price Changes." *International Labor Review* (June): 785–92.

Fisher, Irving, and Herbert W. Fisher. 1942. *Constructive Income Taxation.* New York: Harper & Brothers.

Fisher, Louis. 1975. *Presidential Spending Power.* Princeton: Princeton University Press.

Fisher, Kenneth L. 2000. "Gephardt for Speaker." *Forbes* (September 4): 153.

Flash, Edward S. 1965. *Economic Advice and Presidential Leadership.* New York: Columbia University Press.

Fletcher, Michael. 2005. "Bush Is Keeping Cabinet Secretaries Close to Home: Spending Time at the White House Required." *Washington Post* (March 31).

Forbes, Steve. 2001. "On Tax Cuts, Bush Must Be Bolder." *Wall Street Journal* (April 5).

Francis, Theo. 2004. "Retiree Costs Get Recalculated." *Wall Street Journal* (March 2).

Francois, Joseph F., and Laura Baughman. 2001. *Estimated Economic Effects of Proposed Import Relief Remedies for Steel.* Washington: Consuming Industries Trade Action Coalition.

Francois, Joseph, and Laura Baughman. 2003. *The Unintended Consequences of U.S. Steel Import Tariffs: A Quantification of the Impact during 2002.* Washington: Consuming Industries Trade Action Coalition.

Frank, Robert H. 1999. *Luxury Fever.* New York: Free Press.

Freeman, Richard, and Eileen Appelbaum. 2001. "Instead of a Tax Cut, Send Out Dividends." *New York Times* (February 1).

Freudenheim, Milt. 2003. "Employers Seek to Shift Costs of Drugs to U.S." *New York Times* (July 2).

Friedman, Milton. 1978a. "The Limitations of Tax Limitation." *Policy Review* (summer): 7–14.

Friedman, Milton. 1978b. "The Kemp-Roth Free Lunch." *Newsweek* (August 7).

Friedman, Milton. 2003. "What Every American Wants." *Wall Street Journal* (January 15).

Friedman, Milton, and Rose Friedman. 1998. *Two Lucky People.* Chicago: University of Chicago Press.

Frum, David. 2003. *The Right Man.* New York: Random House.

Fuerbringer, Jonathan. 1992. "Bonds Gain on a Presidential Poll." *New York Times* (October 29).

Fullerton, Don, and Diane Lim Rogers. 1993. *Who Bears the Lifetime Tax Burden?* Washington: Brookings Institution.

Fullerton, Don, John Shoven, and John Whalley. 1983. "Replacing the U.S. Income Tax with a Progressive Consumption Tax." *Journal of Public Economics* (February): 3–23.

Fullerton, Don, A. Thomas King, John Shoven, and John Whalley. 1981. "Corporate Tax Integration in the United States: A General Equilibrium Approach." *American Economic Review* (September): 677–91.

Fund, John. 2005a. "Rush for the Border." www.opinionjournal.com (January 31).

Fund, John. 2005b. "Run for the Border." www.opinionjournal.com (August 15).

Fund, John. 2005c. "Hey, Big Spender." www.opinionjournal.com (September 12).

Furchtgott-Roth, Diana. 1990. "OECD Countries and the VAT: The Historical Experience." American Petroleum Institute Research Study No. 49 (February).

Galbraith, John Kenneth. 1958. *The Affluent Society.* Boston: Houghton Mifflin.

Galbraith, John Kenneth. 1969. *Ambassador's Journal.* Boston: Houghton Mifflin.

Galbraith, John Kenneth. 1970. "Richard Nixon and the Great Socialist Revival." *New York* (September 21): 24–29.

Gale, William G. 1999. "The Required Tax Rate in a National Retail Sales Tax." *National Tax Journal* (September): 443–57.

Gale, William G. 2004. "A Note on the Required Tax Rate in a National Retail Sales Tax: Preliminary Estimates for 2005–2014." Brookings Institution (August 12).

Gale, William G. 2005. "The National Retail Sales Tax: What Would the Rate Have to Be?" Brookings Institution (April).

Gale, William G., Evan F. Koenig, Diane Lim Rogers, and John Sabelhaus. 1998. "Taxing Government in a National Retail Sales Tax." *Tax Notes* (October 5): 97–109.

Gardner, Richard N. 1969. *Sterling-Dollar Diplomacy,* rev. ed. New York: McGraw-Hill.

Gasparino, Charles. 2005. *Blood on the Street.* New York: Free Press.

George, Henry. 1975 (1880). *Progress and Poverty*. New York: Robert Schalkenbach Foundation.

George, Robert A. 2004. "Conscientious Objector: Why I Can't Vote for Bush." *New Republic* (October 25): 20–23.

Gigot, Paul A. 2000. "Bush Has a Tax Credit For You and You, and . . ." *Wall Street Journal* (April 21).

Gigot, Paul. 2001a. "Beltway 101: Teddy Takes George To School." *Wall Street Journal* (May 4).

Gigot, Paul. 2001b. "Two Bushes: One Flips, the Other Doesn't." *Wall Street Journal* (June 22).

Gingrich, Newt. 2003. "Conservatives Should Vote 'Yes' on Medicare." *Wall Street Journal* (November 20).

Glanz, James. 2004. "At the Center of the Storm over Bush and Science." *New York Times* (March 30).

Glazier, Stephen. 1988. "Line-Item Veto Hides Under an Alias." *Wall Street Journal* (March 18).

Gleckman, Howard. 2003a. "From Good Tax Policy to Empty Gesture." *BusinessWeek* (May 26): 42.

Gleckman, Howard. 2003b. "Medicare Reform: No Miracle Drug for the GOP." *BusinessWeek* (September 15): 52.

Gleckman, Howard. 2004. "Why the GOP Has a Medicare Headache." *BusinessWeek* (July 26): 49.

Gleckman, Howard, and David Welch. 2005. "Take the Money and Don't Run." *BusinessWeek* (June 20): 141–42.

Goetz, Michael. 1978. "Tax Avoidance, Horizontal Equity, and Tax Reform: A Proposed Synthesis." *Southern Economic Journal* (April): 798–812.

Goldstein, Amy. 2004a. "Higher Medicare Costs Suspected for Months." *Washington Post* (January 31).

Goldstein, Amy. 2004b. "Foster: White House Had Role in Withholding Medicare Data." *Washington Post* (March 19).

Goldstein, Amy. 2004c. "Medicare Official Cites Cost Warning." *Washington Post* (March 25).

Goldstein, Amy, and Helen Dewar. 2004. "GOP Still Seeking Afterglow of Vote on Drug Benefits." *Washington Post* (February 29).

Gollop, Frank M., and Mark J. Roberts. 1983. "Environmental Regulations and Productivity Growth: The Case of Fossil-fueled Electric Power Generation." *Journal of Political Economy* (August): 654–74.

Goode, Richard. 1977. "The Economic Definition of Income." In *Comprehensive Income Taxation*, ed. Joseph A. Pechman, pp. 1–30. Washington: Brookings Institution.

Goodman, Peter S. 2003. "China Plans to Purchase U.S. Goods in a Big Way." *Washington Post* (October 29).

Gordon, Robert J. 1980. "Postwar Macroeconomics: The Evolution of Events and Ideas." In *The American Economy in Transition,* ed. Martin Feldstein, pp. 101–62. Chicago: University of Chicago Press.

Gottfried, Paul. 1993. *The Conservative Movement,* rev. ed. New York: Twayne Publishers.

Gowa, Joanne. 1983. *Closing the Gold Window: Domestic Politics and the End of Bretton Woods.* Ithaca: Cornell University Press.

Graetz, Michael. 1979. "Implementing a Progressive Consumption Tax." *Harvard Law Review* (June): 1575–1661.

Graetz, Michael. 2002. "100 Million Unnecessary Returns: A Fresh Start for the U.S. Tax System." *Yale Law Journal* (November): 261–310.

Gramlich, Edward, Richard Kasten, and Frank Sammartino. 1989. "Deficit Reduction and Income Redistribution." *American Economic Review* (May): 315–19.

Gray, Wayne B. 1987. "The Cost of Regulation: OSHA, EPA and the Productivity Slowdown." *American Economic Review* (December): 998–1006.

Gray, Wayne B., and Ronald J. Shadbegian. 1995. "Pollution Abatement Costs, Regulation, and Plant-Level Productivity." National Bureau of Economic Research Working Paper No. 4994 (January).

Grayson, C. Jackson. 1974. *Confessions of a Price Controller.* Homewood, IL: Dow Jones-Irwin.

Green Scissors. 2004. *Green Scissors, 2004: Cutting Wasteful & Environmentally Harmful Spending.* www.greenscissors.org.

Greenberg, David. 2003. *Nixon's Shadow.* New York: W. W. Norton.

Greider, William. 1987. *Secrets of the Temple.* New York: Simon & Schuster.

Grimaldi, James V. 2002. "Enron Succeeded in Aid Pursuit." *Washington Post* (March 22).

Grimaldi, James V. 2005. "Abramoff Indictment May Aid D.C. Inquiry." *Washington Post* (August 13).

Gron, Anne, and Alan O. Sykes. 2002–2003. "A Role for Government?" *Regulation* (winter): 44–51.

Grow, Brian. 2005. "Embracing Illegals." *BusinessWeek* (July 18): 56–64.

Gruber, Jon, and Emmanuel Saez. 2002. "The Elasticity of Taxable Income: Evidence and Implications." *Journal of Public Economics* (April): 1–32.

Grunwald, Michael. 2002. "Members of Congress Rally around Ousted Corps Chief: Lawmakers Say Official Punished for Budget Truthfulness." *Washington Post* (March 8).

Grunwald, Michael. 2005. "Money Flowed To Questionable Projects." *Washington Post* (September 8).

Haberler, Gottfried. 1936. *The Theory of International Trade.* London: William Hodge.

Hahn, Robert, and Scott Wallsten. 2003. "Bring the President's Nerds Back in From the Cold." *Financial Times* (October 30).

Haig, Robert M. 1959 (1921). "The Concept of Income—Economic and Legal Aspects." In *Readings in the Economics of Taxation,* ed. Richard A. Musgrave and Carl Shoup, pp. 54–76. Homewood, IL: Richard D. Irwin.

Hale, David. 2003. "Washington's Weak Dollar Policy." *Financial Times* (May 20).

Hall, Robert E. 2004. Statement before the House Budget Committee (October 6).

Hall, Robert E., and Alvin Rabushka. 1995. *The Flat Tax,* 2nd ed. Stanford: Hoover Institution Press.

Hallow, Ralph Z. 2004. "Spending Has GOP Grass Roots Grumbling." *Washington Times* (February 11).

Halstead, Ted, and Maya MacGuineas. 2004. "A Tax Plan for Kerry." *Washington Post* (May 24).

Hamburger, Tom. 2003. "Despite Bush's Credo, Government Grows." *Wall Street Journal* (September 4).

Hanushek, Eric A. 1986. "The Economics of Schooling: Production and Efficiency in Public Schools." *Journal of Economic Literature* (September): 1141–77.

Hanushek, Eric A. 1998. "Conclusions and Controversies about the Effectiveness of School Resources." *Economic Policy Review,* Federal Reserve Bank of New York (March): 11–27.

Hanushek, Eric A., John F. Kain, and Steven G. Rivkin. 1999. "Do Higher Salaries Buy Better Teachers?" National Bureau of Economic Research Working Paper No. 7082 (April).

Harden, Blaine. 2001. "2-Parent Families Rise after Change in Welfare Laws." *New York Times* (August 12).

Harris, Gardiner. 2003. "Some Experts Foresee Revolt by Elderly over Drug Benefits." *New York Times* (November 26).

Harris, John F., and Robin Wright. 2004. "Aid Grows Amid Remarks about the President's Absence." *Washington Post* (December 29).

Harris, Trevor, R. Glenn Hubbard, and Deen Kemsley. 2001. "The Share Price Effects of Dividend Taxes and Tax Imputation Credits." *Journal of Public Economics* (March): 569–96.

Hart, Jeffrey A. 1994. "The Politics of HDTV in the United States." *Policy Studies Journal* (summer): 213–28.

Hartman, Thomas E. 2004. *The Cost of Being Public in the Era of Sarbanes-Oxley.* Chicago: Foley & Lardner.

Hartman, Thomas E. 2005. *The Cost of Being Public in the Era of Sarbanes-Oxley.* Chicago: Foley & Lardner.

Harwood, John. 2003. "Republicans Assess Gingrich's Warning of Medicare Debacle." *Wall Street Journal* (August 27).

Harwood, John. 2005a. "Republicans Splinter on Bush Agenda." *Wall Street Journal* (April 7).

Harwood, John. 2005b. "Immigration Emerges as Republican Divider." *Wall Street Journal* (May 17).

Harwood, John. 2005c. "Washington Wire." *Wall Street Journal* (August 26).

Harwood, John. 2005d. "President's Edge on Education Dwindles." *Wall Street Journal* (August 30).

Harwood, John, and Kathy Chen. 2001. "Under President Bush, Regulatory Rollback Has Major Impact." *Wall Street Journal* (August 3).

Harwood, John, and David Rogers. 1993. "A Plan That's Tailored to Suit the Democrats." *Wall Street Journal* (February 18).

Harwood, John, and David Wessel. 1991 "Bush's Domestic Policy Is in Growing Disarray, Plagued by Flip-Flops." *Wall Street Journal* (November 22).

Hassett, Kevin. 2003a. "The Deficit Club." www.techcentralstation.com (February 6).

Hassett, Kevin. 2003b. "The Dividend Fiasco." www.techcentralstation.com (May 9).

Hassett, Kevin. 2005. "Bring Back Clinton—Just His Spending Habits." www.bloomberg.com (July 18).

Hassett, Kevin, and Maya MacGuineas. 2005. "Fitting the Bill?" www.nationalreview.com (April 13).

Haufler, Andreas. 2001. *Taxation in a Global Economy*. New York: Cambridge University Press.

Hayek, F. A. 1945. "The Use of Knowledge in Society." *American Economic Review* (September): 519–30.

Heller, H. Robert. 2005. "Fair Tax Is a Stealthy Double Hit on Boomers." Letter to the Editor. *Wall Street Journal* (March 16).

Henderson, Nell. 2005. "Greenspan Says He Expects Tax Increases." *Washington Post* (April 22).

Hensley, Scott. 2003. "Money Spent on Latest Drugs Is Worth the Cost, Economist Says." *Wall Street Journal* (September 30).

Hernandez, Raymond. 2003. "Hillary Clinton Taking Fire from the Left as Well as Right." *New York Times* (May 30).

Hetzel, Robert L. 1998. "Arthur Burns and Inflation." *Economic Quarterly,* Federal Reserve Bank of Richmond (winter): 21–44.

Hewitt, Hugh. 2005. *Blog: Understanding the Information Reformation That's Changing Your World*. Nashville: Thomas Nelson.

Hill, Andrew. 2002. " 'There's a Desire to Stay Off the Radar . . . But Companies Have to Take Risks, Make Decisions.' " *Financial Times* (October 10).

Hindley, Brian, and Patrick A. Messerlin. 1996. *Antidumping Industrial Policy.* Washington: American Enterprise Institute.

Hitchens, Christopher. 1994. "Minority Report." *Nation* (December 12): 716.

Hitchens, Christopher. 2004. "Rumble on the Right." *Vanity Fair* (July): 70–75.

Hitt, Greg. 2004. "Bush Woos Voters through Local Projects." *Wall Street Journal* (July 13).

Hitt, Greg. 2005a. "Trade and Aid Clash over Shrimp Tariffs." *Wall Street Journal* (April 25).

Hitt, Greg. 2005b. "Last-Minute Deals Put Cafta over the Top." *Wall Street Journal* (July 29).

Hitt, Greg, and Joel Millman. 2004. "Bush Set to Ease Immigration." *Wall Street Journal* (January 7).

Hoagland, Jim. 2002. "A Tone-Deaf Economic Team." *Washington Post* (July 28).

Hoebeke, C. H. 1995. *The Road to Mass Democracy: Original Intent and the Seventeenth Amendment.* New Brunswick, NJ: Transaction Publishers.

Hoff, Joan. 1994. *Nixon Reconsidered.* New York: Basic Books.

Holcombe, Randall, G., and Jeffrey A. Mills. 1994. "Is Revenue-Neutral Tax Reform Revenue-Neutral?" *Public Finance Quarterly* (January): 65–85.

Holmans, A. E. 1958. "The Eisenhower Administration and the Recession, 1953–55." *Oxford Economic Papers* (February): 34–54.

Holmans, A. E. 1961. *United States Fiscal Policy, 1945–1959.* New York: Oxford University Press.

Holtz-Eakin, Douglas. 2005. Letter to the Honorable Bill Thomas. Congressional Budget Office (February 9).

Holtz-Eakin, Douglas, Whitney Newey, and Harvey S. Rosen. 1989. "The Revenue-Expenditures Nexus: Evidence from Local Government Data." *International Economic Review* (May): 415–29.

Hong, Peter, and Thane Peterson. 1992. "Honk If You Hate the EPA: Car Owners Moan, But Some Businesses Love New Emission-Control Rules." *BusinessWeek* (July 27): 37.

Hook, Janet. 2003. "GOP Puts Its Mark on Congress and Deficit." *Los Angeles Times* (November 30).

Hook, Janet, and Warren Vieth. 2004. "Bush's Cut-and-Spend Plan Is Math-Challenged." *Los Angeles Times* (September 19).

Hoover, Kevin D., and Steven M. Sheffrin. 1992. "Causation, Spending, and Taxes: Sand in the Sandbox or Tax Collector for the Welfare State?" *American Economic Review* (March): 225–48.

Hoover, Kevin D., and Mark V. Siegler. 2000. "Taxing and Spending in the Long View: The Causal Structure of U.S. Fiscal Policy, 1791–1913." *Oxford Economic Papers* (October): 745–73.

House, Christopher L., and Matthew D. Shapiro. 2004. "Phased-In Tax Cuts and Economic Activity." National Bureau of Economic Research Working Paper No. 10415 (April).

House Committee on the Budget and Joint Economic Committee. 1978. *Economic Stabilization Policies:The Historical Record, 1962–76.* Joint Committee Print, 95th Congress, 2nd session. Washington: U.S. Government Printing Office.

House Committee on Standards of Official Conduct. 2004. *Investigation of Certain Allegations Related To Voting on the Medicare Prescription Drug, Improvement, and Modernization Act of 2003* (September 30).

House Committee on Ways and Means. 1963. *Revenue Act of 1963.* House Report 749, 88th Congress, 1st session. Washington: U.S. Government Printing Office.

House Committee on Ways and Means. 2004. *2004 Green Book.* Washington: U.S. Government Printing Office.

Hoxby, Caroline M. 2000. "The Effects of Class Size on Student Achievement: New Evidence from Population Variation." *Quarterly Journal of Economics* (November): 1239–85.

Hsu, Spencer S. 2005. "Leaders Lacking Disaster Experience." *Washington Post* (September 9).

Hubbard, R. Glenn. 1993. "Corporate Tax Integration: A View from the Treasury Department." *Journal of Economic Perspectives* (winter): 115–32.

Hufbauer, Gary Clyde, and Carol Gabyzon. 1996. *Fundamental Tax Reform and Border Tax Adjustments.* Washington: Institute for International Economics.

Hufbauer, Gary Clyde, and Ben Goodrich. 2003. "Next Move in Steel: Revocation or Retaliation?" International Economic Policy Brief No. PB03-10, Institute for International Economics (October).

Hufbauer, Gary Clyde, and Paul Grieco. 2005. "America Badly Needs a Value-Added Tax." *Financial Times* (April 21).

Hulse, Carl. 2003. "Kennedy's Support for Medicare Bill Angers His Allies." *New York Times* (June 22).

Hulse, Carl. 2005. "Did Congress and Bush Fudge the Books on Roads Bill?" *New York Times* (August 4).

Hunt, Albert R. 1980. "As Ronald Reagan's Star Rises, So Does That of the Conservative Newspaper *Human Events.*" *Wall Street Journal* (July 9).

Hutzler, Charles. 2003a. "China Set to Go on Buying Spree for U.S. Goods." *Wall Street Journal* (October 30).

Hutzler, Charles. 2003b. "China Delays Trade Mission as U.S. Curbs Textile Imports." *Wall Street Journal* (November 19).

Hutzler, Charles, and Rebecca Buckman. 2003. "China Makes Sharp Response To New U.S. Textile Restrictions." *Wall Street Journal* (November 20).

Ignatius, David. 2004a. "Mystery of the Missing Jobs." *Washington Post* (March 9).

Ignatius, David. 2004b. "Exit Strategy for a Fiscal Impasses." *Washington Post* (November 9).

Ikenson, Dan. 2004. "Zeroing In: Antidumping's Flawed Methodology under Fire." Cato Institute Free Trade Bulletin No. 11 (April 27).

Ikenson, Dan. 2005. "Nonmarket Nonsense: U.S. Antidumping Policy toward China." Cato Institute Trade Briefing Paper No. 22 (March 7).

Internal Revenue Service. 1993. *A Study of Administrative Issues in Implementing a Federal Value-Added Tax*. Office of the Assistant Commissioner for Planning and Research (May).

Internal Revenue Service. 2005. "New IRS Study Provides Preliminary Tax Gap Estimate." www.irs.ustreas.gov/newsroom (March 29).

International Monetary Fund. 2003. "IMF Concludes 2003 Article IV Consultation with the People's Republic of China." Public Information Notice No. 03/136 (November 18).

Ip, Greg. 2002. "Mood Swings in Favor of Regulation." *Wall Street Journal* (March 29).

Ip, Greg. 2005a. "Bush Adviser Is Named Economic Council Director." *Wall Street Journal* (January 11).

Ip, Greg. 2005b. "Search for Fed Chairman Widens." *Wall Street Journal* (August 4).

Irwin, Douglas A. 1998. "The Smoot-Hawley Tariff: A Quantitative Assessment." *Review of Economics and Statistics* (May): 326–34.

Irwin, Douglas A. 2004. "The Aftermath of Hamilton's 'Report on Manufactures.'" *Journal of Economic History* (September): 800–821.

Jacoby, Jeff. 2005. "The Republican Pork Barrel." *Boston Globe* (August 4).

Jacoby, Neil H. 1964. "The Fiscal Policy of the Kennedy-Johnson Administration." *Journal of Finance* (May): 353–69.

Jacobzone, Stephanie. 2000. "Pharmaceutical Policies in OECD Countries: Reconciling Social and Industrial Goals." Labor Market and Social Policy Occasional Paper No. 40, Organisation for Economic Co-operation and Development (April).

Jenkins, Holman. 2003a. "Don't Sweat It: There's Nothing Wrong with Corporate Governance That the Threat of a Hostile Takeover Couldn't Fix." *Wall Street Journal* (February 24).

Jenkins, Holman. 2003b. "Republicans Learn to Love (Well, Like) the Deficit." *Wall Street Journal* (November 5).

Jenkins, Holman. 2004. "Too Bad He Couldn't Find a Veep Named Gridlock." *Wall Street Journal* (July 7).

Jensen, Michael C. 1984. "Takeovers: Folklore and Science." *Harvard Business Review* (November–December): 109–21.

Jensen, Michael C. 1986. "Agency Costs of Free Cash Flow, Corporate Finance, and Takeovers." *American Economic Review* (May): 323–29.

Jensen, Michael C. 1988. "Takeovers: Their Causes and Consequences." *Journal of Economic Perspectives* (winter): 21–48.

Jensen, Michael C. 1989. "Eclipse of the Public Corporation." *Harvard Business Review* (September–October): 61–74.

Jensen, Michael C., and Richard S. Ruback. 1983. "The Market for Corporate Control." *Journal of Financial Economics* (April): 5–50.

Johnson, David S., Jonathan A. Parker, and Nicholas S. Souleles. 2004. "Household Expenditure and the Income Tax Rebates of 2001." National Bureau of Economic Research Working Paper No. 10784 (September).

Joint Committee on Taxation. 1991. *Factors Affecting the International Competitiveness of the United States.* Washington: U.S. Government Printing Office.

Joint Committee on Taxation. 2000. "Budget Neutral Tax Rate for H.R. 2525." Memorandum from Lindy Paull to John Buckley (April 7).

Joint Committee on Taxation. 2005. *Estimates of Federal Tax Expenditures for Fiscal Years 2005–2009.* Washington: U.S. Government Printing Office.

Joint Economic Committee. 1965. *January 1965 Economic Report of the President.* 89th Congress, 1st session. Washington: U.S. Government Printing Office.

Joint Economic Committee. 1969. *The 1969 Economic Report of the President.* 91st Congress, 1st session. Washington: U.S. Government Printing Office.

Joint Economic Committee. 1973. *Federal Transportation Policy: The SST Again.* Report of the Subcommittee on Priorities and Economy in Government. Joint Committee Print, 93rd Congress, 1st session. Washington: U.S. Government Printing Office.

Jones, Del. 2003. "Sarbanes-Oxley: Dragon or White Knight?" *USA Today* (October 19).

Jorgenson, Dale W., and Peter J. Wilcoxen. 1990. "Environmental Regulation and U.S. Economic Growth." *RAND Journal of Economics* (summer): 314–40.

Jorgenson, Dale W., Mun S. Ho, and Kevin J. Stiroh. 2004. "Will the U.S. Productivity Resurgence Continue?" *Current Issues in Economics and Finance,* Federal Reserve Bank of New York (December).

Jorgenson, Dale W., and Kun-Young Yun. 1991. "The Excess Burden of Taxation in the United States." *Journal of Accounting, Auditing and Finance* (fall): 487–508.

Joulfaian, David, and Rajen Mookerjee. 1990. "The Government Revenue-Expenditure Nexus: Evidence from a State." *Public Finance Quarterly* (January): 92–103.

Kadlec. Daniel. 2000. "Vote for Gridlock." *Time* (August 28): 66.

Kaldor, Nicholas. 1955. *An Expenditure Tax*. London: George Allen & Unwin.

Kaplan, Robert S. 1977. *Indexing Social Security: An Analysis of the Issues*. Washington: American Enterprise Institute.

Karp, Walter. 1979. *The Politics of War*. New York: Harper & Row.

Kaufman, Marc, and Bill Brubaker. 2004. "Higher Prices Erode Value of Medicare Cards." *Washington Post* (May 26).

Keen, Judy. 2004. "Cheney Says It's Too Soon to Tell on Iraqi Arms." *USA Today* (January 19).

Kelly, Kenneth H., and Morris E. Morkre. 2002. *Quantifying Causes of Injury to U.S. Industries Competing with Unfairly Traded Imports: 1989 to 1994*. Bureau of Economics, Federal Trade Commission (December).

Kemp, Murray C. 1960. "The Mill-Bastable Infant-Industry Dogma." *Journal of Political Economy* (February): 65–67.

Kennedy, John F. 1963. *Public Papers of the Presidents of the United States: John F. Kennedy, 1962*. Washington: U.S. Government Printing Office.

Kessler, Glenn. 2002. "2003 Budget Completes Big Jump in Spending." *Washington Post* (April 15).

Kettl, Donald F. 1986. *Leadership at the Fed*. New Haven: Yale University Press.

Keynes, John Maynard. 1973 (1936). *The General Theory of Employment Interest and Money*. The Collected Writings of John Maynard Keynes, vol. 7. London: Macmillan.

Keynes, John Maynard. 1981. *Activities, 1922–1929: The Return to Gold and Industrial Policy*. The Collected Writings of John Maynard Keynes, vol. 19, part 1. London: Macmillan.

Kiefer, Donald W. 1992. "Tax Cuts and Rebates for Economic Stimulus: The Historical Record." *CRS Report for Congress* (January 2).

Kimmel Lance J., and Steven W. Vazquez. 2003. *The Increased Financial and Non-Financial Cost of Staying Public*. Chicago: Foley & Lardner.

Kingdon, John W. 2003. *Agendas, Alternatives, and Public Policies*, 2nd ed. New York: Longman.

Kirkpatrick, David D. 2004a. "Lack of Resolution in Iraq Finds Conservatives Divided." *New York Times* (April 19).

Kirkpatrick, David D. 2004b. "Some Big Conservative Donors, Unhappy with Bush, Say They Won't Back His Campaign." *New York Times* (June 4).

Kirkpatrick, David D. 2004c. "*National Review* Founder Says It's Time to Leave Stage." *New York Times* (June 29).

Kirkpatrick, David D. 2004d. "War Heats Up in the Neoconservative Fold." *New York Times* (August 22).

Kirkpatrick, David D. 2005. "Bush Moved Conservatism Past Reactionary, Rove Says." *New York Times* (February 18).

Koenig, Evan F. 1999. "Achieving 'Program Neutrality' under a National Retail Sales Tax." *National Tax Journal* (December): 683–97.

Koitz, David, and Michelle Harlan. 1994. "Major Deficit-Reduction Measures Enacted in Recent Years." *CRS Report for Congress* (September 8).

Kolb, Charles. 1993. *White House Daze: The Unmaking of Domestic Policy in the Bush Years*. New York: Free Press.

Kolko, Gabriel. 1963. *The Triumph of Conservatism*. Glencoe: Free Press.

Kolko, Gabriel. 1965. *Railroads and Regulation, 1877–1916*. Princeton: Princeton University Press.

Kosterlitz, Julie. 2001. "The O'Neill Enigma." *National Journal* (August 11): 2532–38.

Kosterlitz, Julie. 2003. "The Neoconservative Moment." *National Journal* (May 17): 1540–46.

Kosters, Marvin H. 1975. *Controls and Inflation*. Washington: American Enterprise Institute.

Kottlikoff, Laurence J., and Scott Burns 2004. *The Coming Generational Storm*. Cambridge: MIT Press.

Kristol, Irving. 1978. "Populist Remedy for Populist Abuses." *Wall Street Journal* (August 10).

Kristol, Irving. 1995. *Neoconservatism: The Autobiography of an Idea*. New York: Free Press.

Kronholz, June. 2004. "Bush's Education Law Gets an Incomplete: No Child Left Behind Act, for Those Who Know About It, Hasn't Become a Vote-Getter." *Wall Street Journal* (September 1).

Krueger, Anne O. 1999. "Are Preferential Trading Arrangements Trade-Liberalizing or Protectionist?" *Journal of Economic Perspectives* (fall): 105–24.

Krueger, Anne O., and Baran Tuncer. 1982. "An Empirical Test of the Infant Industry Argument." *American Economic Review* (December): 1142–52.

Krugman, Paul. 1999. "The Ascent of E-man." *Fortune* (May 24): 42.

Kuttner, Bob. 2002. "Enron: A Powerful Blow To Market Fundamentalists." *Business Week* (February 4).

Kuttner, Bob. 2003. "Health Club." *Boston Globe* (June 18).

Ladd, Everett Carl. 1998. "Nixon, Clinton and the Polls." *Wall Street Journal* (April 1).

Lambro, Donald. 2002. "Bush Decisions Rankle Conservatives." *Washington Times* (March 27).

Lambro, Donald. 2005. "Conservative Group Bashes Bush Policies." *Washington Times* (January 10).

Landler, Mark. 2004. "Germans Weigh Taking Stocks Off Wall Street." *New York Times* (November 20).

Langenfeld, James, and James Nieberding. 2005. "The Benefits of Free Trade to U.S. Consumers." *Business Economics* (July): 41–51.

Lardy, Nicholas R. 2003. "The Economic Rise of China: Threat or Opportunity?" *Economic Commentary*, Federal Reserve Bank of Cleveland (August 1).

Lazear, Edward P. 1999. "Educational Production." National Bureau of Economic Research Working Paper No. 7349 (September).

Ledbetter, Mark A. 2004. "Comparison of BEA Estimates of Personal Income and IRS Estimates of Adjusted Gross Income." *Survey of Current Business* (November): 9–14.

Lemann, Nicholas. 2004. "Remember the Alamo." *New Yorker* (October 18): 148–61.

Lenway, Stefanie, Randall Morck, and Bernard Yeung. 1996. "Rent Seeking, Protectionism, and Innovations in the American Steel Industry." *Economic Journal* (March): 410–21.

Leubsdorf, Carl. 2002. "Economy to Decide Winners and Losers in Budget Battle." *Dallas Morning News* (January 10).

Levitt, Steven D. 1994. "Using Repeat Challengers to Estimate the Effect of Campaign Spending on Election Outcomes in the U.S. House." *Journal of Political Economy* (August): 777–98.

Levy, Philip I. 1997. "A Political-Economic Analysis of Free-Trade Agreements." *American Economic Review* (September): 506–19.

Li, Wenli, and Pierre-Daniel Sarte. 2001. "Growth Effects of Progressive Taxes." Finance and Economics Discussion Paper No. 2002-3, Federal Reserve Board (November).

Lichtblau, Eric. 2005. "Profiling Report Leads To a Clash and a Demotion." *New York Times* (August 24).

Lichtenberg, Frank. 2002–2003. "New Drugs: Health and Economic Impacts." *NBER Reporter* (winter): 5–7.

Lichtenberg, Frank. 2003a. "Pharmaceutical Innovation, Mortality Reduction, and Economic Growth." In *Measuring the Gains from Medical Research: An Economic Approach*, ed. Kevin Murphy and Robert Topel, pp. 74–109. Chicago: University of Chicago Press.

Lichtenberg, Frank. 2003b. "The Value of New Drugs: The Good News in Capsule Form." *Milken Institute Review* (fourth quarter): 16–25.

Lichtman, Allan. 2004. "In Plain Sight: with the Public Distracted, George W. Bush Is Building a Big Government—of the Right." *Newsday* (August 7).

Light, Paul C. 1991. *The President's Agenda: Domestic Policy Choice from Kennedy to Reagan,* rev. ed. Baltimore: Johns Hopkins University Press.

Light, Paul C. 1999. *The True Size of Government*. Washington: Brookings Institution.

Light, Paul C. 2003. "Fact Sheet on the New True Size of Government." Brookings Institution (September 5).

Ligos, Melinda. 2004. "When Going Public May Not Be Worth It." *New York Times* (June 3).

Linder, Marc. 1996. "Eisenhower-Era Marxist-Confiscatory Taxation: Requiem for the Rhetoric of Rate Reduction for the Rich." *Tulane Law Review* (March): 905–1040.

Lindsey, Brink, Mark A. Groombridge, and Prakash Loungani. 2000. "Nailing the Homeowner: The Economic Impact of Trade Protection of the Softwood Lumber Industry." Cato Institute Trade Policy Analysis No. 11 (July 6).

Link, Albert N. 1982. "Productivity Growth, Environmental Regulations and the Composition of R&D." *Bell Journal of Economics* (autumn): 548–54.

Lipton, Eric, Eric Schmitt, and Thom Shanker. 2005. "Political Issues Snarled Plans for Troop Aid." *New York Times* (September 9).

Lizza, Ryan. 2005. "The ATM for Bush's America." *New York* (July 25): 35–39, 73.

Los Angeles Times. 2004. "A Drug Deal Gone Sour" (March 18).

Lowry, Rich. 2004. "The Medicare Monstrosity." www.townhall.com (February 2).

Lyon, Andrew B. 1997. *Cracking the Code: Making Sense of the Corporate Alternative Minimum Tax*. Washington: Brookings Institution.

MacDonald, Heather. 2004. "The Illegal-Alien Crime Wave." *City Journal* (winter): 46–57.

MacDonald, Heather. 2005. Statement before the House Judiciary Committee (April 13).

Macomber, Shawn. 2005. "Tax Credit Welfare." *American Spectator* (April): 40–41.

Maggs, John. 2005. "Feeding the Beast." *National Journal* (March 5): 689.

Magnusson, Paul, and Ben Elgin. 2005. "Go Back Where You Came From." *BusinessWeek* (July 4): 86–87.

Mallaby, Sebastian. 2001. "Goodbye to Reaganomics." *Washington Post* (February 19).

Manage, Neela, and Michael L. Marlow. 1986. "The Causal Relation between Federal Expenditures and Receipts." *Southern Economic Journal* (January): 617–29.

Manchester Union Leader. 1999. "Bush Won't Push Tax Reform" (December 2).

Mankiw, N. Gregory, and Phillip L. Swagel. 2005. "Antidumping: The Third Rail of Trade Policy." *Foreign Affairs* (July–August): 107–119.

Manne, Henry G. 2002. "Bring Back the Hostile Takeover." *Wall Street Journal* (June 26).

Martinez, Barbara. 2004. "Drug-Price Surge May Erode Savings from Medicare Card." *Wall Street Journal* (March 24).

Maskell, Jack. 2004. Memorandum To the Honorable Charles Rangel. Congressional Research Service (April 26).

Matusow, Allen J. 1998. *Nixon's Economy: Booms, Busts, Dollars, and Votes.* Lawrence: University Press of Kansas.

Mayhew, David R. 2005. *Divided We Govern*, 2nd ed. New Haven: Yale University Press.

Maynard, Micheline. 2004. "Airline Bailout Fails to Do the Job, Some Experts Contend." *New York Times* (May 14).

McCaffery, Edward J. 2002. *Fair Not Flat.* Chicago: University of Chicago Press.

McCaffery, Edward. J. 2005. "A New Understanding of Tax." *Michigan Law Review* (March): 807–938.

McClellan, Mark. 2001. "Medicare and the Federal Budget: Past Experience, Current Policy, Future Prospects." In *Tax Policy and the Economy*, vol. 15, ed. James M. Poterba, pp. 167–200. Cambridge: MIT Press.

McCoy, Charles F. 1984. "FTC Studies Tactics of Cement Producers in Fighting Imports." *Wall Street Journal* (December 28).

McDonald, Forrest. 1988. "Line-Item Veto: Older Than Constitution." *Wall Street Journal* (March 7).

McGee, Robert W. 1993. "The Case to Repeal the Antidumping Laws." *Northwestern Journal of International Law and Business* (spring): 491–562.

McKinnon, John D. 2004. "Bush Budget Pledge Falls Flat." *Wall Street Journal* (January 22).

McKinnon, John D. 2005a. "Some Republicans Debate Stance on Taxes." *Wall Street Journal* (February 22).

McKinnon, John D. 2005b. "White House to Launch Push for Pro-Business Regulation." *Wall Street Journal* (March 9).

McKinnon, John D. 2005c. "Big Government's Changing Face." *Wall Street Journal* (April 4).

McKinnon, John D. 2005d. "White House to Push for Revised Immigration Plan." *Wall Street Journal* (August 16).

McLean, Bethany, and Peter Elkind. 2003. *The Smartest Guys in the Room: The Amazing Rise and Scandalous Fall of Enron.* New York: Portfolio.

McLure, Charles E. 1979. *Must Corporate Income Be Taxed Twice?* Washington: Brookings Institution.

McLure, Charles E. 1987. *The Value-Added Tax: Key to Deficit Reduction?* Washington: American Enterprise Institute.

McQueen, Michel, and John Harwood. 1991. "Bush's Schedule Shows He Spends Little Time on Domestic Concerns." *Wall Street Journal* (October 28).

McQuillan, Laurence. 2002. "For Bush, Secrecy Is a Matter of Loyalty." *USA Today* (March 14).

McTague, Jim. 2004. "The Unseen Voters." *Barron's* (July 26): 35.

Meckler, Laura. 2005. "Highway Bill Includes U-Turn for $8.5 Billion in State Funds." *Wall Street Journal* (August 4).

Meeropol, Michael. 1998. *Surrender: How the Clinton Administration Completed the Reagan Revolution*. Ann Arbor: University of Michigan Press.

Meese, Edwin, and James Gattuso. 2004. "Votes May Be Hiding in Heap of Regulations." *Los Angeles Times* (February 3).

Melloan, George. 2001. "Scrapping Kyoto May Prove to Be Bush's Finest Act." *Wall Street Journal* (April 3).

Melloan, George. 2004. "Promises, Promises; But Who's Minding the Budget?" *Wall Street Journal* (January 20).

Melloan, George. 2005. "Washington's Spending Spree and the Dangers It Poses." *Wall Street Journal* (July 12).

Merrill, Peter. 2004. Statement before the House Budget Committee (July 22).

Merski, Paul. 1991. "Budget Deal Perpetuates Fiscal Failure." Tax Foundation Issue Brief (November).

Messere, Ken, Flip de Kam, and Christopher Heady. 2003. *Tax Policy: Theory and Practice in OECD Countries*. New York: Oxford University Press.

Meyerson, Harold. 2004. "Democrats in a Divided Land." *Washington Post* (November 5).

Michaels, Adrian. 2004. "AIG 'Forced to Spend' $300m a Year on New Rules." *Financial Times* (May 20).

Michel, Norbert, and Ralph Rector. 2004. "Dividend Policy and the 2003 Tax Cut: Preliminary Evidence." *Tax Notes* (August 23): 853–54.

Micklethwait, John, and Adrian Wooldridge. 2004. "The Right Wing's Deep, Dark Secret." *Los Angeles Times* (July 28).

Milbank, Dana. 2002. "From Bush, Some Flexibility on Election Promises." *Washington Post* (March 25).

Milbank, Dana. 2003a. " 'CEA You Later,' Bush Says." *Washington Post* (May 6).

Milbank, Dana. 2003b. "The Making of the President: The Nixon in Bush." *Washington Post* (November 25).

Mill, John Stuart. 1909 (1848). *Principles of Political Economy*. London: Longmans, Green.

Miller, Matthew. 1997. "Hey, Big Spender: I Mean You, Mr. Nixon." *U.S. News & World Report* (March 24): 30.

Miller, Rich, Mike McNamee, and Lee Walczak. 2004. "Wanted: One Tough Economic Team." *BusinessWeek* (December 13): 40–41.

Miller, Steve. 2004. "Five Bush States Increase Taxes." *Washington Times* (November 29).

Miniter, Brendan. 2005. "The Last Laff?" www.opinionjournal.com (August 16).

Miniter, Richard. 1999. "Real Record of Bush Best Predictor of Presidential Performance." *Manchester Union Leader* (December 2).

Mitchell, Dan. 2004. "Medicare: A Ticking Time Bomb for Tax Increases." www.heritage.org (March 31).

Modigliani, Franco, and Charles Steindel. 1977. "Is a Tax Rebate an Effective Tool for Stabilization Policy?" *Brookings Papers on Economic Activity* (No. 1): 175–203.

Moffitt, Robert A. 2002. "From Welfare To Work: What the Evidence Shows." Welfare Reform and Beyond Policy Brief No. 13, Brookings Institution (January).

Mooney, Chris. 2005. *The Republican War on Science.* New York: Basic Books.

Moore, David W. 2001. "Few Americans Expect to Use Tax Rebate for New Spending." Gallup Organization (July 24).

Moore, Stephen. 2002. "A Little Modesty, Please." *Weekly Standard* (April 8): 19–20.

Morgan, A. R. C. 2005. *Sarbanes-Oxley Implementation Costs: What Companies Are Reporting in their SEC Filings* (February).

Morgan, Dan. 2000. "Clinton's Last Regulatory Rush." *Washington Post* (December 6).

Morin, Richard. 2002. "More Curbs on Business Sought." *Washington Post* (July 2).

Morris, Dick. 2001. "The Politics of Energy: W. Repeats Bill's Mistakes." *New York Post* (May 22).

Morris, Dick. 2005. "How Second Terms Fail." *New York Post* (January 19).

Morton, Fiona M. Scott. 2001. "The Problems of Price Controls." *Regulation* (spring): 50–54.

Mulford, Charles W., and Eugene E. Comiskey. 2002. *The Financial Numbers Game.* New York: John Wiley.

Murray, Alan. 2003a. "Exile on G Street: Bush's Economists Play Peripheral Role." *Wall Street Journal* (May 13).

Murray, Alan. 2003b. "Bush Seems to Lack Will to Shift Course to Correct a Deficit." *Wall Street Journal* (December 2).

Murray, Alan. 2004a. "Bush Speech Shows U.S. Conservatism Has a New Playbook." *Wall Street Journal* (September 7).

Murray, Alan. 2004b. "Treasury Troubles: John Snow, You're No Alexander Hamilton." *Wall Street Journal* (October 19).

Murray, Alan. 2004c. "Microsoft Foe Quits Antitrust Crusade—With Check in Hand." *Wall Street Journal* (December 7).

Murray, Alan. 2005. "Bush Starts to Deliver for Big Business." *Wall Street Journal* (August 3).

Murray, Charles. 1984. *Losing Ground: American Social Policy, 1950–1980.* New York: Basic Books.

Murray, Shailagh, and Jim VandeHei. 2005. "Katrina's Cost May Test GOP Harmony." *Washington Post* (September 21).

Nader, Ralph. 2000. *Cutting Corporate Welfare.* New York: Seven Stories Press.

Nagourney, Adam. 2005. "Squabbles under the Big Tent." *New York Times* (April 3).

National Review. 2003. "Left Turn" (July 28): 8–9.

New York Times. 1971. "Nixon Reportedly Says He Is a Keynesian" (January 7).

New York Times. 1977. "Abolish the Corporate Income Tax" (September 11).

New York Times. 2002. "A Wise Investment in Foreign Aid" (March 16).

New York Times. 2004a. "A Triumph for Big Sugar" (February 14).

New York Times. 2004b. "Political Timing, Outsourced" (February 17).

New York Times. 2004c. "Are We Stingy? Yes." (December 30).

New York Times. 2005. "Who's Minding the Store?" (March 25).

Newton, Maxwell. 1983. *The Fed.* New York: Times Books.

Nichols, Hans. 2003. "Leadership Lines Up with Deficit Doves." *The Hill* (February 6).

Niskanen, William A. 2002. Comment. In *American Economic Policy in the 1990s,* ed. Jeffrey Frankel and Peter Orszag, pp. 184–87. Cambridge: MIT Press.

Niskanen, William A. 2003. "A Case for Divided Government." www.cato.org (May 7).

Niskanen, William A. 2004. " 'Starve the Beast' Does Not Work." *Cato Policy Report* (March–April): 2.

Niskanen, William A. 2005. " 'Starving the Beast' Will Not Work." *Cato Handbook on Policy,* 6th ed., pp. 113–16. Washington: Cato Institute.

Nixon, Richard M. 1962. *Six Crises.* New York: Doubleday.

Nock, Albert Jay. 1935. *Our Enemy, the State.* New York: William Morrow.

Nock, Albert Jay. 1943. *Memoirs of a Superfluous Man.* New York: Harper & Brothers.

Nofziger, Lyn. 2004a. "Don't Forget about Your Conservative Base." *New York Times* (March 28).

Nofziger, Lyn. 2004b. "Bush's Trouble Ahead." *New York Times* (November 7).

Noonan, Peggy. 2005. "Bookends." www.opinionjournal.com (August 11).

Nordhauser, Norman. 1973. "Origins of Federal Oil Regulation in the 1920s." *Business History Review* (spring): 53-71.

Norton, Hugh S. 1991. *The Quest for Economic Stability: Roosevelt To Bush.* Columbia: University of South Carolina Press.

Novak, Robert. 1992. "Staying the Course to GOP Disaster?" *Washington Post* (August 16).

Novak, Robert. 1999. "Capital Gains: An MIA Issue for the GOP." *Washington Post* (December 6).

Novak, Robert. 2002a. *Evans-Novak Political Report* (May 8).

Novak, Robert. 2002b. "Did John DiIulio Say That?" *Washington Post* (December 5).

Novak, Robert. 2003a. "Any Health Bill Will Do." *Washington Post* (July 7).

Novak, Robert. 2003b. "Executive Arrogance." *Washington Post* (July 28).

Novak, Robert. 2004a. "Republican Malaise." *Washington Post* (March 4).

Novak, Robert. 2004b. *Evans-Novak Political Report* (March 24).

Novak, Robert. 2004c. "In Search of a Base Hit." *Washington Post* (June 3).

Novak, Robert. 2004d. "Bush as Reformer?" *Washington Post* (June 14).

Novak, Robert. 2004e. "Dictated by Bush." *Washington Post* (August 26).

Novak, Robert. 2004f. "Torturing Snow." *Washington Post* (December 9).

Novak, Robert. 2005a. "A Less Conservative Bush?" *Washington Post* (January 24).

Novak, Robert. 2005b. "In Indiana, GOP Apostasy." *Washington Post* (March 17).

Novak, Robert. 2005c. "Holes on the Bush Team." *Washington Post* (April 4).

Novak, Robert. 2005d. "The Threat of the Auditors." *Washington Post* (April 7).

Novak, Robert. 2005e. *Evans-Novak Political Report* (June 28).

Novak, Robert. 2005f. "The GOP's Price for Being Right." *Washington Post* (July 11).

Novak, Robert. 2005g. "'Victories' on the Hill." *Washington Post* (August 4).

Oberlander, Jonathan, and Jim Jaffe. 2003. "Next Step: Drug Price Controls." *Washington Post* (December 14).

OECD. 1988. *Taxing Consumption.* Paris: Organisation for Economic Co-operation and Development.

OECD. 1993. *Taxation in OECD Countries.* Paris: Organisation for Economic Co-operation and Development.

OECD. 2004. *Revenue Statistics, 1965–2003.* Paris: Organisation for Economic Co-operation and Development.

Office of Management and Budget. 2002. *Budget of the United States Government: Fiscal Year 2003.* Washington: U.S. Government Printing Office.

Omestad, Thomas. 2004. "Fixin' for a Fight." *U.S. News & World Report* (October 25): 51-55.

O'Neill, June. 2001. "Welfare Reform Worked." *Wall Street Journal* (August 1).

Oreskes, Michael. 1990. "Support for Bush Declines in Poll: Most Disapprove of Reversal on Taxes, Gallup Says, but Deficit Looms Larger." *New York Times* (July 11).

Ornstein, Norman, Thomas Mann, and Michael Malbin. 2002. *Vital Statistics on Congress, 2001–2002*. Washington: American Enterprise Institute.

Orszag, Jonathan M., Peter R. Orszag, and Laura D. Tyson. 2002. "The Process of Economic Policy-Making During the Clinton Administration." In *American Economic Policy in the 1990s*, ed. Jeffrey A. Frankel and Peter R. Orszag, pp. 983–1027. Cambridge: MIT Press.

Panetta, Leon. 1982. "The Income Tax Simplification Act of 1982." *Congressional Record* (April 5): H 1422–23 (daily ed.).

Parmet, Herbert S. 1990. *Richard Nixon and His America*. Boston: Little, Brown.

Paterson, Thomas G. 1976. "Robert A. Taft and American Foreign Policy, 1939–1945." In *Watershed of Empire*, ed. Leonard P. Liggio and James J. Martin, pp. 183–207. Colorado Springs: Ralph Myles.

Pear, Robert. 2004a. "Democrats Demand Inquiry into Charge by Medicare Officer." *New York Times* (March 14).

Pear, Robert. 2004b. "Despite the Sluggish Economy, Welfare Rolls Actually Shrank." *New York Times* (March 22).

Pear, Robert. 2004c. "Medicare Official Testifies on Cost Figures." *New York Times* (March 25).

Pear, Robert. 2004d. "Drug Law Is Seen Causing Big Drop in Retiree Plans." *New York Times* (July 14).

Pear, Robert. 2005. "Estimate Revives Fight on Medicare Costs." *New York Times* (February 10).

Pear, Robert, and Edmund Andrews. 2004. "White House Says Congressional Estimate of New Medicare Costs Was Too Low." *New York Times* (February 2).

Pear, Robert, and Robin Toner. 2003. "A Final Push in Congress." *New York Times* (November 23).

Pechman, Joseph A. 1990. "The Future of the Income Tax." *American Economic Review* (March): 1–20.

Peterson, Peter G. 1999. *Gray Dawn*. New York: Times Books.

Peterson, Peter G. 2004. *Running on Empty*. New York: Farrar, Straus and Giroux.

Peterson, Willis L. 1979. "International Farm Prices and the Social Cost of Cheap Food Policies." *American Journal of Agricultural Economics* (February): 12–21.

Pierce, James L. 1979. "The Political Economy of Arthur Burns." *Journal of Finance* (May): 485–504.

Pinkerton, James. 1992. "Life in Bush Hell." *New Republic* (December 14): 22–27.

Pinkerton, James. 2003. "Bush's War Strategy Looks Like a Steal of Nixon's." *Newsday* (November 18).

Plender, John. 2004. "Counting the Cost of Globalization: How Companies Keep Tax Low and Stay within the Law." *Financial Times* (July 21).

Podhoretz, John. 1993. *Hell of a Ride: Backstage at the White House Follies, 1989–1993*. New York: Simon & Schuster.

Podhoretz, John. 2003a. "Big Gov't Bush." *New York Post* (September 3).

Podhoretz, John. 2003b. "Dems Strike Back." *New York Post* (December 9).

Podhoretz, John. 2005. "2nd Term Disease." *New York Post* (July 15).

Politi, James, Adrian Michaels, and David Wighton. 2004. "Governance 'Burden' Taking Its Toll." *Financial Times* (May 14).

Pollin, Robert. 2003. *Contours of Descent*. New York: Verso.

Ponnuru, Ramesh. 1999. "A Conservative No More." *National Review* (October 11): 34–38.

Ponnuru, Ramesh. 2003. "Swallowed By Leviathan." *National Review* (September 29): 30-33.

Poole, William. 1979. "Burnsian Monetary Policy: Eight Years of Progress?" *Journal of Finance* (May): 473–84.

Porter, Roger. 1983. "Economic Advice To the President: From Eisenhower To Reagan." *Political Science Quarterly* (fall): 403–26.

Porter, Roger. 1997. "Presidents and Economists: The Council of Economic Advisers." *American Economic Review* (May): 103–106.

Powell, Jim. 2000. *The Triumph of Liberty*. New York: Free Press.

Powell, Jim. 2005. *Wilson's War*. New York: Crown Forum.

Power, Stephen, and Susan Carey. 2002. "Should U.S. Prop Up United?" *Wall Street Journal* (August 5).

Power, Stephen, and Jacob Schlesinger. 2002. "Bush's Rules Czar Brings Long Knife To New Regulations." *Wall Street Journal* (June 12).

Pozen Robert. 2004. "How to Escape from an American Listing." *Financial Times* (February 13).

Public Citizen. 2001. *Blind Faith: How Deregulation and Enron's Influence over Government Looted Billions from Americans* (December).

Radelet, Steven. 2003. "Bush and Foreign Aid." *Foreign Affairs* (September–October): 104–17.

Radosh, Ronald. 1975. *Prophets on the Right*. New York: Simon & Schuster.

Rajan, Raghuram G., and Luigi Zingales. 2003. *Saving Capitalism from the Capitalists*. New York: Crown Business.

Raspberry, William. 2001. "Better, Simpler, Fairer." *Washington Post* (February 12).

Rauch, Jonathan. 1994. "What Nixon Wrought." *New Republic* (May 16): 28–31.

Rauch, Jonathan. 2003. "The Accidental Radical." *National Journal* (July 26): 2404–10.

Rauch, Jonathan. 2004a. "Do These Deficits Look Familiar? Meet Richard Milhous Bush." *National Journal* (January 24): 218–19.

Rauch, Jonathan. 2004b. "Divided We Stand." *Atlantic Monthly* (October): 39–40.

Rawls, John. 1999. *A Theory of Justice,* rev. ed. Cambridge: Harvard University Press.

Razin, Assaf, and Efraim Sadka. 2004. "Capital Income Taxation in the Globalized World." National Bureau of Economic Research Working Paper No. 10630 (July).

Reagan, Ronald. 1982. *Public Papers of the Presidents of the United States: Ronald Reagan, 1981.* Washington: U.S. Government Printing Office.

Reagan, Ronald. 1984. *Public Papers of the Presidents of the United States: Ronald Reagan, 1983.* Washington: U.S. Government Printing Office.

Reagan, Ronald. 1988. *Public Papers of the Presidents of the United States: Ronald Reagan, 1985.* Washington: U.S. Government Printing Office.

Reagan, Ronald. 1989. *Public Papers of the Presidents of the United States: Ronald Reagan, 1987.* Washington: U.S. Government Printing Office.

Reagan, Ronald. 1993. "Hurry Up and Wait." *Wall Street Journal* (July 8).

Reddy, Anitha. 2001. "Retailers Zero in on Tax Refund Checks." *Washington Post* (July 13).

Reed, Bruce. 2004. "Bush's War against Wonks." *Washington Monthly* (March): 14–16.

Reich, Robert. 1999. "Use Budget Surpluses for People's Real Needs." *Los Angeles Times* (January 22).

Reich, Robert. 2000. "Coolidge's Democratic Disciples." *New York Times* (February 8).

Reich, Robert. 2001. "Subsidies Aren't a Wartime Necessity." *Wall Street Journal* (October 16).

Reid, T. R. 2005. "GOP Governors Fight Tax Limits." *Washington Post* (March 27).

Reinhardt, Uwe. 2001. Letter to the Editor. *Wall Street Journal* (March 12).

Republican Study Committee. 2003. *Letter to Dennis Hastert, Tom DeLay, and Roy Blunt* (October 29).

Republican Study Committee. 2005. *RSC Budget Options, 2005: Operation Offset* (September 21).

Reston, James. 1972. "The Conservative Tide." *New York Times* (November 1).

Revkin, Andrew C. 2002. "U.S. Sees Problems in Climate Change." *New York Times* (June 3).

Revkin, Andrew C. 2004. "Bush vs. the Laureates: How Science Became a Partisan Issue." *New York Times* (October 19).

Reynolds, Alan. 2001. "Tax Cut 2001: A Little Bang for a Lot of Buck." *Wall Street Journal* (May 30).

Reynolds, Alan. 2003. "Tax Cut Priorities." *Washington Times* (May 11).

Reynolds, Alan. 2004. "Fed Tutorial of 1972." *Washington Times* (May 16).

Ribstein, Larry E. 2002. "Market vs. Regulatory Responses To Corporate Fraud: A Critique of the Sarbanes-Oxley Act of 2002." *Journal of Corporation Law* (fall): 1–67.

Ribstein, Larry E. 2003. "Bubble Laws." *Houston Law Review* (spring): 77–97.

Rich, Jennifer L. 2002. "U.S. Admits That Politics Was Behind Steel Tariffs." *New York Times* (March 14).

Richardson, Valerie. 2004. "Aliens Program Costs Bush." *Washington Times* (August 3).

Riedl, Brian. 2002. "How Washington Increased Spending by Nearly $800 Billion in Just Four Years." Heritage Foundation Backgrounder No. 1581 (September 4).

Riedl, Brian. 2003. "The Quiet Earthquake in Spending." Heritage Foundation Commentary (November 23).

Riekhof, Gina M., and Michael E. Sykuta. 2004. "Regulating Wine by Mail." *Regulation* (fall): 30–36.

Roberts, Paul Craig. 1987a. "How the Defeat of Inflation Wrecked the U.S. Budget." *Los Angeles Times* (January 27).

Roberts, Paul Craig. 2000. "What Really Happened in 1981." *Independent Review* (fall): 279–81.

Roberts, Paul Craig. 2005. "Private Accounts: Right Idea, Wrong Time." *Business-Week* (March 7): 39–40.

Rockoff, Hugh. 1984. *Drastic Measures: A History of Wage and Price Controls in the United States.* New York: Cambridge University Press.

Roe, Mark J. 1994. *Strong Managers, Weak Owners.* Princeton: Princeton University Press.

Rogers, David. 2001. "House GOP Undoes Bush Budget Cuts." *Wall Street Journal* (June 7).

Rogers, David. 2002. "Bush Budget Chief Fails to Cut Capitol Hill's Appetite for Pork." *Wall Street Journal* (January 22).

Rogers, David. 2004. "Medicare Actuary Reveals E-Mail Warning." *Wall Street Journal* (March 18).

Romano, Roberta. 2005. "The Sarbanes-Oxley Act and the Making of Quack Corporate Governance." *Yale Law Journal* (May): 1521–1611.

Rose, Sanford. 1974. "The Agony of the Federal Reserve." *Fortune* (July): 90–93, 180–90.

Rosenbaum, David. 2002a. "Official Forced to Step Down after Testifying on Budget Cuts." *New York Times* (March 7).

Rosenbaum, David. 2002b. "Wary Eye on Wall St. and Washington: No Strong Voice Is Heard on Bush's Economic Team." *New York Times* (July 21).

Rosenbaum, David E. 2003a. "Embracing Deficits to Deter Spending." *New York Times* (February 9).

Rosenbaum, David E. 2003b. "Spending Discipline Proves Unfashionable This Year." *New York Times* (November 25).

Rosenthal, Andrew. 1992. "Tax Increase Was Mistake, Bush Admits." *Wall Street Journal* (June 26).

Rossum, Ralph A. 2001. *Federalism, the Supreme Court, and the Seventeenth Amendment: The Irony of Constitutional Democracy.* Lanham, MD: Lexington Books.

Rubin, Robert E., and Jacob Weisberg. 2003. *In an Uncertain World.* New York: Random House.

Rutenberg, Jim. 2004. "The Right Has Begun Standing a Little Less Behind Bush." *New York Times* (February 10).

Sabelhaus, John. 1993. "What Is the Distributional Burden of Taxing Consumption?" *National Tax Journal* (September): 331–44.

Saddler, Jeanne. 1991. "Small-Business Owners Feel They've Been Betrayed." *Wall Street Journal* (November 20).

Safire, William. 1975. *Before the Fall.* New York: Belmont Tower Books.

Safire, William. 2003. "Nixon on Bush." *New York Times* (July 7).

Sager, Ryan. 2005a. "Cuckolded by the Conservative State." www.techcentralstation.com (April 1).

Sager, Ryan. 2005b. "GOP: Party of Bloat." *New York Post* (May 8).

Salins, Peter D., and Gerard C. S. Mildner. 1992. *Scarcity by Design: The Legacy of New York City's Housing Policies.* Cambridge: Harvard University Press.

Samuel, Terence. 2004. "Spending Spree." *U.S. News & World Report* (January 26): 21–22.

Samuelson, Robert J. 1992. "Hey, Vote for Me." *Washington Post* (October 28).

Samuelson, Robert J. 2003. "Bush, Nixon and History." *Newsweek* (October 20): 38.

Sanger, David E. 2003. "Mr. Deregulation's Regulations: Stuff of Politics, Mad Cows and Dietary Pills to Die For." *New York Times* (December 31).

Satel, Sally. 2004. "Science Fiction." *Weekly Standard* (April 12 & 19): 15–16.

Sawicky, Max. 2003. "Don't Kid Yourself—Whoever Wins, Taxes Will Rise." *Charlotte Observer* (December 17).

Scarborough, Joe. 2004. "Pork." *Wall Street Journal* (September 23).

Scheiber, Noam. 2002. "Numbers Game: Bush's War on Honest Economics." *New Republic* (May 6): 21–24.

Scheiber, Noam. 2003a. "Buried Treasury: Is Snow Worse than O'Neill?" *New Republic* (August 11): 17–21.

Scheiber, Noam. 2003b. "Loose Change." *New Republic* (December 22): 8.

Scheiber, Noam. 2004. "Out of Depth: Can Greg Mankiw Survive Politics?" *New Republic* (April 12 & 19): 14–17.

Schlesinger, Arthur. 1959. *The Coming of the New Deal*. Boston: Houghton Mifflin.

Schlesinger, Arthur. 1983. "Should Conservatives Embrace Big Government?" *Wall Street Journal* (February 3).

Schlesinger, Arthur. 1997. "Rating the Presidents: Washington to Clinton." *Political Science Quarterly* (summer): 179–90.

Schlesinger, Jacob. 1999. "Bush's Economic Guru Talks Like a Bear." *Wall Street Journal* (December 6).

Schmalz, Jeffrey. 1992. "Words on Bush's Lips in '88 Now Stick in Voters' Craw." *New York Times* (June 14).

Schmitt, Eric. 2001. "Bush Aides Weigh Legalizing Status of Mexicans in U.S." *New York Times* (July 15).

Schmitt, Eric, and Robert Pear. 2004. "Plan Omits Costs in Iraq and Afghanistan." *New York Times* (February 3).

Schneider, Friedrich, and Dominik Enste. 2002. *The Shadow Economy:An International Survey*. New York: Cambridge University Press.

Schneider, William. 2005. "What Political Dividend?" *National Journal* (January 15): 154.

Schultz, Ellen E., and Theo Francis. 2004. "How Cuts in Retiree Benefits Fatten Companies' Bottom Lines." *Wall Street Journal* (March 16).

Schultze, Charles. 2004. "Offshoring, Import Competition, and the Jobless Recovery." Brookings Institution Policy Brief No. 136 (August).

Schultze, Charles. 2005. "2005: A Space Odious." *Washington Examiner* (June 9).

Senate Committee on Governmental Affairs. 1989. *Nomination of Richard G. Darman*. 101st Congress, 1st session. Washington: U.S. Government Printing Office.

Senate Library. 2001. *Presidential Vetoes, 1989–2000*. Senate Publication 107-10. Washington: U.S. Government Printing Office.

Shaffer, Butler. 1997. *In Restraint of Trade:The Business Campaign against Competition, 1918–1938*. London: Associated University Presses.

Shah, Angela, and David Jackson. 2005. "Treasury Strapped for Clout." *Dallas Morning News* (April 24).

Shane, Scott. 2005. "Since 2001, Sharp Increases in the Number of Documents Classified by the Government." *New York Times* (July 3).

Shapiro, Matthew D., and Joel Slemrod. 2003a. "Consumer Response To Tax Rebates." *American Economic Review* (March): 381–96.

Shapiro, Matthew D., and Joel Slemrod. 2003b. "Did the 2001 Tax Rebate Stimulate Spending? Evidence from Taxpayer Surveys." In *Tax Policy and the Economy*, vol. 17, ed. James M. Poterba, pp. 83–109. Cambridge: MIT Press.

Shapiro, Robert J., and Chris J. Soares. 1997. "Cut and Invest to Grow." Policy Report No. 26, Progressive Policy Institute (July).

Shaviro, Daniel. 2004a. "The New Age of Big Government." *Regulation* (spring): 36–42.

Shaviro, Daniel. 2004b. "Replacing the Income Tax with a Progressive Consumption Tax." *Tax Notes* (April 5): 91–113.

Shear, Michael, and Chris Jenkins. 2004. "Va. Passes Landmark Increases in Taxes." *Washington Post* (April 28).

Shirouzu, Norihiko. 2003. "China, in 'Buy American' Flurry, To Set Deals for Cars, Jet Engines." *Wall Street Journal* (November 12).

Shlaes, Amity. 2001. "O'Neill Lays Out Radical Vision for Tax." *Financial Times* (May 19).

Shlaes, Amity. 2004a. "A Republican Sacred Cow Is Led To Slaughter." *Financial Times* (January 5).

Shlaes, Amity. 2004b. "The Right Kind of Uncertainty." *Financial Times* (November 9).

Shoup, Carl S. 1973. "Factors Bearing on an Assumed Choice Between a Federal Retail-Sales Tax and a Federal Value-Added Tax." In *Broad-Based Taxes: New Options and Sources*, pp. 215–26. Baltimore: Johns Hopkins University Press.

Simendinger, Alexis. 2003. "The Broker's Burden." *National Journal* (April 26): 1306–1308.

Simon, William E. 1978. *A Time for Truth*. New York: McGraw-Hill.

Simons, Henry C. 1938. *Personal Income Taxation*. Chicago: University of Chicago Press.

Simons, Henry C. 1950. *Federal Tax Reform*. Chicago: University of Chicago Press.

Simpson, Glenn R. 2002. "Deals That Took Enron Under Had Many Supporters." *Wall Street Journal* (April 10).

Singer, Paul. 2005. "By the Horns." *National Journal* (March 26): 898–904.

Skinner, Kiron K., Annelise Anderson, and Martin Anderson. 2001. *Reagan in His Own Hand*. New York: Free Press.

Skinner, Kiron K., Annelise Anderson, and Martin Anderson. 2003. *Reagan: A Life in Letters*. New York: Free Press.

Skinner, Kiron K., Annelise Anderson, and Martin Anderson. 2004. *Reagan's Path to Victory*. New York: Free Press.

Skrzycki, Cindy. 2000. "The Regulators: The Party's Almost Over." *Washington Post* (November 7).

Slemrod, Joel. 1996. "Which Is the Simplest Tax System of Them All?" In *Economic Effects of Fundamental Tax Reform*, ed. Henry J. Aaron and William G. Gale, pp. 355–91. Washington: Brookings Institution.

Slemrod, Joel. 1997. "Deconstructing the Income Tax." *American Economic Review* (May): 151–55.

Slivinski, Stephen. 2001. "The Corporate Welfare Budget: Bigger Than Ever." Cato Institute Policy Analysis No. 415 (October 10).

Slivinski, Stephen. 2005. "The Grand Old Spending Party: How Republicans Became Big Spenders." Cato Institute Policy Analysis No. 543 (May 3).

Small, Melvin. 1999. *The Presidency of Richard Nixon.* Lawrence: University Press of Kansas.

Smith, Adam. 1937 (1776). *The Wealth of Nations.* New York: Modern Library.

Smith, Dan Throop. 1965. "The Value-Added Tax as an Alternative To the Corporate Income Tax." *National Tax Association Proceedings, 1964,* pp. 424–30.

Smith, Daniel. 2005. "Political Science." *New York Times Magazine* (September 4): 37–41.

Smith, Vernon L. 1963. "Tax Depreciation Policy and Investment Theory." *International Economic Review* (January): 80–91.

Snee, John, and Mary Ross. 1978. "Social Security Amendments of 1977: Legislative History and Summary of Provisions." *Social Security Bulletin* (March): 3–20.

Solomon, Deborah. 2005. "Donaldson Ends an SEC Tenure Marked by Active Regulation." *Wall Street Journal* (June 2).

Solomon, Ira, and Mark E. Peecher. 2004. "SOX 404—A Billion Here, a Billion There . . ." *Wall Street Journal* (November 9).

Starobin, Paul. 1995. "No Returns." *National Journal* (March 18): 666–71.

Starr, Paul. 2005. "Winning Cases, Losing Voters." *New York Times* (January 26).

Stein, Herbert. 1984. *Presidential Economics.* New York: Simon & Schuster.

Stein, Herbert. 1991. "My Price-Control Days with Nixon." *Wall Street Journal* (August 16).

Stein, Herbert. 1996. "Wage and Price Controls: 25 Years Later." *Wall Street Journal* (August 15).

Steindel, Charles. 2001. "The Effect of Tax Changes on Consumer Spending." *Current Issues in Economics and Finance,* Federal Reserve Bank of New York (December).

Steinfels, Peter. 1979. *The Neoconservatives: The Men Who Are Changing America's Politics.* New York: Simon & Schuster.

Stern, Philip M. 1964. *The Great Treasury Raid.* New York: Random House.

Stevenson, Richard. 2001. "White House Balks at Further Bailouts." *New York Times* (October 17).

Stevenson, Richard. 2002. "Enron Received Many Loans From U.S. for Foreign Projects During the 1990s." *New York Times* (February 21).

Stevenson, Richard. 2004. "Conservative Republicans Push for Slowdown in U.S. Spending." *New York Times* (January 22).

Stevenson, Richard. 2005. "Bush Names Longtime Friend to Head Economic Council." *New York Times* (January 11).

Stigler, George. 1975. *The Citizen and the State*. Chicago: University of Chicago Press.

Stiglitz, Joseph. 2003. *The Roaring Nineties*. New York: W. W. Norton.

Stockfisch, J. A. 1985. "Value-Added Taxes and the Size of Government: Some Evidence." *National Tax Journal* (December): 547–52.

Stolberg, Sheryl Gay, and David D. Kirkpatrick. 2005. "G.O.P. Senators Balk at Tax Cuts in Bush's Budget." *New York Times* (March 10).

Stolberg, Sheryl Gay, and Robert Pear. 2004. "Mysterious Fax Adds To Intrigue Over Drug Bill." *New York Times* (March 18).

Strine, Leo. 2005. "Sarbanes-Oxley's Creeping Intrusion." *Financial Times* (July 6).

Stuart, Charles. 1984. "Welfare Costs per Dollar of Additional Tax Revenue in the United States." *American Economic Review* (June): 352–60.

Sugin, Linda. 2004. "Theories of Distributive Justice and Limitations on Taxation: What Rawls Demands from Tax Systems." *Fordham Law Review* (April): 1991–2014.

Sullivan, Andrew. 2000. "Far Gone." *New Republic* (November 6): 8.

Sullivan, Andrew. 2004. "If It Could Happen to Churchill . . ." *Time* (March 8): 88.

Sullivan, Andrew. 2005a. "Bush's Triumph Conceals the Great Conservative Crack-Up." *London Times* (March 20).

Sullivan, Andrew. 2005b. "How Fundamentalism Is Splitting the GOP." *New Republic* (May 2 & 9): 16–23.

Sullivan, Martin. 1999. "Taxes in Texas: Bush's Record." *Tax Notes* (December 27): 1622–26.

Sullivan, Martin. 2004. "Data Show Dramatic Shift of Profits to Tax Havens." *Tax Notes* (September 13): 1190–1200.

Super, David A. 2004. "The Political Economy of Entitlement." *Columbia Law Review* (April): 633–729.

Surowiecki, James. 2004. "Hail To the Geek." *New Yorker* (April 19 & 26): 70.

Surrey, Stanley S. 1973. *Pathways To Tax Reform*. Cambridge: Harvard University Press.

Suskind, Ron. 2003. "Why Are These Men Laughing?" *Esquire* (January): 96–105.

Suskind, Ron. 2004a. *The Price of Loyalty*. New York: Simon & Schuster.

Suskind, Ron. 2004b. "Without a Doubt." *New York Times Magazine* (October 17): 44–51, 54, 102, 106.

Suskind, Ron. 2004c. "The Cabinet of Incuriosities." *New York Times* (December 28).

Sustainable Energy & Economy Network. 2002. *Enron's Pawns: How Public Institutions Bankrolled Enron's Globalization Game*. Washington: Institute for Policy Studies (March 22).

Swarns, Rachel L. 2004. "Outcry on Right over Bush Plan on Immigration." *New York Times* (February 21).

Taft, Robert A. 1951. *A Foreign Policy for Americans*. New York: Doubleday.

Tait, Alan A. 1988. *Value Added Tax: International Practice and Problems*. Washington: International Monetary Fund.

Tampa Tribune. 2004. "Why We Cannot Endorse President Bush for Re-Election" (October 19).

Tanenhaus, Sam. 2003. "Is Bush Conservative Enough?" *Los Angeles Times* (July 22).

Tanzi, Vito. 1995. *Taxation in an Integrating World*. Washington: Brookings Institution.

Tanzi, Vito. 2000. "Globalization and the Future of Social Protection." International Monetary Fund Working Paper No. 00/12 (January).

Taylor, Jerry. 2002. "Enron Was No Friend To Free Markets." *Wall Street Journal* (January 21).

Taylor, Timothy. 2004. "The Economy in Perspective." *Public Interest* (fall): 85–99.

Tempalski, Jerry. 2003. "Revenue Effects of Major Tax Bills." Office of Tax Analysis Working Paper No. 81, U.S. Treasury Department (July).

Thernstrom, Stephan, and Abigail Thernstrom. 1997. *America in Black and White*. New York: Simon & Schuster.

Thomas, Rich. 1992. "One Issue, Two Fantasies." *Newsweek* (September 7): 32.

Thornton, Emily. 2004. "A Little Privacy, Please." *Business Week* (May 24): 74–75.

Thuronyi, Victor. 1990. "The Concept of Income." *Tax Law Review* (fall): 45–105.

Time. 1965. "U.S. Business in 1965" (December 31): 64–67.

Touré, Amadou Toumani, and Blaise Compaoré. 2003. "Your Farm Subsidies Are Strangling Us." *New York Times* (July 11).

Trueheart, Charles. 1991. "Buchanan, on the Firing Line; Buckley Calls on Candidate to Recant Antisemitic Statements." *Washington Post* (December 12).

Tucker, Sundeep, and Andrew Parker. 2005. "Sarbanes-Oxley Law Goes Too Far, Admits One of Its Architects." *Financial Times* (July 8).

Tumulty, Karen, Mark Thompson, and Mike Allen. 2005. "How Many More Mike Browns Are Out There?" *Time* (October 3): 49–54.

Ture, Norman. 1974. "Tax Treatment of Savings and Capital Recovery." *George Washington Law Review* (March): 501–15.

Unger, Irwin. 1996. *The Best of Intentions.* New York: Doubleday.

U.S. Department of Commerce. 2001. *The Effect of Imports of Iron Ore and Semi-Finished Steel on the National Security.* Bureau of Export Administration (October).

U.S. Department of Health & Human Services. 2004. *Statement of Dara Corrigan, Acting Principal Deputy Inspector General, Department of Health and Human Services, on Thomas Scully and Richard Foster Investigation.* Office of Inspector General (July 6).

U.S. General Accounting Office. 1992. *Prescription Drugs: Companies Typically Charge More in the United States Than in Canada.* Report GAO/HRD-92-110 (September).

U.S. General Accounting Office. 1993a. *Implications of Replacing the Corporate Income Tax with a Consumption Tax.* Report GGD-93-55 (May).

U.S. General Accounting Office. 1993b. *Value-Added Tax: Administrative Costs Vary with Complexity and Number of Businesses.* Report GAO/GGD-93-78 (May).

U.S. General Accounting Office. 2000. *Supporting Sugar Prices Has Increased Users' Costs While Benefiting Producers.* Report GAO/RCED-00-126 (June).

U.S. General Accounting Office. 2001. *Tax Administration: Interim Report on Advance Tax Refunds.* Report GAO-02-257 (December).

U.S. General Accounting Office. 2004. *Implementation of the Terrorism Risk Insurance Act of 2002.* Report GAO-04-307 (April).

U.S. Government Accountability Office. 2005a. *Twenty-first Century Challenges: Reexamining the Base of the Federal Government.* Report GAO-05-325SP (February).

U.S. Government Accountability Office. 2005b. *Summary of Estimates of the Costs of the Federal Tax System.* Report GAO-05-878 (August).

U.S. Government Accountability Office. 2005c. *Issues and Effects of Implementing the Continued Dumping and Subsidy Offset Act.* Report GAO-05-979 (September).

U.S. International Trade Commission. 1995. *The Economic Effects of Antidumping and Countervailing Duty Orders and Suspension Agreements.* Publication 2900 (June).

U.S. International Trade Commission. 1998. *Implications for U.S. Trade and Competitiveness of a Broad-Based Consumption Tax.* Publication 3110 (June).

U.S. International Trade Commission. 2001. *Steel.* Publication 3479 (December).

U.S. International Trade Commission. 2003. *Steel-Consuming Industries: Competitive Conditions with Respect To Steel Safeguard Measures.* Publication 3632 (September).

U.S. Treasury Department. 1977. *Blueprints for Basic Tax Reform.* Washington: U.S. Government Printing Office.

U.S. Treasury Department. 1982. *United States Participation in the Multilateral Development Banks in the 1980s.* Washington: U.S. Government Printing Office.

U.S. Treasury Department. 1984. *Tax Reform for Fairness, Simplicity, and Economic Growth,* 3 vols. Washington: U.S. Government Printing Office.

U.S. Treasury Department. 1992. *Integration of the Individual and Corporate Tax Systems: Taxing Business Income Only Once.* Washington: U.S. Government Printing Office.

University of Michigan. 2001. News Release (October 9).

VandeHei, Jim. 2005a. "Blueprint Calls for Bigger, More Powerful Government." *Washington Post* (February 9).

VandeHei, Jim. 2005b. "Tax Cuts Lose Spot on GOP Agenda." *Washington Post* (March 7).

VandeHei, Jim. 2005c. "Business Sees Gain in GOP Takeover." *Washington Post* (March 27).

Vatter, Harold G. 1963. *The U.S. Economy in the 1950s: An Economic History.* Chicago: University of Chicago Press.

Vedder, Richard, Lowell Gallaway, and Christopher Frenze. 1991. *Taxes and Deficits: New Evidence.* Washington: Joint Economic Committee.

Vernon, John A. 2002–2003. "Drug Research and Price Controls." *Regulation* (winter): 22–25.

Vernon, John A. 2004. "New Evidence on Drug Price Controls." *Regulation* (fall): 13–14.

Vickrey, William. 1993. "Today's Task for Economists." *American Economic Review* (March): 1–10.

Vieth, Warren. 2005. "A Traveling Salesman Far from Treasury." *Los Angeles Times* (May 2).

Vietor, Richard H. K. 1990. "Contrived Competition: Airline Regulation and Deregulation, 1925–1988." *Business History Review* (spring): 61–108.

Viner, Jacob. 1923. *Dumping: A Problem in International Trade.* Chicago: University of Chicago Press.

Viner, Jacob. 1950. *The Customs Union Issue.* New York: Carnegie Endowment for International Peace.

Vogan, Christine R. 1996. "Pollution Abatement and Control Expenditures, 1972–94." *Survey of Current Business* (September): 48–67.

Vogel, Thomas T. 1992. "Bonds Fall on Outlook for Clinton." *Wall Street Journal* (October 21).

Von Furstenberg, George M. 1991. "Taxes: A License to Spend or a Late Charge?" In *The Great Fiscal Experiment,* ed. Rudolph Penner, pp. 155–91. Washington: Urban Institute.

Von Furstenberg, George M., R. Jeffery Green, and Jin-Ho Jeong. 1985. "Have Taxes Led Government Expenditures? The United States as a Test Case." *Journal of Public Policy* (August): 321–48.

Von Furstenberg, George M., R. Jeffery Green, and Jin-Ho Jeong. 1986. "Tax and Spend, or Spend and Tax?" *Review of Economics and Statistics* (May): 179–88.

Wall Street Journal. 1978a. "Mr. Mondale in the Wings" (January 4).

Wall Street Journal. 1978b. "Schmidt Says Germany Won't Stimulate Economy as U.S. Wants; Inflation Feared" (January 20).

Wall Street Journal. 1985. "Excerpts from the Interview with Ronald Reagan" (February 8).

Wall Street Journal. 2001. "Fiscal Primer" (September 28).

Wall Street Journal. 2002. "Let Bush Be Bush" (April 17).

Wall Street Journal. 2003a. "The GOP's Spending Spree" (November 25).

Wall Street Journal. 2003b. "Lessons of Steel" (December 2).

Wall Street Journal. 2004a. "GOP Spending Spree" (January 20).

Wall Street Journal. 2004b. "Bad Medicare Math" (March 17).

Wall Street Journal. 2005a. "Hubbard's Council" (January 11).

Wall Street Journal. 2005b. "The Tax That France Built" (March 4).

Walsh, Kenneth T. 1991. "George Bush's Idea-Free Zone." *U.S. News & World Report* (January 14): 34–35.

Washington, Wayne. 2004. "Republicans Waiting for Bush to Sharpen His Focus." *Boston Globe* (February 20).

Washington Post. 2002. "Mr. Bush and Foreign Aid" (March 15).

Washington Post. 2004a. "Mr. O'Neill and Iraq" (January 15).

Washington Post. 2004b. "Mr. Mankiw Is Right" (February 13).

Washington Post. 2005. "Big-Government Conservatives" (August 15).

Weidenbaum, Murray. 1986. "The Role of the President's Council of Economic Advisers: Theory and Reality." *Presidential Studies Quarterly* (summer): 460–66.

Weisberg, Jacob. 2005. "Interest-Group Conservatism." www.slate.com (May 4).

Weisman, Jonathan. 2002. "Treasury Departures Hurt Staff Morale." *Washington Post* (August 23).

Weisman, Jonathan. 2003a. "Government Outgrows Cap Set by President." *Washington Post* (November 12).

Weisman, Jonathan. 2003b. "Alarms Sounded on Cost of GOP Bills." *Washington Post* (November 24).

Weisman, Jonathan. 2003c. "Bush Economic Aide Says Government Lacks Vision." *Washington Post* (December 13).

Weisman, Jonathan. 2004. "Bush, Adviser Assailed for Stance on 'Offshoring' Jobs." *Washington Post* (February 11).

Weisman, Jonathan. 2005a. "Dropping Report's Iraq Chapter Was Unusual, Economists Say." *Washington Post* (February 23).

Weisman, Jonathan. 2005b. "Conservatives Splitting on Social Security." *Washington Post* (March 29).

Weisman, Jonathan. 2005c. "Lawmakers Keeping Treasury Depleted." *Washington Post* (July 20).

Weisman, Jonathan. 2005d. "In Congress, the GOP Embraces Its Spending Side." *Washington Post* (August 4).

Wells, Wyatt C. 1994. *Economist in an Uncertain World: Arthur F. Burns and the Federal Reserve, 1970–1978.* New York: Columbia University Press.

Wessel, David. 1992. "Economic Security Council Stirs Debate." *Wall Street Journal* (November 10).

Wessel, David. 1993. "Clinton 'Economic Stimulus' Would Aid Projects Democrats Have Long Favored." *Wall Street Journal* (February 23).

Wessel, David. 2003. "There Is No Denying the Math: Taxes Will Rise." *Wall Street Journal* (November 20).

Wessel, David. 2005. "Bush Budget Aide Weighs Cut in Benefit Outlays." *Wall Street Journal* (September 26).

Wessel, David, and Michel McQueen. 1992. "In a Three-Way Race, Conservative Criticism Could Hurt Bush Badly." *Wall Street Journal* (July 6).

Wessel, David, and Gerald Seib. 1992. "Comments on Bush's Economic Team Spur Purge Rumors." *Wall Street Journal* (October 13).

White House. 1985. *The President's Tax Proposals To the Congress for Fairness, Growth, and Simplicity.* Washington: U.S. Government Printing Office.

Wighton, David, and James Harding. 2004. "Wall St. Republicans Grow Cool on Bush's Campaign." *Financial Times* (August 27).

Wildavsky, Aaron. 1980. *How to Limit Government Spending.* Berkeley: University of California Press.

Wildavsky, Aaron. 1991. "A President without Policies." *Wall Street Journal* (November 25).

Will, George. 1992a. "Vacuum vs. Resentment." *Newsweek* (March 9): 74.

Will, George. 1992b. "Twilight along the Potomac?" *Newsweek* (October 19): 80.

Will, George. 2002a. "Virtue at Last! (In November)." *Newsweek* (February 25): 64.

Will, George. 2002b. "Bending for Steel." *Washington Post* (March 7).

Will, George. 2002c. " 'Reforming' Free Speech." *Washington Post* (March 30).

Will, George. 2003a. "Campaign by Tax Cut." *Washington Post* (June 1).

Will, George. 2003b. "A Questionable Kind of Conservatism." *Washington Post* (July 24).

Will, George. 2004. "Contemptuous Collaboration." *Washington Post* (August 31).

Wolffe, Richard. 2000. "Bush Admits Dispute with Greenspan on Tax Cuts." *Financial Times* (January 25).

Wonacott, Peter. 2002. "Trade Chief Steels China for Tariffs." *Wall Street Journal* (April 11).

Wood, Donna J. 1985. "The Strategic Use of Public Policy: Business Support for the 1906 Food and Drug Act." *Business History Review* (autumn): 403–32.

Woodward, Bob. 1992a. "The Origin of the Tax Pledge." *Washington Post* (October 4).

Woodward, Bob. 1992b. "No-Tax Vow Scuttled Anti-Deficit Mission." *Washington Post* (October 5).

Woodward, Bob. 1992c. "Primary Heat Turned Deal into a 'Mistake.'" *Washington Post* (October 6).

Woodward, Bob. 1992d. "The President's Key Men: Splintered Trio, Splintered Policy." *Washington Post* (October 7).

Woodward, Bob. 1994. *The Agenda*. New York: Simon & Schuster.

Woolley, John T. 1984. *Monetary Politics: The Federal Reserve and the Politics of Monetary Policy*. New York: Cambridge University Press.

Wreszin, Michael. 1971. *The Superfluous Anarchist: Albert Jay Nock*. Providence: Brown University Press.

Yago, Glenn. 1991. *Junk Bonds: How High Yield Securities Restructured Corporate America*. New York: Oxford University Press.

Yardley, William. 2005. "Connecticut Restores Estate Tax in Move to Balance Budget." *New York Times* (June 8).

Yoo, John. 2005. "What Became of Federalism?" *Los Angeles Times* (June 21).

York, Byron. 2001. "George Bush's House Training." *National Review* (August 20): 17–18.

Zepezauer, Mark. 2004. *Take the Rich Off Welfare*. Cambridge, MA: South End Press.

Zhang, Ivy Xiying. 2005. "Economic Consequences of the Sarbanes-Oxley Act of 2002." AEI-Brookings Joint Center for Regulatory Studies (June).

Zodrow, George R. 1999. "The Sales Tax, the VAT, and Taxes in Between—or, Is the Only Good NRST a 'VAT in Drag'?" *National Tax Journal* (September): 439–42.

Zywicki, Todd J. 1997. "Beyond the Shell and Husk of History: The History of the Seventeenth Amendment and Its Implications for Current Reform Proposals." *Cleveland State Law Review* (No. 2): 165–234.

INDEX

ABC News polls, 13, 75
Abramoff, Jack, 17
Affirmative action, 153, 154
Agricultural subsidies, 19, 86,
 91–92
AIG, 115
Airline industry, post-September 11
 aid package for, 118
Alcoa, 78
Alesina, Alberto, 172
Alternative Minimum Tax (AMT),
 184, 185
Altman, Daniel, 74
American Airlines, 78
American Association of Retired
 Persons (AARP), 75, 80, 81
American Conservative, 173
American Conservative Union,
 12–13
American Institute for International
 Steel, 87
Amtrak, 155
Antle, Jim, 173
Aquaslide 'N' Dive Corporation, 104
Archer, Bill, 55
Armey, Dick, 80
Arrogance of Bush Administration,
 16, 40–41

Arthur Andersen, 111
Atlantic Monthly, 144
Australia
 trade with, 92, 96, 97–98
 VAT in, 187

Baby boomers, retirement of, 167,
 169, 173, 185
Bagehot, Walter, 112
Bahrain, trade with, 97
Baicker, Katherine, 36
Bainbridge, Stephen, 113, 205, 208
Baker, James, 28–29
Bandow, Doug, 13
Barnes, Fred, 11, 92, 132, 134, 200
Barringer, William, 87
Barro, Robert, 57, 165, 203
Bartlett, Roscoe, 65
Bartley, Bob, 49, 53
Bastable, C. F., 87
Baughman, Laura, 88, 90
Becker, Gary S., 165
Bell, Steve, 125
BellSouth, 78
Bentsen, Lloyd, 126
Berle, Adolf, 110
Bernanke, Ben, 36
Bernstein, David, 143

Berthoud, John, 11
Bhagwati, Jagdish, 97
Big business, *see* Corporate interests
Birnbaum, Jeffrey, 38, 173
Blair, Tony, 33, 116
Blinder, Alan, 53
Blodget, Henry, 112
Blumenthal, Sid, 144
Bodman, Samuel, 37
Bolivia, trade with, 97
Boot, Max, 37, 130
Boozman, John, 66
Borjas, George, 206
Boskin, Michael, 23
Botswana, trade with, 97
Bradley, Bill, 178
Brady, Kevin, 66
Brady, Nicholas, 6
Brinkley, Alan, 120
Broder, David, 9–10
Brookhiser, Rick, 43
Brookings Institution, 133, 176
Brown, Michael, 38, 40
Bubbles, economic, 112–13
Buchanan, Patrick, 49, 84
Buckley, William F., 13
Budget Act of 1974, 159
Budgets
  balanced, 158, 159, 164, 173
  Bush Administration, 14, 15, 61,
    102, 131–39, 170, 173, 192, 199,
    200
  Clinton Administration, 13, 18, 51,
    122–30, 140
  deficit reduction, *see* Deficit
    reduction
  Reagan, 133, 138–39, 163
Burgess, Michael, 65
Burns, Arthur, 34, 145, 146, 147
Bush, George H. W., 135

economic policy, disinterest in, 23
  no–new–taxes pledge,
    abandonment of, 7, 48, 49,
    124–25, 171
  presidential election of 1992, 12,
    23, 48, 122–23, 124–25, 156
  Reagan-style conservativism and,
    5–7
  trade policy, 84
Bush, George W., and Bush
  Administration. *See specific policies
  and individuals.*
Business interests, *see* Corporate
  interests
BusinessWeek, 57, 78
Butler, Stuart, 170
Byrd Amendment, 101

Caldwell, Christopher, 143
California, Proposition 13 in,
  160–61
Campaign finance reform, 9, 11,
  12, 17
  backfiring of, 14
Canada
  drug prices in, 79
  trade with, 91, 92, 96
  VAT in, 187
Capital formation, 152
  tax policy and, 47, 58–59, 149,
    177–78
Capital gains tax, 61, 128, 149, 179
Carter, Jimmy, and Carter
  Administration, 58, 84, 123,
    135, 196
Carter, John, 66
Casse, Daniel, 12
Cato Institute, 137
Centers for Medicare & Medicaid
  Services (CMS), 67, 69

Central American Free Trade
  Agreement (CAFTA), 98
Chait, Jonathan, 17
Cheney, Dick, 102, 193
  O'Neill and, 27, 29
Child tax credit, 57, 175, 179
Chile, trade with, 96
China
  exchange rate, 93, 94
  trade with, 89, 93–94
Chocola, Chris, 66
Citizens Against Government Waste,
  131–32, 167
Civil Aeronautics Board, 105
Clarke, Richard, 41
Clinton, Bill, and Clinton
  Administration, 13, 119–20, 135
  budget surpluses, 13, 51, 128, 168
  deficit reduction under, 18, 51,
    122–30, 140
  Enron and, 117, 118
  entitlement programs under, 18,
    127, 128–29
  health plan, 126
  leaking of information by, 5
  Lewinsky scandal, 147, 168
  "midnight regulations," 107
  National Economic Council and,
    23–24
  pork barrel spending during, 131–32
  presidential election of 1992, 23
  Social Security and, 167–68
  tax policy, 49, 51, 126
  trade policy, 84–85
  the veto, use of, 18, 127
  welfare reform, 128–29
Clinton, Hillary, 140
Club for Growth, 13, 199–200
Collender, Stan, 136
Colombia, trade with, 97

Commerce Department, U.S.,
  87–88, 100, 184
Competitive Enterprise Institute, 120
Comprehensive income tax, 176–77,
  178, 180
Concorde, 154
Congress elections of 2002, 9
Congressional Budget and
  Impoundment Control Act of
  1974, 151
Congressional Budget Office, 67,
  68, 69, 91, 167, 173, 185
Connally, John, 146
Conservatism and conservatives,
  1–19
  "big government conservatism,"
    Bush's, 2, 8, 10–11, 14, 15, 17,
    92, 132
  Bush, Sr. and, 5–7, 12
  "compassionate conservatism,"
    7–8, 143, 195
  core beliefs of, 1–2
  foreign policy, 3
  revolt of, 194–96
Conservative Political Action
  Conference, 15
Consolidated Omnibus Budget
  Reconciliation Act of 1985, 163
Constitution, conservative
  interpretation of the, 1
Consumer Product Safety
  Commission, 104, 152, 156
Consumption-based taxation,
  177–78, 179–81
  retail sales tax, 171, 181
  VAT, see Value-added tax (VAT)
Continuing Resolution for 1987, 163
Continuing Resolution for 1988, 163
Contract with America, 120
Cook, Charlie, 74

Coolidge, Calvin, 120
Corporate Alternative Minimum
    Tax, 56, 58
Corporate income tax, 60–61, 128,
    148, 176
  VAT to replace, 183–85
Corporate interests
  "big government conservatism"
    and, 17
  Byrd Amendment and, 101
  Medicare prescription drug bill
    and, 77–78
  Nixon and, 154–55
  pro-business policies of Bush
    Administration, 106, 117–20, 206
  regulation and, 103–6, 107, 120
Corporate scandals, 109–13
Costa Rica, trade with, 96
Council of Economic Advisers
    (CEA), 24, 34–36, 39
  Bush, Sr. and, 23
  Economic Report of the President,
    36, 95
Cowen, Tyler, 130
Crane, Ed, 8, 133
Crane, Phil, 66
Culberson, John, 65
Czech Republic, VAT in, 187

Daniels, Mitch, 171
Darman, Dick, 4–5, 124–25
Dean, Howard, 195
Decision-making process, Bush,
    40–41
Defense Department, U.S., 24,
    87–88
Deficit reduction, 160, 164, 165, 196
  Bush Administration and, 136
  Clinton Administration and, 18,
    51, 122–30, 140

financial crises and demands for,
    171–72
  Johnson Administration and, 148
  Reagan Administration and, 161
  VAT and, 184, 185–86, 188
Deficit Reduction Act of 1984, 163
DeHaven, Tad, 133
DeLay, Tom, 66
Delphi, 78
Denison, Edward, 152
Department of Education, U.S.,
    133
Department of Health & Human
    Services, U.S., 69, 70
De Rugy, Veronique, 133, 138, 199
Deutsche Post, 104
Devine, Don, 11, 12–13
Dewar, Helen, 76
DiIulio, John, 25
Dionne, E. J., 52
Dissent
  Bush Administration's intolerance
    of, 3, 16, 31, 34
  leaks and, 4–5
Dividends, tax treatment of, 35,
    59–62, 179
Doha Round of multilateral trade
    negotiations, 19, 86, 88, 90, 91,
    92, 96, 98
Doherty, Brian, 13
Doherty, Jacqueline, 142
Dole, Bob, 49, 193
Dominican Republic, trade with, 97
Donaldson, William, 114
Donlan, Tom, 55
Dooley, Calvin, 65
Dreher, Rod, 204–5
DRI, 46
Drucker, Peter, 90
Dudley, Susan, 107, 108

"Dumping" and antidumping
  statutes, 93, 98–100, 101

Earned Income Tax Credit, 57
Easterbrook, Gregg, 136
Economic Report of the President,
  36, 95
Ecuador, trade with, 97
Education legislation, Bush's, 8, 9,
  11, 12, 13, 131, 137
Eisenhower, Dwight D., 83, 144–45
  balanced budgets and, 158
Elections, presidential, see
  Presidential elections
Emanuel, Rahm, 76
Energy and Water Appropriations
  Act of 2000, 127
Energy Policy Act of 2005, 12, 63, 203
Enron, 3, 102, 107, 108, 109, 111,
  113, 114, 117–18
Entitlement programs, 167, 173, 198
  under Bush, 18, 137
  under Clinton, 18, 127, 128–29
  deficit reduction and cuts in, 172
  Republican attitude toward, 72–73
Environmental Protection Agency
  (EPA), 151, 153, 155, 156
Ephedra, 109
Esquire, 26
Estate tax, 56, 179
European Union, 90
Evans, Don, 93
Export-Import Bank, 117

Fair, Ray, 14
Fast-track authority, 85, 88, 89–90
Federal Emergency Management
  Agency (FEMA), 38, 204–5
Federalism, 1, 3, 197
  assaults on, 114, 120

Federal Reserve, 36, 62, 102, 126,
  147, 160, 162
  Nixon and, 145–46, 156
Federal Trade Commission, 106
FedEx, 104
Feldstein, Martin, 54–55
Ferguson, Andrew, 12, 15, 58, 136,
  195
Financial Executives International,
  115, 116
Financial Times, 33, 61, 91, 97
Finland, VAT in, 187
Finn, Chester, 131
Fisher, Kenneth, 198–99
527 groups, 14
Flake, Jeff, 138
Flat tax, 49, 50, 62, 177, 178, 180
Foley & Lardner, 115, 116
Forbes, Kristin, 36
Forbes, Randy, 66
Forbes, Steve, 49, 50, 53
Ford, Gerald R., and Ford
  Administration, 12, 27, 135, 159,
  193, 195, 196
Ford Motor Company, 56
Foreign aid, 132–33
Foreign policy, traditional
  conservative, 3
Foreign Sales Corporation, 101
Foster, Richard, 67–68, 69, 70
Franc, Michael, 131
Francois, Joseph, 88, 90
Frank, Robert H., 181
Franks, Trent, 65
Free markets, 2, 13, 105, 106, 119,
  120
Free speech, campaign finance
  reform and, 9, 12, 17
Free trade. See Trade policy,
  international.

Frenze, Christopher, 164
Friedman, Milton, 105, 146, 155, 160–61, 165–66, 167
Friedman, Stephen, 30, 31
Frum, David, 26–27
Fund, John, 14, 205
Furchtgott-Roth, Diana, 187

Galbraith, John Kenneth, 46, 154, 181
Gallaway, Lowell, 164
Gasoline tax, 162
Gattuso, James, 109, 119
General Accounting Office (GAO), 101
General Agreement on Tariffs and Trade (GATT), 83
General Electric, 94, 115, 162
General Motors, 78
George, Henry, 190
George, Robert, 13
Gephardt, Richard, 178, 199
Gigot, Paul, 9, 50
Gingrich, Newt, 74, 172
Gleckman, Howard, 74, 77
Global Crossing, 109
Global warming, 38, 106
Goldberg, Jonah, 195
Gold standard, 146
Goldstein, Amy, 69, 76
Goode, Virgil, 65
Gore, Al, 8, 129
Government, role of
  Bush's "big government conservatism," 2, 8, 10–11, 14, 15, 17, 92, 132, 208
  Clinton Administration and, 129–30
  conservative view of, 1, 2
  liberal view of, 1, 2

Government Accountability Office, U.S., 167, 173
Government Printing Office, 22
Graham, John D., 106, 107
Graham, Lindsey, 76
Gramm, Phil, 113
Great Depression, 82
Greenberg, Hank, 115
Greenspan, Alan, 34, 36, 161, 165, 172
Gridlock, government spending and, 127, 134, 140, 196–99, 200
Guatemala, trade with, 96
Gutierrez, Carlos, 39–40

Haig-Simons definition of income, 176
Hale, David, 37
Hall, Robert, 177
Hall-Rabushka flat tax proposal, 177
Hamilton, Alexander, 86–87
Hart-Teeter poll, 197
Hassett, Kevin, 62, 138, 173
Hastert, Dennis, 95–96
Hastings, Doc, 64
Health Savings Accounts, 201
Highway bill of 2005, 138, 139, 199, 205
Highway Revenue Act of 1982, 162
Hoekstra, Pete, 66
Honduras, trade with, 96
Hook, Janet, 134
Hoover, Herbert, 82
Hostile corporate takeovers, 111
House, Christopher, 55
Howard, John, 97
Howard, John L., Jr., 40
"How Uncurbed Entitlements Will Force Large Tax Increases," 170

Hubbard, R. Glenn, 25, 31, 34–35, 61
Hufbauer, Gary, 90, 98
Human Events, 5
Humphrey, Hubert, 193

IBM, 56
Ignatius, David, 115–16
Immigration policy, 9, 14, 15, 16, 107, 205–7
Income tax, comprehensive, *see* Comprehensive income tax
Indian gambling interests, 17
Inflation, 45, 47, 126, 162
  indexing of Social Security benefits to, 149–50
  during Johnson Administration, 148
  during Nixon Administration, 146, 147
Inside Politics, 75
Interest rates, 62, 102, 126
Internal Revenue Service, 33, 181
  "tax gap" estimate, 184
International Monetary Fund, 33, 94, 184
International Trade Commission, U.S. (ITC), 86, 88, 90, 101
Investment Tax Credit, 148, 149
Iraq, invasion and occupation of, 1, 2, 10, 17, 18, 142, 156, 205
  conservative criticism of, 13, 207–8
  interagency coordination and, 37
  Lindsey's cost estimate for, 30
  neoconservatives and, 10
  supplemental appropriation requests for, 135
  WMDs, failure to find, 11, 207–8
Ireland, VAT in, 187
Isakson, Johnny, 66
Israel, trade with, 96

Issues and Answers, 73
Istook, Ernest, 65, 66

Jacoby, Jeff, 138
Jacoby, Neil, 158–59
Japan, VAT in, 187
Jenkins, Holman, 165, 199
Jepsen, Roger, 119
John Birch Society, 154–55
John Deere, 78
Johnson, Lyndon B., and Johnson Administration, 46, 84, 135, 148
Joint Committee on Taxation, 45, 63
Jordan, trade with, 96
Junk bonds, 110–11

Kadlec, Daniel, 198
Kasten, Robert Walter, Jr., 178
Katrina, Hurricane, 38, 40, 80, 139, 204–5
Keating, Dave, 199
Kemp, Jack, 160, 178
Kemp-Roth tax bill, 160, 162
Kennedy, Edward, 8, 74–75
Kennedy, John F., 144, 148, 160
  tax cut of 1963, 45–46, 158–59
  trade policy, 83–84
Kennedy, Mark, 66
Kerry, John, 13, 14, 36, 62, 77, 136, 137, 196
Keynes, John Maynard, and Keynesian economics, 45, 46, 48, 51–52, 58, 148, 155–56, 177
King, Steve, 66
Kline, John, 65
Kristol, Irving, 161
Krugman, Paul, 102
Kuttner, Bob, 81
Kyoto Treaty, 106, 107

Laffer Curve, 160, 161, 203
Lamie, Hugh, 124
Lay, Ken, 117
Lazear, Edward P., 165
Leaks, 4–5
Leavitt, Michael, 79
Lesotho, trade with, 97
Lewinsky, Monica, 147, 168
Liberal view of role of government, 1, 2
Lichtenberg, Frank, 73–74
Lichtman, Allan, 17
Light, Paul, 39
Limbaugh, Rush, 142–43
Lindsey, Larry, 24–25, 29–31, 35, 49, 50, 51
Lockheed Corporation, bailout of, 154
Long, Michael, 11
Los Angeles Times, 70
Lowry, Richard, 76
Loyalty, Bush Administration demands for, 3, 18, 30, 31, 39–40

Macomber, Shawn, 58
"Mad cow" disease, 109
Maggs, John, 137–38
Mallaby, Sebastian, 52
Managers, corporate, 109–11
Manchester Union Leader, 7, 50
Mandates on the states, unfunded federal, 120
Mankiw, N. Gregory, 35–36, 95, 96
Manzullo, Donald, 66, 89
Mars, manned mission to, 136
Marshall, Jim, 65
Marshall Plan, 83
Martin, William McChesney, 145–46
McCain, John, 80, 199
McKinnon, Mark, 3
McNealy, Scott, 114

McTague, Jim, 130
Means, Gardiner, 110
Medicare, 72, 189
  trustees, annual reports of, 70, 71–72, 168
  unfunded liability for, 70–72, 168–69, 202
"Medicare: A Ticking Time Bomb for Tax Increases," 170
Medicare Prescription Drug, Improvement, and Modernization Act of 2003, 13, 16, 36, 64–81, 143, 174, 192, 200, 201, 202
  corporations, benefits for, 77–78
  costs of, 17, 65, 67–72, 80
  future tax increases and, see Tax increases, future
  House vote on, 64–66
  political backlash, 75–77, 80
  political rationale for, 73–74, 156
  unfunded liability for, 4, 11, 71, 79, 168
Meese, Ed, 119
Melloan, George, 135, 138
Mexico, trade with, 96
Meyerson, Harold, 77
Milbank, Dana, 143
Milken, Michael, 111
Mill, John Stuart, 87, 208
Miller, Jeff, 65
Milliken, Roger, 93
Minimum tax, 149
Miniter, Brendan, 203
Miniter, Richard, 7
Missile defense, 38
Mitchell, Dan, 170
Modern Corporation and Private Property, The (Berle and Means), 110

Modigliani, Franco, 53
Moffit, Robert, 70
Moore, Steve, 59, 133
Morgenthau, Henry, 27
Morocco, trade with, 97
Morris, Dick, 197, 202–3
"Murder board," 42
Muris, Tim, 106
Murphy, Kevin M., 165
Murphy, Tim, 66
Murray, Alan, 37, 106, 120, 143, 170
Myrick, Sue, 66

NAFTA, 84, 85, 96
Namibia, trade with, 97
National Conference of State
    Legislatures, 120
National debt, 50, 102
    interest on, 127–28
National Economic Council (NEC),
    23–25, 29–31, 35
    under Rubin, 24, 31, 126
National Educational Association, 138
National Review, 11, 29
National Security Council, 24
National Tax Journal, 187
National Taxpayers Union, 138
Neoconservatives, 10
Neugebauer, Randy, 65
Newmark, Kathryn, 138
Newsweek, 160–61
New York Post, 134
New York Times, 5, 40, 60, 74, 78, 93,
    96, 98, 109, 124, 130, 132, 170
Nicaragua, trade with, 96
Nicholson, Jim, 15
Niskanen, William, 166, 198
Nixon, Richard M., and Nixon
    Administration, 84, 121, 135,
    141–56, 193

balanced federal budget and, 159
Bush compared to, 1, 19, 141–44,
    153, 156, 194
federal spending under, 149–51
government regulation under,
    151–54, 155, 156
"industrial policy," 154–55
presidential campaigns, 144–45,
    147, 149, 155, 156, 194
Social Security spending and,
    149–50, 151, 155, 156
tax policy, 148–49, 159, 189
wage and price controls, 146, 147,
    152, 155
Watergate scandal, 147, 193
Nock, Albert Jay, 11
Nofziger, Lyn, 12, 14
Noonan, Peggy, 15
North American Free Trade
    Agreement (NAFTA), 84, 85, 96
Novak, Robert, 3, 11, 16, 30, 40,
    50, 76–77, 117, 201
Nunes, Devin, 66

Occupational Health and Safety
    Administration (OSHA), 151–52,
    153, 155, 156
Office of Faith-Based and
    Community Initiatives, 25
Office of Management and Budget
    (OMB), 24, 106, 107, 108
    powers of, 21–22
Office of Policy Development
    (OPD), 22, 23, 24
Omnibus Budget Reconciliation Act
    of 1987, 163
O'Neill, Paul, 27–29, 30, 53, 59, 61,
    102
Organisation for Economic Co-
    operation and Development, 83

Otter, Butch, 65, 66
Outsourcing, 90, 94–96, 115
Overseas Private Investment
    Corporation, 117
Oxley, Michael, 113, 117

Panagariya, Arvind, 97
Panetta, Leon, 126, 181
Parker, Mike, 3
Payroll taxes, 128, 163, 183
Penn Central Railroad, bailout of,
    154
Perot, Ross, 23, 49, 84, 122
Perotti, Roberto, 172
Personal income tax, 60–61
    VAT to replace, 184–85
Peru, trade with, 97
Peterson, Pete, 167
"Philadelphia Plan," 154
Pierce, Kenneth, 87
Pinkerton, Jim, 142
Pitts, Joe, 65
Podhoretz, John, 3, 11, 134, 200
Policy development process, 20–43
    Bush Administration and, 18, 20,
        24–43, 200–201
    historically, 20–23
    National Economic Council and,
        23–25, 29–31
Politicization of policy analysis, 30,
    38–40
    economic policy, 37
    science policy, 38
Pollock, Ron, 75–76
Pollution abatement and control,
    expenditures for, 152–53
Ponnuru, Ramesh, 42–43
Pork barrel spending, 11, 98,
    131–32, 138–39, 167, 199, 203,
    205, 208, 213

Powell, Colin, 132, 193
Presidential elections
    1960, 144–45, 156
    1968, 145, 194
    1972, 142, 147, 155, 193
    1976, 12, 149, 159, 196
    1980, 12, 195, 209
    1992, 12, 23, 48, 122–23, 124–25,
        156
    1996, 49
    2000, 8, 42, 51
    2004, 12–14, 36, 62, 77, 119, 136,
        137, 144, 194, 196, 206
    2008, 19, 140, 193, 194, 195, 196,
        208–9
Press, Bush and the, 41–42, 143
Price controls
    on drugs, 78–79
    under Nixon, 146, 147, 152, 155
Price of Loyalty, The (Suskind), 28
Productivity, regulation and, 152–53
Progress and Poverty (George), 190
Progressive tax rates, 177, 180
Proposition 13 in California, 160–61
Protectionism, 84, 156
    agricultural subsidies, 19, 86, 91–92
    antidumping statutes, 98–100, 101
    bilateral trade agreements and,
        96, 97
    Chinese textiles, restrictions on
        imports of, 93–94
    dangers of, 82–83, 100, 101
    history of U.S., 82–83, 86–87
    for infant industries, 86–87
    Nixon and, 153–54, 156
    steel tariffs, 9, 11, 19, 35, 85–91, 101

Rabushka, Alvin, 177
Rauch, Jonathan, 144, 198
Rawls, John, 181

Rayburn, Sam, 82–83
Reagan, Ronald, and Reagan
   Administration, 76, 120
discretionary spending under, 133,
   135, 138–39, 161
on foreign aid, 132–33
leaks, tolerance of, 4–5
Nixon's policies and, 19
outside advisors, 41
presidential election of 1980, 12,
   195, 209
supply-side economics, 48, 157
tax policy, 23, 48, 60–61, 161–64,
   173, 186, 214
trade policy, 84
Regulation, government, 103–9,
   112–17, 119–20, 129, 151–54,
   156
Reich, Robert, 96, 118, 128
Reinhardt, Uwe, 52
Reston, James, 155
Retail sales tax, 177, 181
Revenue sharing, 149, 155
Reynolds, Alan, 55, 62
Ribstein, Larry, 112–13
Rice, Condoleezza, 193
Richards, Ann, 117
Riedl, Brian, 169
Right Man, The (Frum), 26–27
Roach, Stephen, 123
Rockefeller, Nelson, 193
Romano, Roberta, 113–14
Roosevelt, Franklin D., 27, 83,
   193, 205
Rosen, Harvey, 36
Roth, Bill, 160
Rove, Karl, 15, 142, 143
Rubin, Robert
   National Economic Council
   headed by, 24, 31, 126

as Secretary of the Treasury, 24,
   28–29, 31

"Safe harbor leasing," 162
Safire, William, 141–42
Sager, Ryan, 137
Sales tax, retail, 177, 181
Samuelson, Robert, 123, 142
Santorum, Rick, 165
Sarbanes-Oxley Act (SOX), 113–17,
   156, 199
Sawicky, Max, 169–70
Scarborough, Joe, 136–37
Schatz, Tom, 167
Scheiber, Noam, 144
Schiavo, Terri, 1
Schlesinger, Arthur, 27
Schmitz, John, 155
Schultze, Charles, 136
Schwab, Charles, 59–60
Science policy, 38
Scott, David, 65
Scowcroft, Brent, 41
Scully, Tom, 69, 70
Securities and Exchange
   Commission, 110, 114–15
September 11, 2001
   conservatives' criticism of Bush
   and, 9, 14
   new regulations after, 107
   subsidies to big business after,
   118–20
Shapiro, Matthew, 55
Shareholders, corporate, 110–11
Shaviro, Dan, 171
Shlaes, Amity, 170
Simon, Bill, 105–6
Simons, Henry, 178
Singapore, trade with, 96
Slaughter, Matthew, 36

Slovakia, VAT in, 187
Small Business Administration, 108
Smith, Adam, 103–4, 110
Smith, Brad, 66
Smith, Chris, 15
Smith, Howard K., 155
Smith, Nick, 66
Smith, Vernon L., 59
Smoot-Hawley Tariff, 82, 83
Snow, John, 31–34
Socialism, 154
Social Security
  Clinton Administration efforts to
    save, 167–68
  indexing of benefits to inflation,
    149–50
  1983 changes to, 162–63, 189
  Nixon and, 149–50, 151, 155, 156
  payroll taxes, 163, 183
  unfunded liability for, 71, 79,
    169, 202
Social Security reform, 15, 16, 18,
  79–80, 200, 202–3
  policy development for, 32,
    200–201
  raising the wage cap, 172
Social Security trust fund, 32
Soros, George, 14
Souder, Mark, 66
South Africa, trade with, 97
Starve-the-beast theory of taxation,
  157, 159–61, 164–67
State Department, U.S., 24
Statement of Administration Policy
  (SAP), 22
Steel tariffs, 9, 11, 19, 35, 85–91,
  101
Stein, Herb, 146, 152, 161
Steindel, Charles, 53
Stem cell research, 38

Stevens, Ted, 167
Stigler, George, 105
Stiglitz, Joseph, 34, 128, 129–30
Stockfisch, J. A., 187
Stockman, David, 72–73
Strine, Leo, 113
Stuttaford, Andrew, 7–8
Successor to George W. Bush,
  193–94
Sullivan, Andrew, 137
Summers, Lawrence, 34
Superfund Amendments of 1986,
  163
Supersonic jet aircraft, 154, 155
Supply-side economics, 48, 52,
  59, 157
Surrey, Stanley, 47
Suskind, Ron, 26, 28, 40–41
Swaziland, trade with, 97

Tampa Tribune, 13
Tancredo, Tom, 206
Tanenhaus, Sam, 10
Tariffs, see Protectionism
Tax brackets, 180
  "bracket creep," 47–48, 128, 173
  changes in the, 49, 50, 53, 54–55,
    56, 126, 178–79, 188
  progressive, 177, 178
  tax reform and, 178–79, 188
Tax credits, 57–58
  child credit, 57, 175, 179
  Investment Tax Credit, 148, 149
Tax Equity and Fiscal Responsibility
  Act of 1982 (TEFRA), 162
Tax increases, future, 157, 168–91
  economists predicting, 169–70
  inevitability of, 168–70, 189
  Republican Party antipathy for,
    170–71

tax reform to achieve, 176–91
trigger for, 18, 171–72, 188, 192
Tax policy
Bush, Jr. *See* Tax policy, Bush
Administration.
Bush, Sr., 7, 48, 49, 124–25, 171
Carter Administration, 58
Clinton Administration, 49, 51, 126
Eisenhower Administration, 158
Ford Administration, 159
future tax increases, *see* Tax
increases, future
Johnson Administration, 148
Kennedy Administration, 45–46,
158–59
Nixon Administration, 148–49,
159, 189
postwar economic view of, 44–47
Reagan Administration, 23, 48,
60–61, 161–64, 173, 186, 214
starve-the-beast theory of taxation,
157, 159–61, 164–67
Tax policy, Bush Administration,
29–30, 33, 35, 44, 48–63
bonus depreciation provision, 35,
58–59, 179
dividend relief, 35, 59–62
tax credits, 57–58
tax cuts, 1, 8, 18, 44, 49–52, 53,
54–56, 59–62, 157, 173, 174,
203–4
tax rebates, 52–54, 56–57
Tax rebates, 52–54, 56–57, 159
Tax reform, 47–48, 62–63, 176–91
basic approaches to, 176–78
comprehensive income tax,
176–77, 178, 180
consumption-based taxation, *see*
Consumption-based taxation
tax rate schedule and, 178–79, 188

Tax Reform Act of 1969, 47, 149,
176
Tax Reform Act of 1986, 23, 125,
163, 178–79, 188
Taylor, Timothy, 37
Telecommunications companies,
government regulation of, 104
Tempalski, Jerry, 162
Terrorism insurance, 118–19
Thomas, Bill, 61–62
Thomas, Rich, 123
Thompson, Tommy, 70
Thornberry, Mac, 66
Time magazine, 46, 155
Tobin, James, 34
Tokyo Round of multilateral trade
negotiations, 84
Trade policy, international, 82–101
agricultural subsidies, 19, 86,
91–92
bilateral trade agreements, 19,
96–97, 101
Bush Administration, 18–19, 82,
85–101
Chinese textiles, imports of, 93–94
conservative philosophy, 1
"dumping" and, 93, 98–100
history of U.S., 82–85, 86–87
outsourcing, 90, 94–96
protectionism, *see* Protectionism
small groups of countries, free
trade agreements with, 96–98
steel tariffs, 9, 11, 19, 35, 85–91,
101
Treasury Department, U.S., 23,
27–29, 31–34, 39
studies by, 148, 149, 162, 177
transition from Reagan to Bush,
Sr., 6
Truman, Harry, 83, 205

Tsunami of 2005, Asian, 132, 133
Ture, Norman, 59
Tyson, Laura, 96

Ullman, Al, 189
United Airlines, 78, 118
UPS, 104
Uruguay Round of multilateral
    trade negotiations, 84, 85
U.S. Steel, 78

Value-added tax (VAT), 181–91, 192
    benefits of, 182, 189
    classic example of, 182
    deficit reduction and, 184, 185–86,
        188
    in Europe, 177, 187, 189, 215–16
    "money machine" fears, 186–88
    options for use of, 183–85
    start-up costs of, 190
    trade, effect on, 182–83
Vedder, Richard, 164
Verizon, 78
Vetoes, presidential, 211–12
    Bush's failure to use, 79, 131, 139,
        199
    Clinton's use of, 18, 127
    line-item veto power, 151, 159
Vickrey, William, 60
Vietnam War, 142, 156
Viguerie, Richard, 11
Virginia legislature, 171

Wall Street Journal, 9, 14, 38, 56, 58,
    69, 74, 78, 91, 107, 123–24, 134,
    135, 161, 163, 169, 186, 197

Warner, Mark, 171
Washington, George, Farewell
    Address of, 3
Washington Post, 5, 14, 28, 32, 39,
    69, 76, 96, 124, 173
    polls, 13, 75
Washington Times, 9, 11–12
Watergate scandal, 147, 193
Wealth of Nations, The (Smith),
    103–4
Weekly Standard, 15, 59, 92, 195
Weisberg, Jacob, 17
Weldon, Dave, 66
Welfare reform, 128–29
Wessel, David, 169
Wharton Economic Forecasting
    Associates, 46
Will, George, 9, 11, 14, 88, 155,
    161, 165
Wilson, Woodrow, 2–3
Wittmann, Marshall, 131
Wolfowitz, Paul, 33–34
Wonacott, Peter, 89
Woodward, Bob, 125
World Bank, 117
    Wolfowitz's appointment as
        president of, 33–34
WorldCom, 107, 109, 113
World Trade Organization, 90,
    100–101, 182

Yellen, Janet, 96

"Zeroing," 99
Zhang, Ivy Xiying, 117
Zoellick, Robert, 12, 85, 88–89

ABOUT THE AUTHOR

BRUCE BARTLETT is the author of *Reaganomics,* which was named one of the *Wall Street Journal*'s best business books of the year in 1981. In the 1980s he was executive director of the Joint Economic Committee of Congress, and later worked in the Reagan White House and the first Bush Treasury Department. Bartlett writes a nationally syndicated newspaper column, and his work has appeared in the *New York Times,* the *Wall Street Journal, Fortune, Commentary,* and other national publications. He was a Senior Fellow at the National Center for Policy Analysis from 1995 to 2005, until he was fired for writing this book. He lives in Great Falls, Virginia.